5th Workshop on Asian Translation (WAT-5)

Hong Kong, China
1 – 3 December 2018

ISBN: 978-1-5108-8908-8

TABLE OF CONTENTS

OVERVIEW OF THE 5TH WORKSHOP ON ASIAN TRANSLATION 1
Toshiaki Nakazawa , Katsuhito Sudoh , Shohei Higashiyama , Chenchen Ding , Raj Dabre , Hideya Mino , Isao Goto , Win Pa Pa , Anoop Kunchukuttan , Sadao Kurohashi

CUNI NMT SYSTEM FOR WAT 2018 TRANSLATION TASKS 42
Tom Kocmi , Shantipriya Parida , Ondrej Bojar

NICT'S PARTICIPATION IN WAT 2018: APPROACHES USING MULTILINGUALISM AND RECURRENTLY STACKED LAYERS 49
Raj Dabre , Anoop Kunchukuttan , Atsushi Fujita , Eiichiro Sumita

SRCB NEURAL MACHINE TRANSLATION SYSTEMS IN WAT 2018 58
Yihan Li , Boyan Liu , Yixuan Tong , Shanshan Jiang , Bin Dong

SMT RERANKED NMT (2) 63
Terumasa Ehara

ENGLISH-MYANMAR NMT AND SMT WITH PRE-ORDERING: NICT'S MACHINE TRANSLATION SYSTEMS AT WAT-2018 69
Rui Wang , Chenchen Ding , Masao Utiyama , Eiichiro Sumita

COMBINATION OF STATISTICAL AND NEURAL MACHINE TRANSLATION FOR MYANMAR-ENGLISH 72
Benjamin Marie , Atsushi Fujita , Eiichiro Sumita

TMU JAPANESE-CHINESE UNSUPERVISED NMT SYSTEM FOR WAT 2018 TRANSLATION TASK 78
Longtu Zhang , Yuting Zhao , Mamoru Komachi

STATISTICAL MACHINE TRANSLATION USING 5-GRAMS WORD SEGMENTATION IN DECODING 85
Aye Thida , Nway Nway Han , Sheinn Thawtar Oo

CVIT-MT SYSTEMS FOR WAT-2018 90
Jerin Philip , Vinay P. Namboodiri , C. V. Jawahar

THE RGNLP MACHINE TRANSLATION SYSTEMS FOR WAT 2018 95
Atul Kr. Ojha , Koel Dutta Chowdhury , Chao-Hong Liu , Karan Saxena

IITP-MT AT WAT2018: TRANSFORMER-BASED MULTILINGUAL INDIC-ENGLISH NEURAL MACHINE TRANSLATION SYSTEM 100
Sukanta Sen , Kamal Kumar Gupta , Asif Ekbal , Pushpak Bhattacharyya

MULTILINGUAL INDIAN LANGUAGE TRANSLATION SYSTEM AT WAT 2018: MANY-TO-ONE PHRASE-BASED SMT 105
Tamali Banerjee , Anoop Kunchukuttan , Pushpak Bhattacharya

TMU JAPANESE-ENGLISH NEURAL MACHINE TRANSLATION SYSTEM USING GENERATIVE ADVERSARIAL NETWORK FOR WAT 2018 109
Yukio Matsumura , Satoru Katsumata , Mamoru Komachi

OSAKA UNIVERSITY MT SYSTEMS FOR WAT 2018: REWARDING, PREORDERING, AND DOMAIN ADAPTATION 117
Yuki Kawara , Yuto Takebayashi , Chenhui Chu , Yuki Arase

UCSYNLP-LAB MACHINE TRANSLATION SYSTEMS FOR WAT 2018 124
Yi Mon Shwe Sin , Thazin Myint Oo , Hsu Myat Mo , Win Pa Pa , Khim Mar Soe , Ye Kyaw Thu

XMU NEURAL MACHINE TRANSLATION SYSTEMS FOR WAT2018 MYANMAR-ENGLISH TRANSLATION TASK 130
Boli Wang , Jinming Hu , Yidong Chen , Xiaodong Shi

Author Index

Foreword

The 32nd Pacific Asia Conference on Language, Information and Computation (PACLIC) was held at The Hong Kong Polytechnic University on December 1-3, 2018, in conjunction with the 25th Joint Workshop on Linguistics and Language Processing (JWLLP) and the 5th Workshop on Asian Translation (WAT). JWLLP was held as a special session within PACLIC, and WAT was held separately at the same time as PACLIC. One of the goals of PACLIC is to emphasize and foster interdisciplinary cross-talk between linguistic and computational research. For example, while the papers presented at that conference can roughly be categorized into "linguistic" and "computational" papers, the conference organizers intentionally avoided arranging them into "linguistic" and "computational" sessions; rather, almost all the oral and poster sessions were arranged to include both types of papers, to create more opportunities for people of these backgrounds to learn about one another's work.

We received 194 submissions from around the world for PACLIC-32, JWLLP-25 and WAT-5 together. For the main conference and JWLLP workshop, 57 papers (32.2%) were accepted for oral presentations and 50 (28.2%) for poster presentations; for WAT-5 workshop, 17 papers were accepted. For these papers, we received reviews from over 180 ad-hoc reviewers outside of the programme committee (plus reviews from members of the programme committee). We would like to express our sincere gratitude to all the authors who submitted their work and to all the reviewers who volunteered their time for reviewing. Without you, this conference could not have been possible.

We were also fortunate to have keynote talks by Laurent Prévot (Aix Marseille Université), Emily M. Bender (University of Washington), and Alan C. L. Yu (University of Chicago), as well as invited talks by Helen Mei-Ling Meng (University of Hong Kong), Yashuhiro Katagiri (Future University Hakodate), Qi Su (Peking University), and Thi Minh Huyen Nguyen (VNU University of Science). Finally, we would like to thank the PACLIC Steering Committee and the local co-chairs (David C. S. Li, Qin Lu, and Hans J. Ladegaard) for their support.

Chu-ren Huang & Min Zhang (Programme Committee Honorary Chairs)
Yu-Yin Hsu & Guohong Fu (Programme Committee Chairs)
The PACLIC 32 Programme Committee

Tak-Sum Wong
Dekai Wu
Chen-hui Wu
Doreen Wu
Jiun-Shiung Wu
Ming Xiang
Shufeng Xiong
Hongzhi Xu
Ruifeng Xu
Nianwen Xue
Yun Xue
Cheng-Zen Yang
Chung-Lin Martin Yang
Jie Yang
Liner Yang
Muyun Yang
Foongha Yap
Satoru Yokoyama
James Hye Suk Yoon
Alan Yu
Liang-Chih Yu
Xue Yun
Hongying Zan
Caicai Zhang
Chengzhi Zhang
Jiajun Zhang
Meishan Zhang
Niina Ning Zhang
Peng Zhang
Hai Zhao
Deyu Zhou
Hao Zhou
Junsheng Zhou
Muhua Zhu
Michael Zock

Overview of the 5th Workshop on Asian Translation

Toshiaki Nakazawa
The University of Tokyo
nakazawa@logos.t.u-tokyo.ac.jp

Katsuhito Sudoh
Nara Institute of Science and Technology
sudoh@is.naist.jp

Shohei Higashiyama and **Chenchen Ding** and **Raj Dabre**
National Institute of
Information and Communications Technology
{shohei.higashiyama, chenchen.ding, raj.dabre}@nict.go.jp

Hideya Mino and **Isao Goto**
NHK
{mino.h-gq, goto.i-es}@nhk.or.jp

Win Pa Pa
University of Conputer Study, Yangon
winpapa@ucsy.edu.mm

Anoop Kunchukuttan
Microsoft AI and Research
anoop.kunchukuttan@gmail.com

Sadao Kurohashi
Kyoto University
kuro@i.kyoto-u.ac.jp

Abstract

This paper presents the results of the shared tasks from the 5th workshop on Asian translation (WAT2018) including Ja↔En, Ja↔Zh scientific paper translation subtasks, Zh↔Ja, K↔Ja, En↔Ja patent translation subtasks, Hi↔En, My↔En mixed domain subtasks and Bn/Hi/Ml/Ta/Te/Ur/Si↔En Indic languages multilingual subtasks. For the WAT2018, 17 teams participated in the shared tasks. About 500 translation results were submitted to the automatic evaluation server, and selected submissions were manually evaluated.

1 Introduction

The Workshop on Asian Translation (WAT) is a new open evaluation campaign focusing on Asian languages. Following the success of the previous workshops WAT2014-WAT2017 (Nakazawa et al., 2014; Nakazawa et al., 2015; Nakazawa et al., 2016; Nakazawa et al., 2017), WAT2018 brings together machine translation researchers and users to try, evaluate, share and discuss brand-new ideas of machine translation. We have been working toward practical use of machine translation among all Asian countries.

For the 5th WAT, we adopted new translation subtasks with Myanmar ↔ English mixed domain corpus[1] and Bengali/Hindi/Malayalam/Tamil/Telugu/Urdu/Sinhalese ↔ English OpenSubtitles corpus[2] in addition to the subtasks at WAT2017.

WAT is the uniq workshop on Asian language transration with the following characteristics:

- Open innovation platform
  Due to the fixed and open test data, we can repeatedly evaluate translation systems on the same dataset over years. WAT receives submissions at any time; i.e., there is no submission deadline of translation results w.r.t automatic evaluation of translation quality.

- Domain and language pairs
  WAT is the world's first workshop that targets scientific paper domain, and Chinese↔Japanese and Korean↔Japanese language pairs. In the future, we will add more Asian languages such as Vietnamese, Thai and so on.

- Evaluation method
  Evaluation is done both automatically and manually. Firstly, all submitted translation results

[1] http://lotus.kuee.kyoto-u.ac.jp/WAT/my-en-data/
[2] http://lotus.kuee.kyoto-u.ac.jp/WAT/indic-multilingual/

Lang	Train	Dev	DevTest	Test
JE	3,008,500	1,790	1,784	1,812
JC	672,315	2,090	2,148	2,107

Table 1: Statistics for ASPEC

Lang	Train	Dev	DevTest	Test-N
zh-ja	1,000,000	2,000	2,000	5,204
ko-ja	1,000,000	2,000	2,000	5,230
en-ja	1,000,000	2,000	2,000	5,668

Lang	Test-N1	Test-N2	Test-N3	Test-EP
zh-ja	2,000	3,000	204	1,151
ko-ja	2,000	3,000	230	–
en-ja	2,000	3,000	668	–

Table 2: Statistics for JPC

are automatically evaluated using three metrics: BLEU, RIBES and AMFM. Among them, selected translation results are assessed by two kinds of human evaluation: pairwise evaluation and JPO adequacy evaluation.

2 Dataset

2.1 ASPEC

ASPEC was constructed by the Japan Science and Technology Agency (JST) in collaboration with the National Institute of Information and Communications Technology (NICT). The corpus consists of a Japanese-English scientific paper abstract corpus (ASPEC-JE), which is used for ja↔en subtasks, and a Japanese-Chinese scientific paper excerpt corpus (ASPEC-JC), which is used for ja↔zh subtasks. The statistics for each corpus are shown in Table 1.

2.1.1 ASPEC-JE

The training data for ASPEC-JE was constructed by NICT from approximately two million Japanese-English scientific paper abstracts owned by JST. The data is a comparable corpus and sentence correspondences are found automatically using the method from (Utiyama and Isahara, 2007). Each sentence pair is accompanied by a similarity score that are calculated by the method and a field ID that indicates a scientific field. The correspondence between field IDs and field names, along with the frequency and occurrence ratios for the training data, are described in the README file of ASPEC-JE.

The development, development-test and test data were extracted from parallel sentences from the Japanese-English paper abstracts that exclude the sentences in the training data. Each dataset consists of 400 documents and contains sentences in each field at the same rate. The document alignment was conducted automatically and only documents with a 1-to-1 alignment are included. It is therefore possible to restore the original documents. The format is the same as the training data except that there is no

similarity score.

2.1.2 ASPEC-JC

ASPEC-JC is a parallel corpus consisting of Japanese scientific papers, which come from the literature database and electronic journal site J-STAGE by JST, and their translation to Chinese with permission from the necessary academic associations. Abstracts and paragraph units are selected from the body text so as to contain the highest overall vocabulary coverage.

The development, development-test and test data are extracted at random from documents containing single paragraphs across the entire corpus. Each set contains 400 paragraphs (documents). There are no documents sharing the same data across the training, development, development-test and test sets.

2.2 JPC

JPO Patent Corpus (JPC) for the patent tasks was constructed by the Japan Patent Office (JPO) in collaboration with NICT. The corpus consists of Chinese-Japanese, Korean-Japanese and English-Japanese patent descriptions whose International Patent Classification (IPC) sections are chemistry, electricity, mechanical engineering, and physics.

At WAT2018, the patent tasks has two subtasks: normal subtask and expression pattern subtask. Both subtasks uses common training, development and development-test data for each language pair. The normal subtask for three language pairs uses four test data with different characteristics:

- test-N: union of the following three sets;

- test-N1: patent documents from patent families published between 2011 and 2013;

Lang	Train	Dev	DevTest	Test
en-ja	200,000	2,000	2,000	2,000

Table 3: Statistics for JIJI Corpus

Lang	Train	Dev	Test	Mono
hi-en	1,492,827	520	2,507	–
hi-ja	152,692	1,566	2,000	–
hi	–	–	–	45,075,279

Table 4: Statistics for IITB Corpus. "Mono" indicates monolingual Hindi corpus.

Lang	TextType	Train	Dev	DevTest	Test
	Title	14,779	500	500	500
en-ja	Ingredient	127,244	4,274	4,188	3,935
	Step	108,993	3,303	3,086	2,804

Table 5: Statistics for Recipe Corpus

- test-N2: patent documents from patent families published between 2016 and 2017; and

- test-N3: patent documents published between 2016 and 2017 where target sentences are manually created by translating source sentences.

The expression pattern subtask for zh→ja pair uses test-EP data. The test-EP data consists of sentences annotated with expression pattern categories: title of invention (TIT), abstract (ABS), scope of claim (CLM) or description (DES). The corpus statistics are shown in Table 2. Note that training, development, development-test and test-N1 data are the same as those used in WAT2017.

2.3 JIJI Corpus

JIJI Corpus was constructed by Jiji Press Ltd. in collaboration with NICT. The corpus consists of news text that comes from Jiji Press news of various categories including politics, economy, nation, business, markets, sports and so on. The corpus is partitioned into training, development, development-test and test data, which consists of Japanese-English sentence pairs. The statistics for each corpus are shown in Table 3.

The sentence pairs in each data are identified in the same manner as that for ASPEC using the method from (Utiyama and Isahara, 2007).

2.4 IITB Corpus

IIT Bombay English-Hindi Corpus contains English-Hindi parallel corpus as well as monolingual Hindi corpus collected from a variety of sources and corpora. This corpus had been developed at the Center for Indian Language Technology, IIT Bombay over the years. The corpus is used for mixed domain tasks hi↔en. The statistics for the corpus are shown in Table 4.

2.5 Recipe Corpus

Recipe Corpus was constructed by Cookpad Inc. Each recipe consists of a title, ingredients, steps, a description and a history. Every text in titles, ingredients and steps consists of a parallel sentence while one in descriptions and histories is not always a parallel sentence. Although all of the texts in the training set can be used for training, only titles, ingredients and steps in the test set is used for evaluation. The statistics for each corpus are described in Table 5.

2.6 ALT and UCSY Corpus

The parallel data for Myanmar-English translation tasks at WAT2018 consists of two corpora, the ALT corpus and UCSY corpus.

- The ALT corpus is one part from the Asian Language Treebank (ALT) project (Riza et al., 2016), consisting of twenty thousand Myanmar-English parallel sentences from news articles.

- The UCSY corpus (Yi Mon Shwe Sin and Khin Mar Soe, 2018) is constructed by the NLP Lab, University of Computer Studies, Yangon (UCSY), Myanmar. The corpus consists of 200 thousand Myanmar-English parallel sentences collected from different domains, including news articles and textbooks.

The released Myanmar textual data have been tokenized into writing units and Romanized. The script for tokenization and recovery is also provided for participants,[3] so that they can make use of their own data and tools for further processing. The automatic

---

[3] http://www2.nict.go.jp/astrec-att/
member/mutiyama/ALT/myan2roma.py

Corpus	Train	Dev	Test
ALT	17,965	993	1,007
UCSY	208,638	–	–
All	226,603	993	1,007

Table 6: Statistics for the data used in Myanmar-English translation tasks

Lang	Train	Dev	Test	Mono (src)
bn-en	337,428	500	1,000	453,859
hi-en	84,557	500	1,000	104,967
ml-en	359,423	500	1,000	402,761
ta-en	26,217	500	1,000	30,268
te-en	22,165	500	1,000	24,750
ur-en	26,619	500	1,000	29,086
si-en	521,726	500	1,000	705,793
en	–	–	–	2,891,079

Table 7: Statistics for Indic Languages Corpus

evaluation of Myanmar translation results is based on the tokenized writing units, and the human evaluation is based on the recovered Myanmar text.

The detailed composition of training, development, and test data of the Myanmar-English translation tasks are listed in Table 6.

2.7 Indic Languages Corpus

The Indic Languages Corpus covers 8 languages, namely: Bengali, Hindi, Malayalam, Tamil, Telugu, Sinhalese, Urdu and English. The corpus has been collected from OPUS[4] and belongs to the spoken language (OpenSubtitles) domain. This corpus is used for the pilot as well as multilingual English↔Indic Languages sub-tasks. The corpus is a collection of 7 bilingual parallel corpora of varying sizes, one for each Indic language and English. The parallel corpora are also accompanied by monolingual corpora from the same domain. The statistics of the parallel and monolingual corpora are given in Table 7.

3 Baseline Systems

Human evaluations were conducted as pairwise comparisons between the translation results for a specific baseline system and translation results for each participant's system. That is, the specific baseline system was the standard for human evaluation. At WAT 2018, we adopted a neural machine translation (NMT) with attention mechanism as a baseline system except for the IITB tasks. We used a phrase-based statistical machine translation (SMT) system, which is the same system as that at WAT 2017, as the baseline system for the IITB tasks.

The NMT baseline systems consisted of publicly available software, and the procedures for building the systems and for translating using the systems were published on the WAT web page.[5] We used OpenNMT (Klein et al., 2017) as the implementation of the baseline NMT systems. In addition to the NMT baseline systems, we have SMT baseline systems for the tasks that started at last year or before last year. The baseline systems are shown in Tables 8, 9, and 10.

SMT baseline systems are described in the previous WAT overview paper (Nakazawa et al., 2017). The commercial RBMT systems and the online translation systems were operated by the organizers. We note that these RBMT companies and online translation companies did not submit themselves. Because our objective is not to compare commercial RBMT systems or online translation systems from companies that did not themselves participate, the system IDs of these systems are anonymous in this paper.

---

[4] http://opus.nlpl.eu

[5] http://lotus.kuee.kyoto-u.ac.jp/WAT/ WAT2018/baseline/baselineSystems.html

System ID	System	Type	ASPEC				JPC					
			ja-en	en-ja	ja-zh	zh-ja	ja-en	en-ja	ja-zh	zh-ja	ja-ko	ko-ja
NMT	OpenNMT's attention-based NMT	NMT	✓	✓	✓	✓	✓	✓	✓	✓	✓	✓
SMT Phrase	Moses' Phrase-based SMT	SMT	✓	✓	✓	✓	✓	✓	✓	✓	✓	✓
SMT Hiero	Moses' Hierarchical Phrase-based SMT	SMT	✓	✓	✓	✓	✓	✓	✓	✓	✓	✓
SMT S2T	Moses' String-to-Tree Syntax-based SMT and Berkeley parser	SMT	✓		✓		✓		✓			
SMT T2S	Moses' Tree-to-String Syntax-based SMT and Berkeley parser	SMT		✓		✓		✓		✓		
RBMT X	The Honyaku V15 (Commercial system)	RBMT	✓	✓			✓	✓				
RBMT X	ATLAS V14 (Commercial system)	RBMT	✓	✓			✓	✓				
RBMT X	PAT-Transer 2009 (Commercial system)	RBMT	✓	✓			✓	✓				
RBMT X	PC-Transer V13 (Commercial system)	RBMT										
RBMT X	J-Beijing 7 (Commercial system)	RBMT			✓	✓			✓	✓		
RBMT X	Hohrai 2011 (Commercial system)	RBMT			✓	✓				✓		
RBMT X	J Soul 9 (Commercial system)	RBMT									✓	✓
RBMT X	Korai 2011 (Commercial system)	RBMT									✓	✓
Online X	Google translate	Other	✓	✓	✓	✓	✓	✓	✓	✓	✓	✓
Online X	Bing translator	Other	✓	✓	✓	✓	✓	✓	✓	✓	✓	✓
AIAYN	Google's implementation of "Attention Is All You Need"	NMT	✓	✓								

Table 8: Baseline Systems I

System ID	System	Type	JIJI		IITB				Recipe		ALT	
			ja-en	en-ja	hi-en	en-hi	hi-ja	ja-hi	ja-en	en-ja	my-en	en-my
NMT	OpenNMT's NMT with attention	NMT	✓	✓	✓	✓	✓	✓	✓	✓	✓	✓
SMT Phrase	Moses' Phrase-based SMT	SMT	✓	✓	✓	✓	✓	✓	✓	✓		
SMT Hiero	Moses' Hierarchical Phrase-based SMT	SMT	✓	✓								
SMT S2T	Moses' String-to-Tree Syntax-based SMT and Berkeley parser	SMT	✓									
SMT T2S	Moses' Tree-to-String Syntax-based SMT and Berkeley parser	SMT		✓								
RBMT X	The Honyaku V15 (Commercial system)	RBMT	✓	✓					✓	✓		
RBMT X	PC-Transer V13 (Commercial system)	RBMT	✓	✓					✓	✓		
Online X	Google translate	Other	✓	✓	✓	✓	✓	✓	✓	✓	✓	✓
Online X	Bing translator	Other	✓	✓	✓	✓	✓	✓	✓	✓		

Table 9: Baseline Systems II

System ID	System	Type	Indic	
			{bn,hi,ml,ta,te,ur,si}-en	en-{bn,hi,ml,ta,te,ur,si}
NMT	OpenNMT's NMT with attention	NMT	✓	✓
NMT M2O	OpenNMT's NMT with attention and multilingual tags (many to one)	NMT	✓	
NMT O2M	OpenNMT's NMT with attention and multilingual tags (one to many)	NMT		✓
NMT M2M	OpenNMT's NMT with attention and multilingual tags (many to many)	NMT	✓	✓

Table 10: Baseline Systems III

3.1 Training Data

We used the following data for training the NMT baseline systems.

- All of the training data for each task were used for training except for the ASPEC Japanese–English task. For the ASPEC Japanese–English task, we only used train-1.txt, which consists of one million parallel sentence pairs with high similarity scores.
- All of the development data for each task was used for validation.

3.2 Tokenization

We used the following tools for tokenization.

- Juman version 7.0[6] for Japanese segmentation.
- Stanford Word Segmenter version 2014-01-04[7] (Chinese Penn Treebank (CTB) model) for Chinese segmentation.
- The Moses toolkit for English and Indonesian tokenization.
- Mecab-ko[8] for Korean segmentation.
- Indic NLP Library[9] for Indic language segmentation.
- subword-nmt[10] for all languages.

When we built BPE-codes, we merged source and target sentences and we used 100,000 for -s option. We used 10 for vocabulary-threshold when subword-nmt applied BPE.

3.3 NMT with attention

We used the following OpenNMT configuration for the NMT with attention system.

- encoder_type = brnn
- brnn_merge = concat
- src_seq_length = 150
- tgt_seq_length = 150
- src_vocab_size = 100000
- tgt_vocab_size = 100000
- src_words_min_frequency = 1
- tgt_words_min_frequency = 1

The default values were used for the other system parameters.

For many to one, one to many, and many to many multilingual NMT (Johnson et al., 2017), we add <2XX> tags, which indicate the target language (XX is replaced by the language code), to the head of the source language sentences.

4 Automatic Evaluation

4.1 Procedure for Calculating Automatic Evaluation Score

We evaluated translation results by three metrics: BLEU (Papineni et al., 2002), RIBES (Isozaki et al., 2010) and AMFM (Banchs et al., 2015). BLEU scores were calculated using `multi-bleu.perl` in the Moses toolkit (Koehn et al., 2007). RIBES scores were calculated using `RIBES.py` version 1.02.4.[11] AMFM scores were calculated using scripts created by the technical collaborators listed in the WAT2018 web page.[12] All scores for each task were calculated using the corresponding reference translations.

Before the calculation of the automatic evaluation scores, the translation results were tokenized or segmented with tokenization/segmentation tools for each language. For Japanese segmentation, we used three different tools: Juman version 7.0 (Kurohashi et al., 1994), KyTea 0.4.6 (Neubig et al., 2011) with full SVM model[13] and MeCab 0.996 (Kudo, 2005) with IPA dictionary 2.7.0.[14] For Chinese segmentation, we used two different tools: KyTea 0.4.6 with full SVM Model in MSR model and Stanford Word Segmenter (Tseng, 2005) version 2014-06-16 with Chinese Penn Treebank (CTB) and Peking University (PKU) model.[15] For Korean segmentation, we

---

[6] http://nlp.ist.i.kyoto-u.ac.jp/EN/index.php?JUMAN

[7] http://nlp.stanford.edu/software/segmenter.shtml

[8] https://bitbucket.org/eunjeon/mecab-ko/

[9] https://bitbucket.org/anoopk/indic_nlp_library

[10] https://github.com/rsennrich/subword-nmt

[11] http://www.kecl.ntt.co.jp/icl/lirg/ribes/index.html

[12] lotus.kuee.kyoto-u.ac.jp/WAT/WAT2018/

[13] http://www.phontron.com/kytea/model.html

[14] http://code.google.com/p/mecab/downloads/detail?name=mecab-ipadic-2.7.0-20070801.tar.gz

[15] http://nlp.stanford.edu/software/segmenter.shtml

used mecab-ko.[16] For English tokenization, we used `tokenizer.perl`[17] in the Moses toolkit. For Hindi, Bengali, Malayalam, Tamil, Telugu, Urdu and Sinhalese tokenization, we used Indic NLP Library.[18] The detailed procedures for the automatic evaluation are shown on the WAT2018 evaluation web page.[19]

4.2 Automatic Evaluation System

The automatic evaluation system receives translation results by participants and automatically gives evaluation scores to the uploaded results. As shown in Figure 1, the system requires participants to provide the following information for each submission:

- Human Evaluation: whether or not they submit the results for human evaluation;

- Publish the results of the evaluation: whether or not they permit to publish automatic evaluation scores on the WAT2018 web page.

- Task: the task you submit the results for;

- Used Other Resources: whether or not they used additional resources; and

- Method: the type of the method including SMT, RBMT, SMT and RBMT, EBMT, NMT and Other.

Evaluation scores of translation results that participants permit to be published are disclosed via the WAT2018 evaluation web page.[20] Participants can also submit the results for human evaluation using the same web interface.

This automatic evaluation system will remain available even after WAT2018. Anybody can register an account for the system by the procedures described in the registration web page. [21]

---

[16] `https://bitbucket.org/eunjeon/mecab-ko/`
[17] `https://github.com/moses-smt/ mosesdecoder/tree/RELEASE-2.1.1/scripts/ tokenizer/tokenizer.perl`
[18] `https://bitbucket.org/anoopk/indic_nlp_ library`
[19] `http://lotus.kuee.kyoto-u.ac.jp/WAT/ evaluation/index.html`
[20] `lotus.kuee.kyoto-u.ac.jp/WAT/ evaluation/index.html`
[21] `http://lotus.kuee.kyoto-u.ac.jp/WAT/ WAT2018/registration/index.html`

5 Human Evaluation

In WAT2018, we conducted two kinds of human evaluations: *pairwise evaluation* and *JPO adequacy evaluation*.

5.1 Pairwise Evaluation

We conducted pairwise evaluation for participants' systems submitted for human evaluation. The submitted translations were evaluated by a professional translation company and *Pairwise* scores were given to the submissions by comparing with baseline translations (described in section 3).

5.1.1 Sentence Selection and Evaluation

For the pairwise evaluation, we randomly selected 400 sentences from the test set of each task. We used the same sentences as the last year for the continuous subtasks. Baseline and submitted translations were shown to annotators in random order with the input source sentence. The annotators were asked to judge which of the translations is better, or whether they are on par.

5.1.2 Voting

To guarantee the quality of the evaluations, each sentence is evaluated by 5 different annotators and the final decision is made depending on the 5 judgements. We define each judgement $j_i(i = 1, \cdots, 5)$ as:

$$j_i = \begin{cases} 1 & \text{if better than the baseline} \\ -1 & \text{if worse than the baseline} \\ 0 & \text{if the quality is the same} \end{cases}$$

The final decision D is defined as follows using $S = \sum j_i$:

$$D = \begin{cases} win & (S \geq 2) \\ loss & (S \leq -2) \\ tie & (otherwise) \end{cases}$$

5.1.3 Pairwise Score Calculation

Suppose that W is the number of *wins* compared to the baseline, L is the number of *losses* and T is the number of *ties*. The Pairwise score can be calculated by the following formula:

$$Pairwise = 100 \times \frac{W - L}{W + L + T}$$

From the definition, the Pairwise score ranges between -100 and 100.

WAT
The Workshop on Asian Translation
Submission

SUBMISSION

Logged in as: ORGANIZER

Logout

Submission:

Human Evaluation: ☐ human evaluation

Publish the results of the evaluation: ☑ publish

Team Name: ORGANIZER

Task: en-ja ▼

Submission File: ファイルを選択 選択されていません

Used Other Resources: ☐ used other resources such as parallel corpora, monolingual corpora and parallel dictionaries in addition to official corpora

Method: SMT ▼

System Description (public): 100 characters or less

System Description (private): 100 characters or less

Submit

Guidelines for submission:

- System requirements:
  - The latest versions of Chrome, Firefox, Internet Explorer and Safari are supported for this site.
  - Before you submit files, you need to enable JavaScript in your browser.
- File format:
  - Submitted files should NOT be tokenized/segmented. Please check the automatic evaluation procedures.
  - Submitted files should be encoded in UTF-8 format.
  - Translated sentences in submitted files should have one sentence per line, corresponding to each test sentence. The number of lines in the submitted file and that of the corresponding test file should be the same.
- Tasks:
  - en-ja, ja-en, zh-ja, ja-zh indicate the scientific paper tasks with ASPEC.
  - HINDENen-hi, HINDENhi-en, HINDENja-hi, and HINDENhi-ja indicate the mixed domain tasks with IITB Corpus.
  - JIJIen-ja and JIJIja-en are the newswire tasks with JIJI Corpus.
  - RECIPE{ALL,TTL,STE,ING}en-ja and RECIPE{ALL,TTL,STE,ING}ja-en indicate the recipe tasks with Recipe Corpus.
  - ALTen-my and ALTmy-en indicate the mixed domain tasks with UCSY and ALT Corpus.
  - INDICen-{bn,hi,ml,ta,te,ur,si} and INDIC{bn,hi,ml,ta,te,ur,si}-en indicate the Indic languages multilingual tasks with Indic Languages Multilingual Parallel Corpus.
  - JPC{N,N1,N2,N3,EP}zh-ja ,JPC{N,N1,N2,N3}ja-zh, JPC{N,N1,N2,N3}ko-ja, JPC{N,N1,N2,N3}ja-ko, JPC{N,N1,N2,N3}en-ja, and JPC{N,N1,N2,N3}ja-en indicate the patent tasks with JPO Patent Corpus. JPCN1{zh-ja,ja-zh,ko-ja,ja-ko,en-ja,ja-en} are the same tasks as JPC{zh-ja,ja-zh,ko-ja,ja-ko,en-ja,ja-en} in WAT2015-WAT2017. AMFM is not calculated for JPC{N,N2,N3} tasks.
- Human evaluation:
  - If you want to submit the file for human evaluation, check the box "Human Evaluation". Once you upload a file with checking "Human Evaluation" you cannot change the file used for human evaluation.
  - When you submit the translation results for human evaluation, please check the checkbox of "Publish" too.
  - You can submit two files for human evaluation per task.
  - One of the files for human evaluation is recommended not to use other resources, but it is not compulsory.
- Other:
  - Team Name, Task, Used Other Resources, Method, System Description (public) , Date and Time(JST), BLEU, RIBES and AMFM will be disclosed on the Evaluation Site when you upload a file checking "Publish the results of the evaluation".
  - You can modify some fields of submitted data. Read "Guidelines for submitted data" at the bottom of this page.

Back to top

Figure 1: The interface for translation results submission

5.1.4 Confidence Interval Estimation

There are several ways to estimate a confidence interval. We chose to use bootstrap resampling (Koehn, 2004) to estimate the 95% confidence interval. The procedure is as follows:

1. randomly select 300 sentences from the 400 human evaluation sentences, and calculate the Pairwise score of the selected sentences

2. iterate the previous step 1000 times and get 1000 Pairwise scores

3. sort the 1000 scores and estimate the 95% confidence interval by discarding the top 25 scores and the bottom 25 scores

5.2 JPO Adequacy Evaluation

We conducted JPO adequacy evaluation for the top two or three participants' systems of pairwise evalution for each subtask.[22] The evaluation was carried out by translation experts based on the JPO adequacy evaluation criterion, which is originally defined by JPO to assess the quality of translated patent documents.

5.2.1 Sentence Selection and Evaluation

For the JPO adequacy evaluation, the 200 test sentences were randomly selected from the 400 test sentences used for the pairwise evaluation. For each test sentence, input source sentence, translation by participants' system, and reference translation were shown to the annotators. To guarantee the quality of the evaluation, each sentence was evaluated by two annotators. Note that the selected sentences are the same as those used in the previous workshops except for the new subtasks at WAT2018.

5.2.2 Evaluation Criterion

Table 11 shows the JPO adequacy criterion from 5 to 1. The evaluation is performed subjectively. "Important information" represents the technical factors and their relationships. The degree of importance of each element is also considered to evaluate. The percentages in each grade are rough indications for the

5	All important information is transmitted correctly. (100%)
4	Almost all important information is transmitted correctly. (80%–)
3	More than half of important information is transmitted correctly. (50%–)
2	Some of important information is transmitted correctly. (20%–)
1	Almost all important information is NOT transmitted correctly. (–20%)

Table 11: The JPO adequacy criterion

transmission degree of the source sentence meanings. The detailed criterion is described in the JPO document (in Japanese). [23]

6 Participants

Table 12 shows the participants in WAT2018. The table lists 17 organizations from various countries, including Japan, China, India, Myanmar, Czech and Ireland.

More than 500 translation results by 17 teams were submitted for automatic evaluation and about 70 translation results by 16 teams were submitted for pairwise evaluation. We selected about 40 translation results for JPO adequacy evaluation according to the pairwise evaluation scores. Table 13 shows tasks for which each team submitted results by the submission deadline. Unfortunately, there were no submissions to Recipe and JIJI tasks this year.

7 Evaluation Results

In this section, the evaluation results for WAT2018 are reported from several perspectives. Some of the results for both automatic and human evaluations are also accessible at the WAT2018 website.[24]

7.1 Official Evaluation Results

Figures 2, 3, 4 and 5 show the official evaluation results of ASPEC subtasks, Figures 6, 7, 8, 9, 10, 11, 12 and 13 show those of JPC subtasks, Figures 14 and 15 show those of IITB subtasks, Figures 16 and 17 show those of ALT subtasks and Figures 18,

---

[22]The number of systems varies depending on the subtasks.

[23]http://www.jpo.go.jp/shiryou/toushin/
chousa/tokkyohonyaku_hyouka.htm

[24]http://lotus.kuee.kyoto-u.ac.jp/WAT/
evaluation/

19, 20 and 21 show those of INDIC subtasks. Each figure contains automatic evaluation results (BLEU, RIBES, AM-FM), the pairwise evaluation results with confidence intervals, correlation between automatic evaluations and the pairwise evaluation, the JPO adequacy evaluation result and evaluation summary of top systems. Some of the figures for some subtasks are omitted because the pairwise evaluation was not conducted or none of the human evaluation was conducted.

The detailed automatic evaluation results are shown in Appendix A. The detailed JPO adequacy evaluation results for the selected submissions are shown in Table 14. The weights for the weighted κ (Cohen, 1968) is defined as $|Evaluation1 - Evaluation2|/4$.

7.2 Statistical Significance Testing of Pairwise Evaluation between Submissions

Tables 15 and 16 show the results of statistical significance testing of ASPEC subtasks, Table 17 shows that of IITB subtasks, Table 18 shows that of ALT subtasks and Tables 19 and 20 show those of INDIC subtasks. $\ggg$, $\gg$ and $>$ mean that the system in the row is *better* than the system in the column at a significance level of $p < 0.01, 0.05$ and 0.1 respectively. Testing is also done by the bootstrap resampling as follows:

1. randomly select 300 sentences from the 400 pairwise evaluation sentences, and calculate the Pairwise scores on the selected sentences for both systems

2. iterate the previous step 1000 times and count the number of wins (W), losses (L) and ties (T)

3. calculate $p = \frac{L}{W+L}$

Inter-annotator Agreement

To assess the reliability of agreement between the workers, we calculated the Fleiss' κ (Fleiss and others, 1971) values. The results are shown in Table 21. We can see that the κ values are larger for X $\rightarrow$ J translations than for J $\rightarrow$ X translations. This may be because the majority of the workers for these language pairs are Japanese, and the evaluation of one's mother tongue is much easier than for other languages in general. The κ values for Hindi languages are relatively higt. This might be because the overall translation quality of the Hindi languages are low, and the evaluators can easily distinguish better translations from worse ones.

8   Conclusion and Future Perspective

This paper summarizes the shared tasks of WAT2018. We had 17 participants worldwide, and collected a large number of useful submissions for improving the current machine translation systems by analyzing the submissions and identifying the issues.

For the next WAT workshop, we plan to conduct documen-level evaluation using the new dataset with context for some translation subtasks and we would like to consider how to realize context-aware evaluation in WAT. Also, we are planning to do extrinsic evaluation of the translations.

Appendix A   Submissions

Tables 23 to 37 summarize translation results submitted for WAT2018 human evaluation. Type, RSRC, Pair, and Adeq columns indicate type of method, use of other resources, pairwise evaluation score, and JPO adequacy evaluation score, respectively.

The tables also include results by the organizers' baselines, which are listed in Table 10. For ALT tasks, we also evaluated outputs of Online-A system and its post-processed version where the western comma (,) is replaced into Myanmar native comma (0x104a). We conducted the post-processing because Myanmar native punctuation marks are consistently used in the WAT 2018 dataset.

Team ID	Organization	Country
srcb (Li et al., 2018)	RICOH Software Research Center Beijing Co.,Ltd	China
Osaka-U (Kawara et al., 2018)	Osaka University	Japan
RGNLP (Ojha et al., 2018)	Jawaharlal Nehru University / Dublin City University	India, Ireland
TMU (Zhang et al., 2018), (Matsumura et al., 2018)	Tokyo Metropolitan University	Japan
EHR (Ehara, 2018)	Ehara NLP Research Laboratory	Japan
NICT (Wang et al., 2018b)	NICT	Japan
NICT-4 (Marie et al., 2018)	NICT	Japan
NICT-5 (Dabre et al., 2018)	NICT	Japan
XMUNLP (Wang et al., 2018a)	Xiamen University	China
UCSYNLP (Mo et al., 2018)	University of Computer Studies, Yangon	Myanmar
UCSMNLP (Thida et al., 2018)	University of Computer Studies, Mandalay	Myanmar
kmust88	Kunming University of Science and Technology	China
USTC	University of Science and Technology of China	China
CUNI (Kocmi et al., 2018)	Charles University, Prague	Czech
Anuvaad (Banerjee et al., 2018)	IIT Bombay / Microsft AI and Research, India	India
IITP-MT (Sen et al., 2018)	Indian Institute of Technology Patna	India
cvit-mt (Philip et al., 2018)	International Institute of Information Technology, Hyderabad	India

Table 12: List of participants in WAT2018

Team ID	ASPEC				JPC (N/N1/N2/N3)				JPC (EP)	IITB		ALT	
	EJ	JE	CJ	JC	EJ	CJ	JC	KJ	CJ	EH	HE	E-My	My-E
srcb	✓	✓		✓									
Osaka-U	✓	✓										✓	✓
TMU	✓	✓	✓										
EHR	✓				✓	✓		✓	✓				
NICT												✓	✓
NICT-4												✓	✓
NICT-5	✓	✓	✓	✓									✓
XMUNLP												✓	✓
UCSYNLP												✓	✓
UCSMNLP												✓	✓
kmust88												✓	
USTC						✓	✓						
CUNI										✓	✓		
cvit-mt										✓	✓		

Team ID	Indic													
	EB	BE	EH	HE	E-Ml	Ml-E	E-Ta	Ta-E	E-Te	Te-E	EU	UE	ES	SE
RGNLP	✓	✓	✓	✓	✓	✓	✓	✓	✓	✓	✓	✓	✓	✓
NICT-5	✓	✓	✓	✓	✓	✓	✓	✓	✓	✓	✓	✓	✓	✓
Anuvaad	✓	✓	✓	✓	✓	✓	✓	✓	✓	✓	✓	✓	✓	✓
IITP-MT	✓	✓	✓	✓	✓	✓	✓	✓	✓	✓	✓	✓	✓	✓

Table 13: Submissions for each task by each team. E, J, C, K, H, B, U, and S denote English, Japanese, Chinese, Korean, Hindi, Bengali, Urdu, and Sinhalese language, respectively.

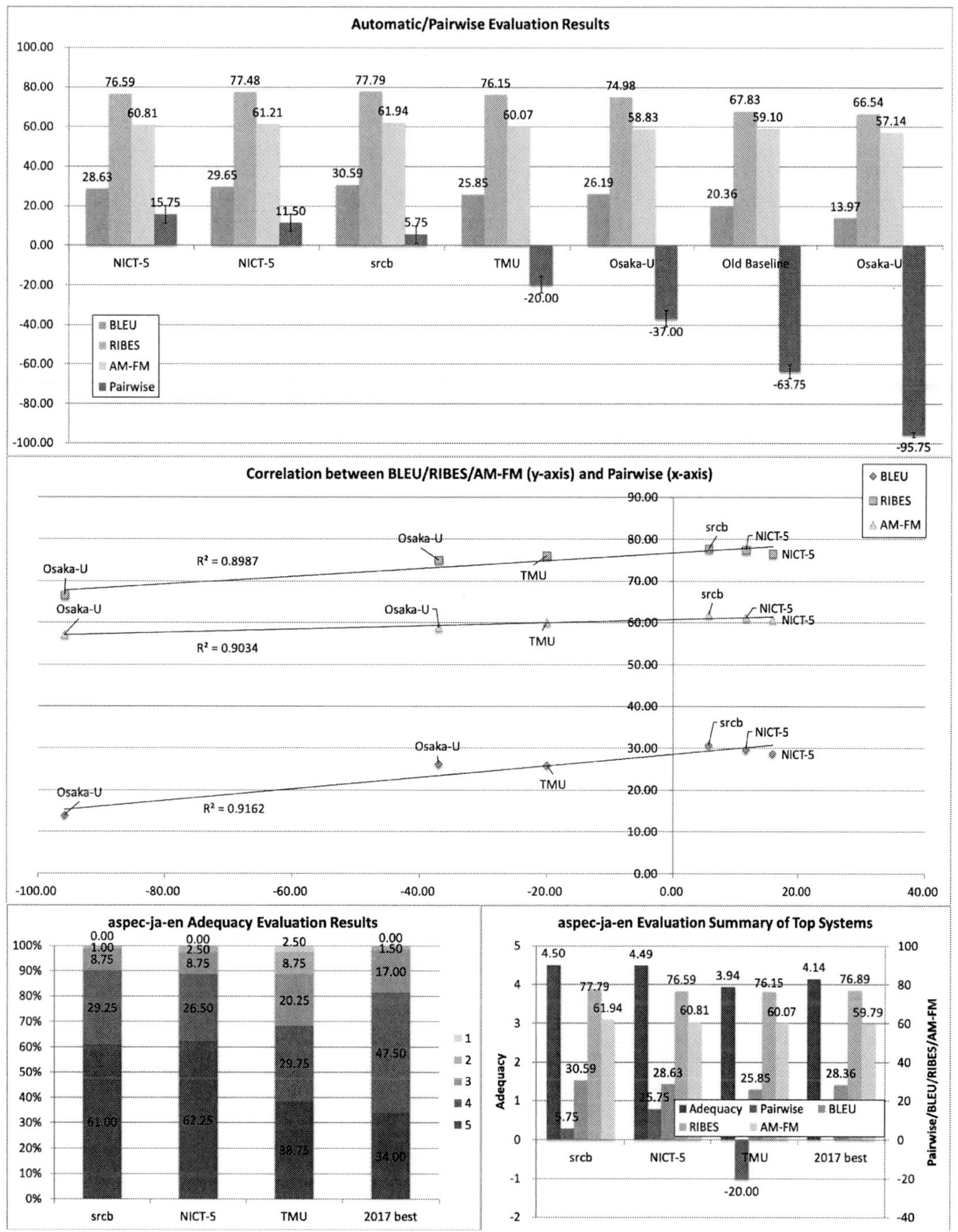

Figure 2: Official evaluation results of aspec-ja-en.

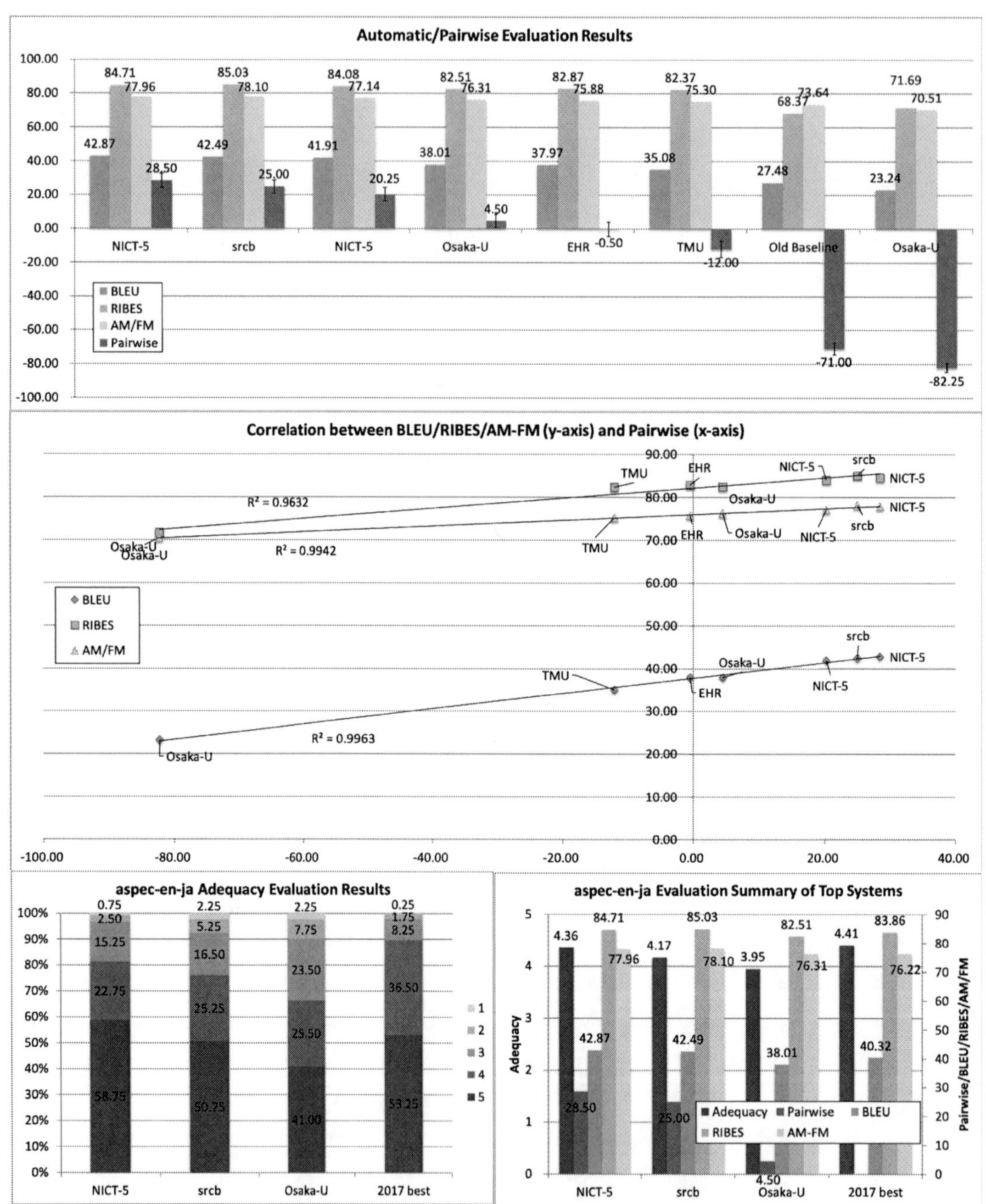

Figure 3: Official evaluation results of aspec-en-ja.

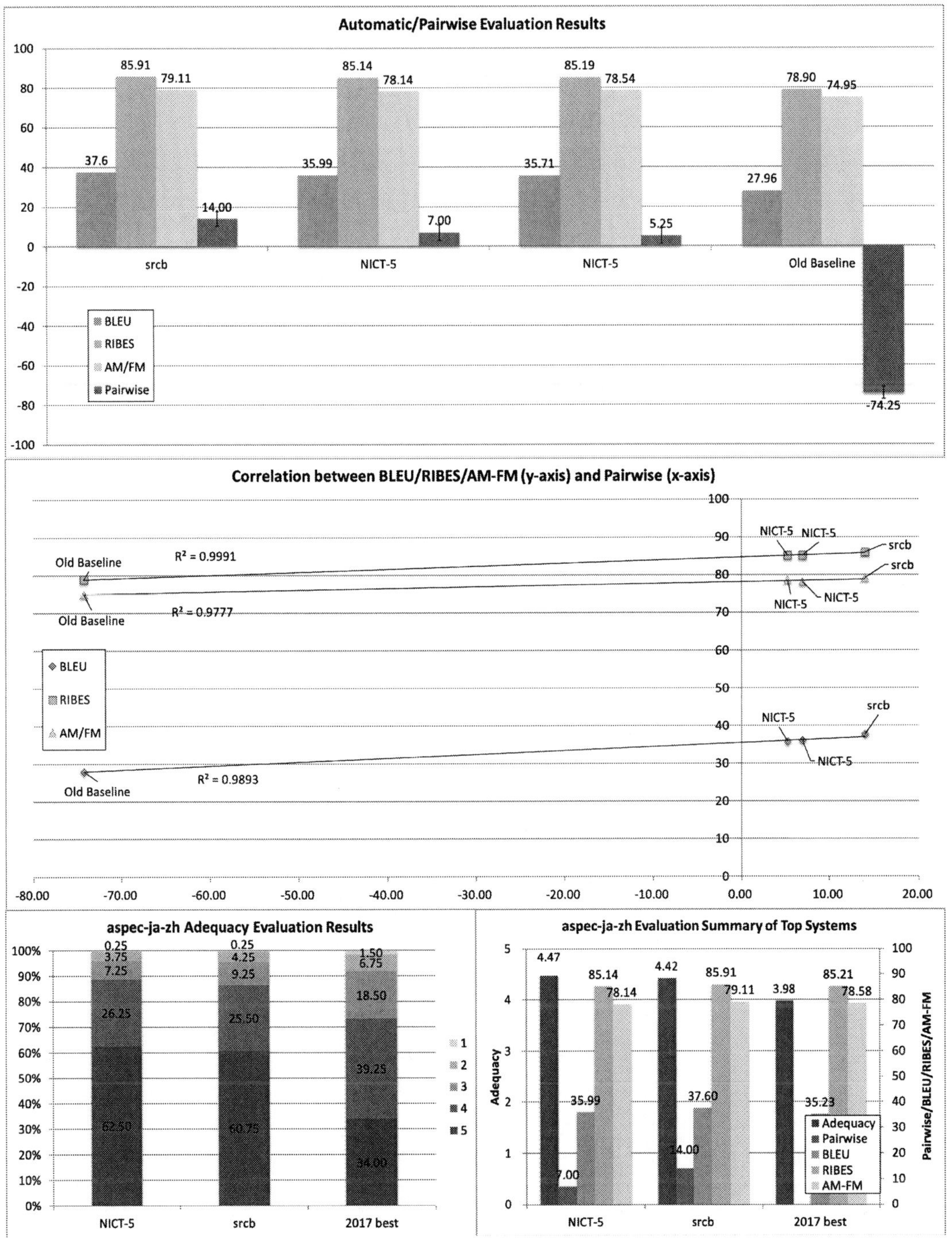

Figure 4: Official evaluation results of aspec-ja-zh.

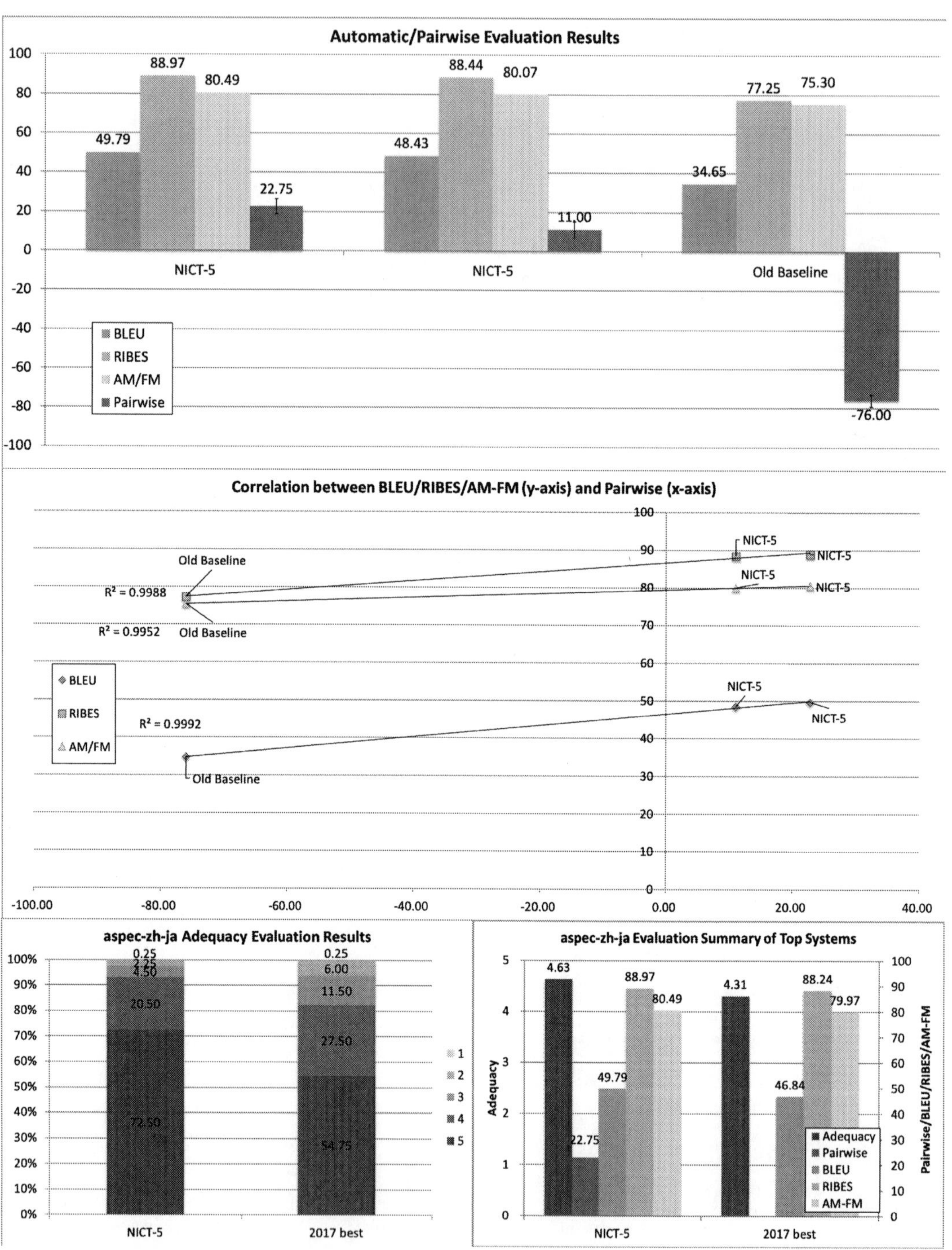

Figure 5: Official evaluation results of aspec-zh-ja.

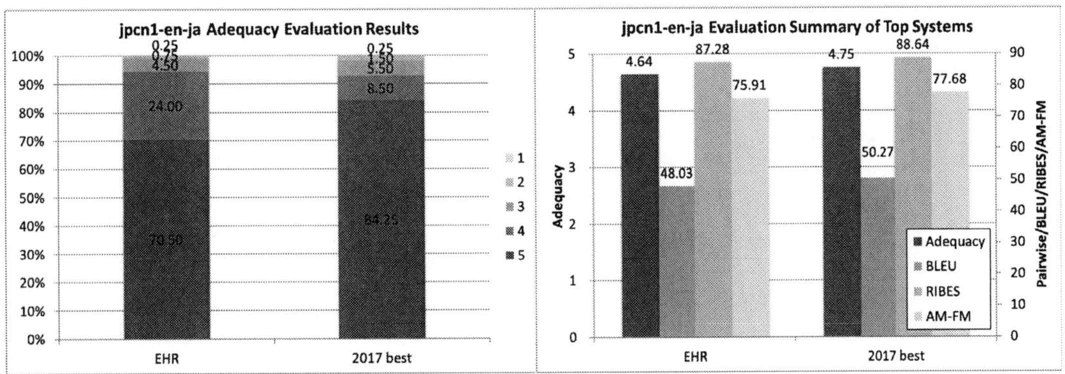

Figure 6: Official evaluation results of jpcn1-en-ja.

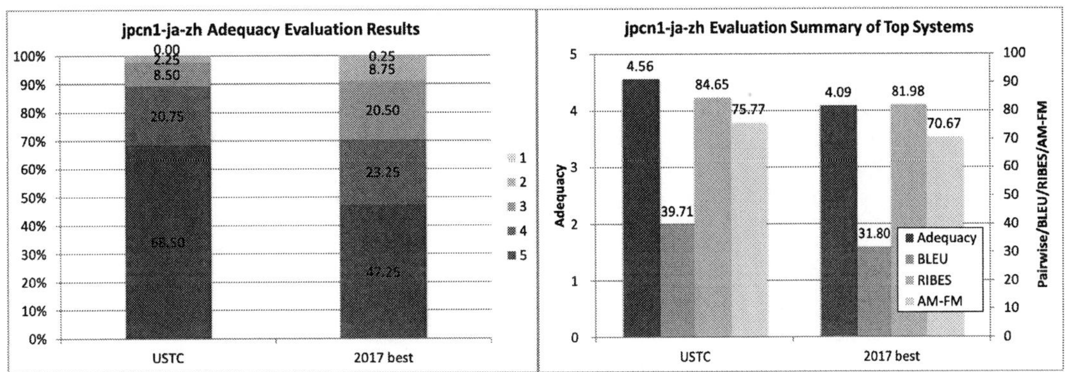

Figure 7: Official evaluation results of jpcn1-ja-zh.

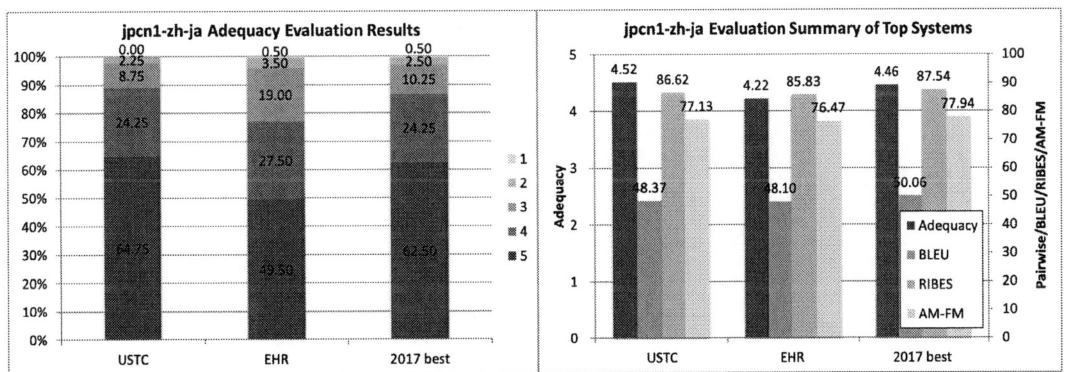

Figure 8: Official evaluation results of jpcn1-zh-ja.

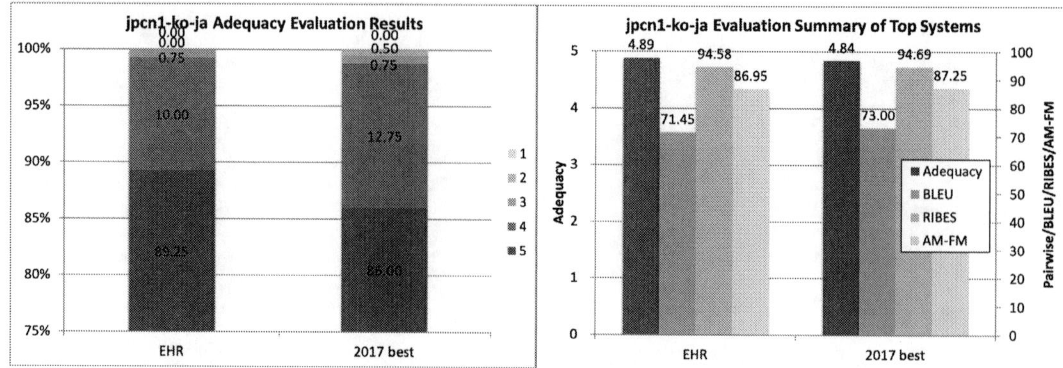

Figure 9: Official evaluation results of jpcn1-ko-ja.

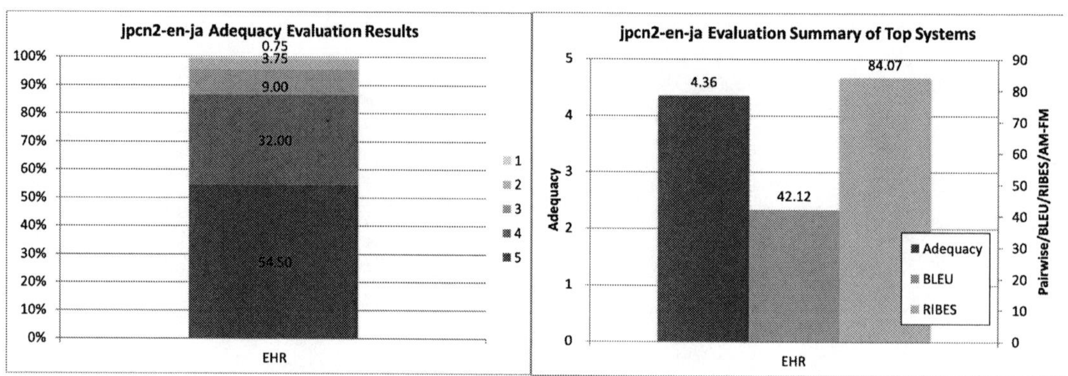

Figure 10: Official evaluation results of jpcn2-en-ja.

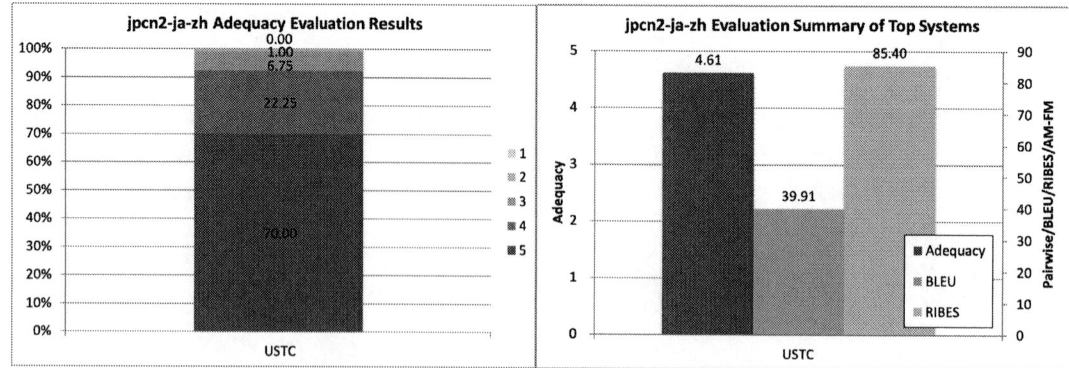

Figure 11: Official evaluation results of jpcn2-ja-zh.

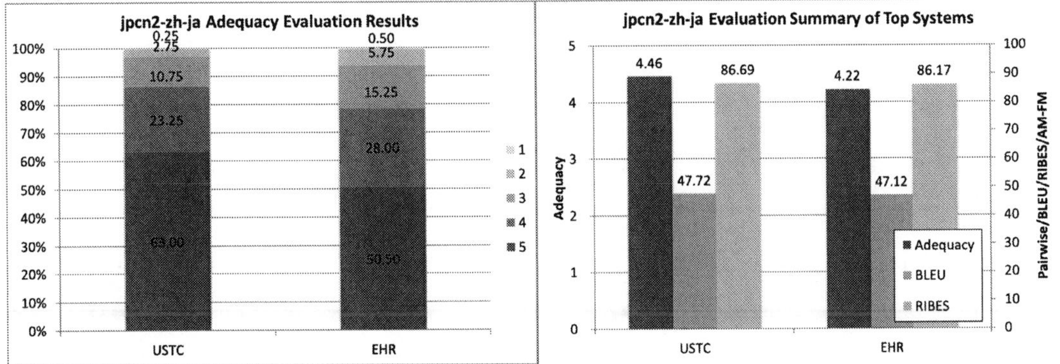

Figure 12: Official evaluation results of jpcn2-zh-ja.

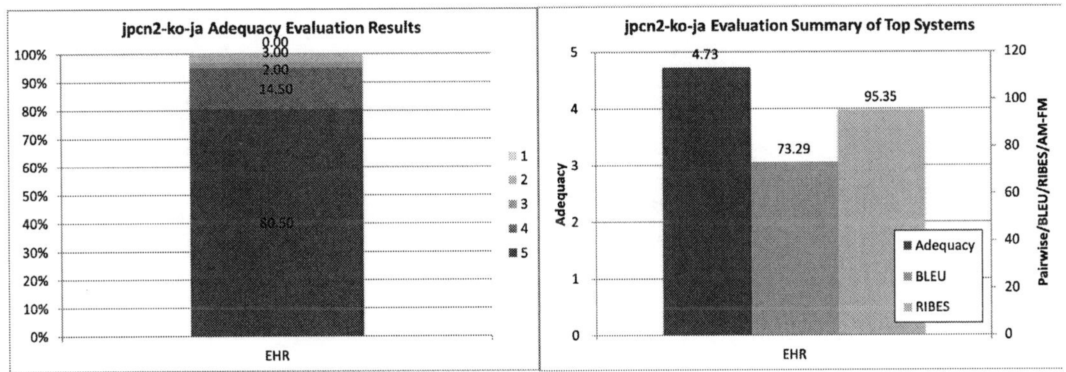

Figure 13: Official evaluation results of jpcn2-ko-ja.

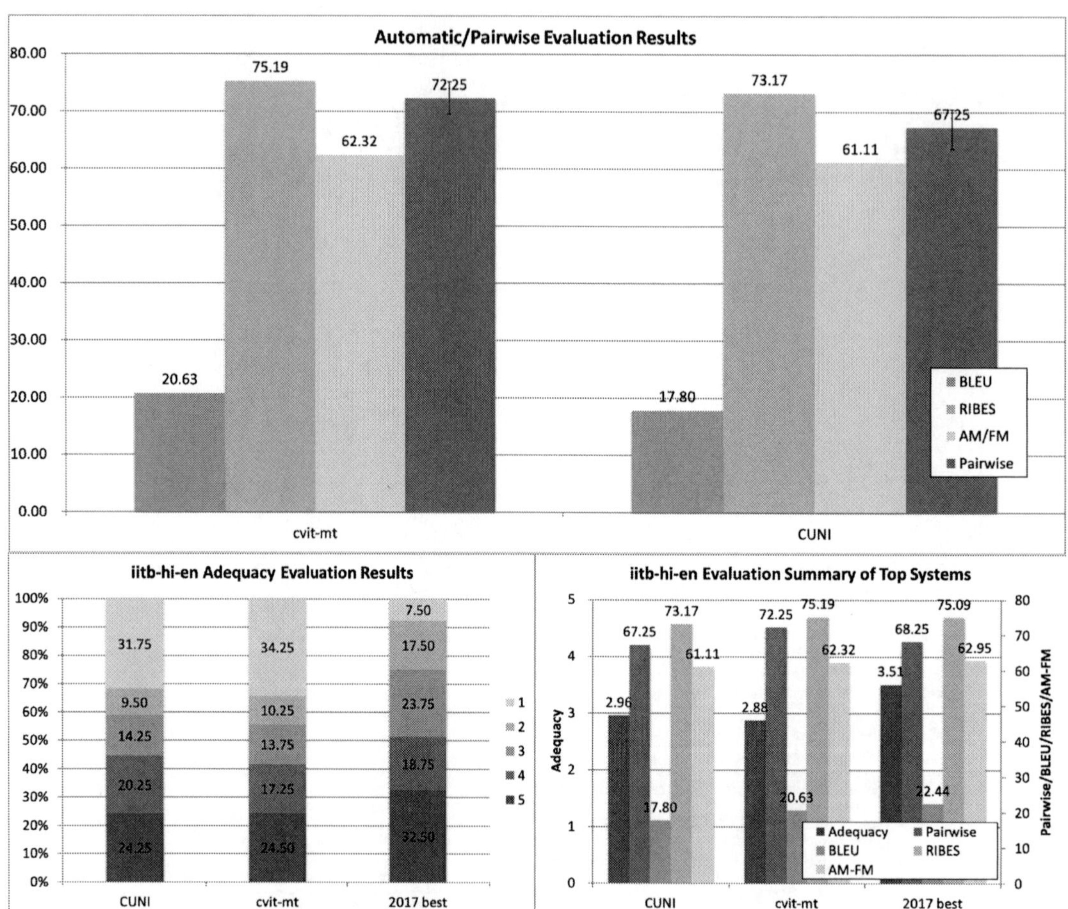

Figure 14: Official evaluation results of iitb-hi-en.

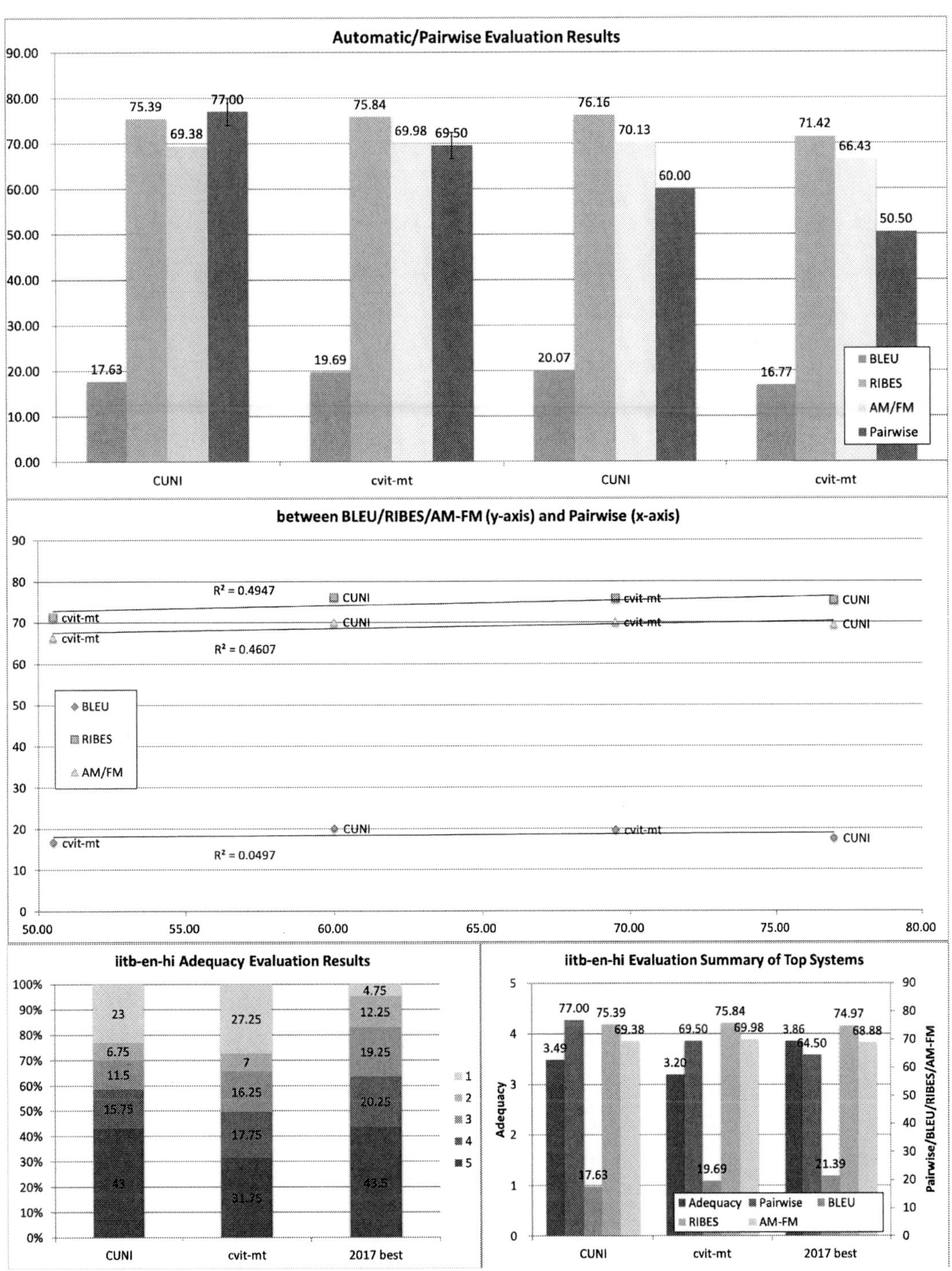

Figure 15: Official evaluation results of iitb-en-hi.

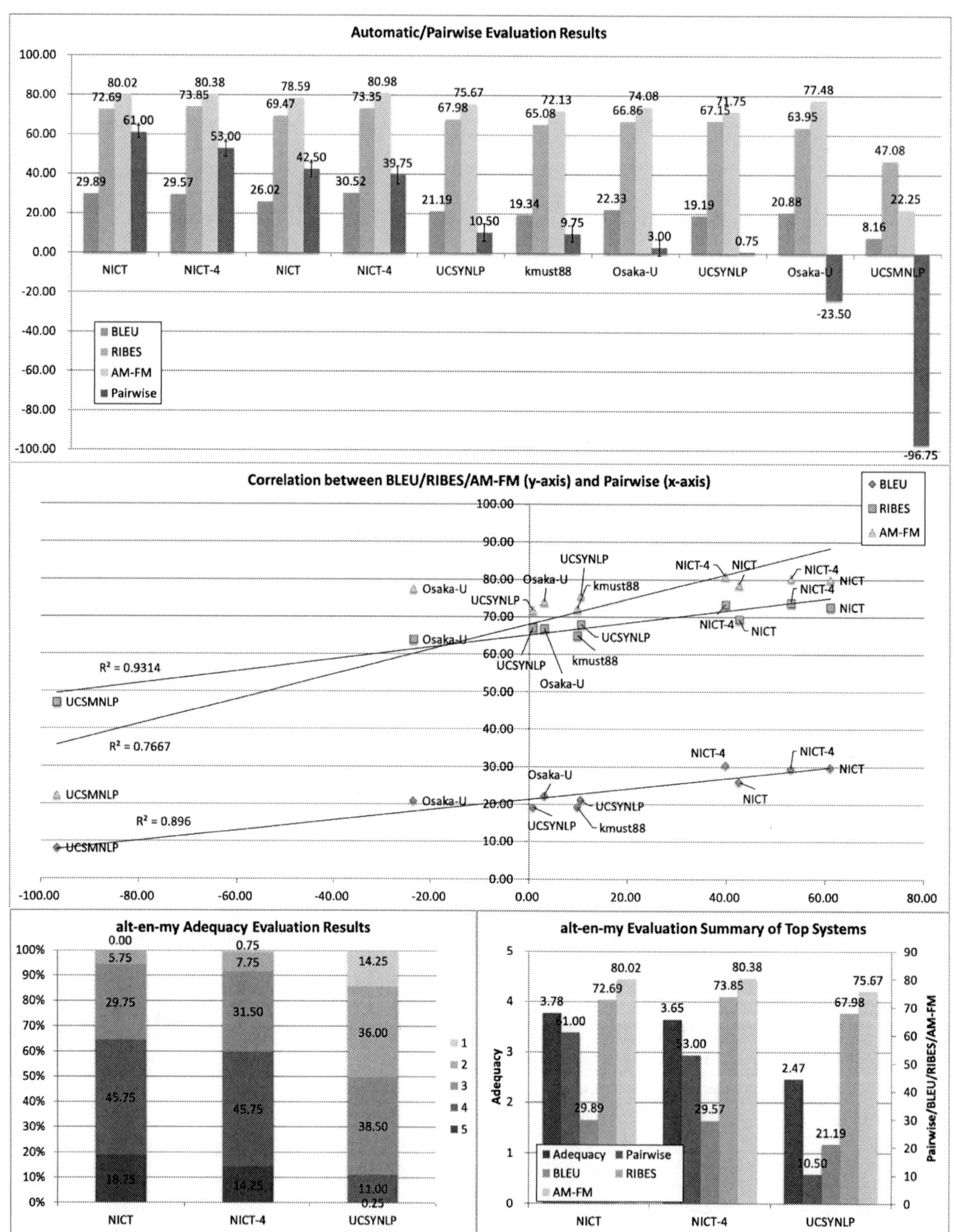

Figure 16: Official evaluation results of alt-en-my.

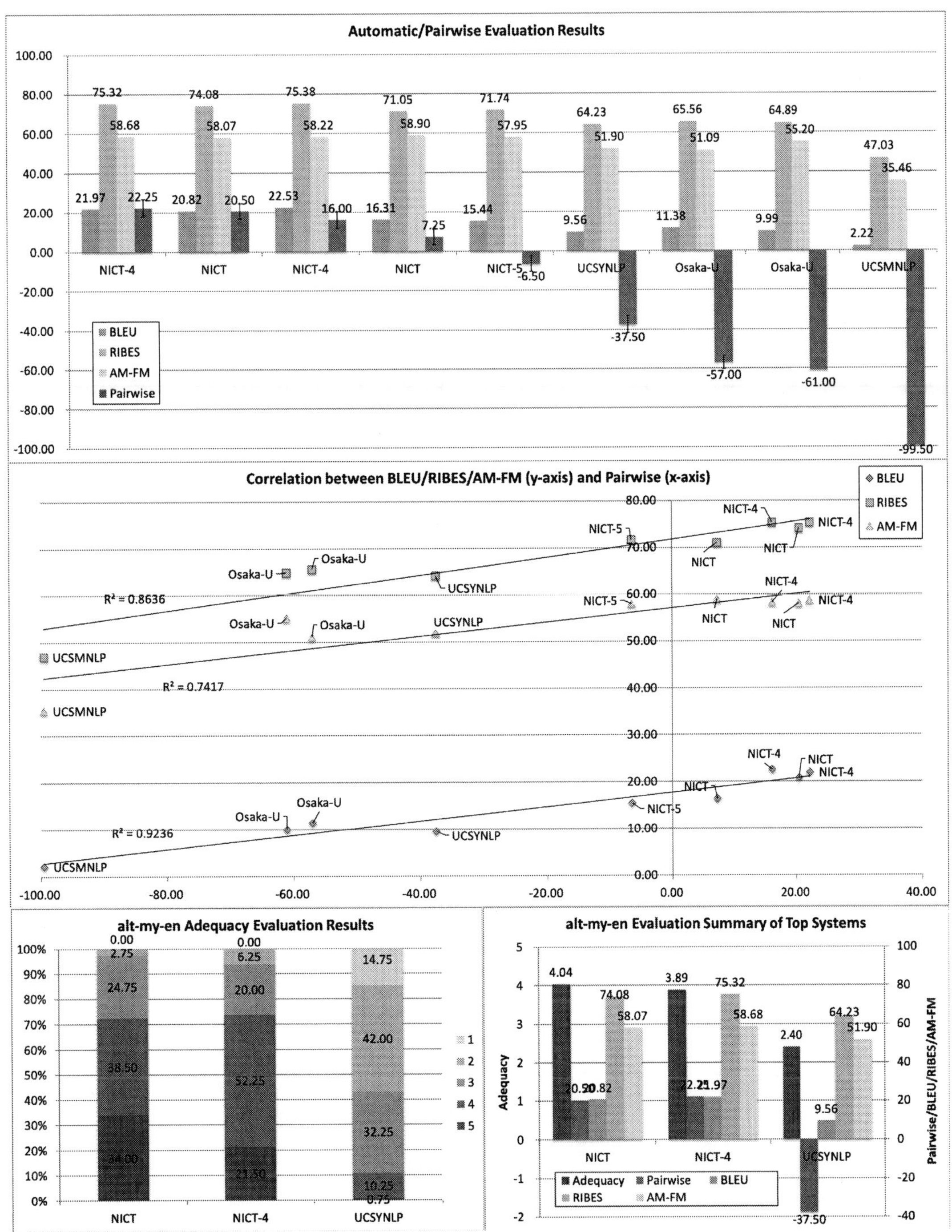

Figure 17: Official evaluation results of alt-my-en.

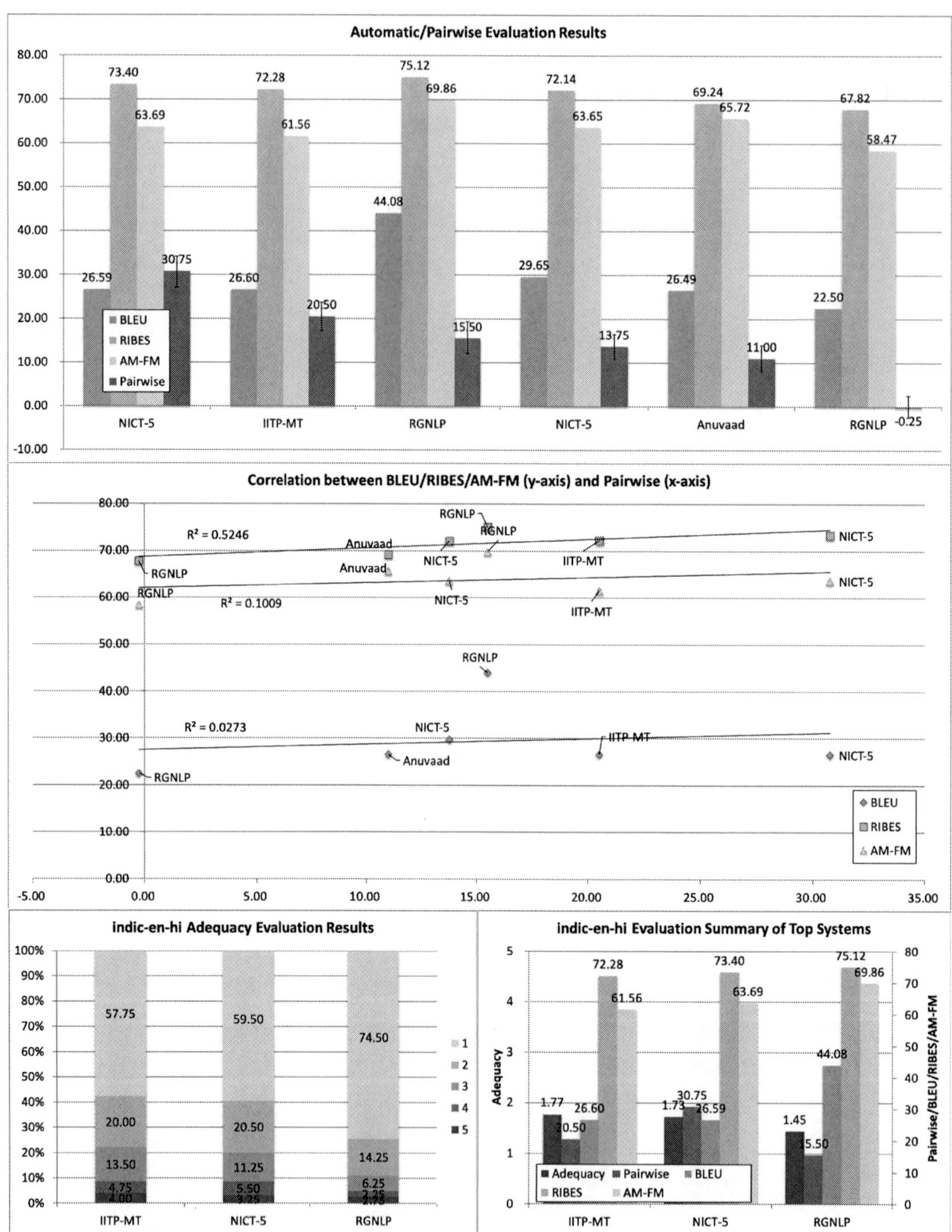

Figure 18: Official evaluation results of indic-en-hi.

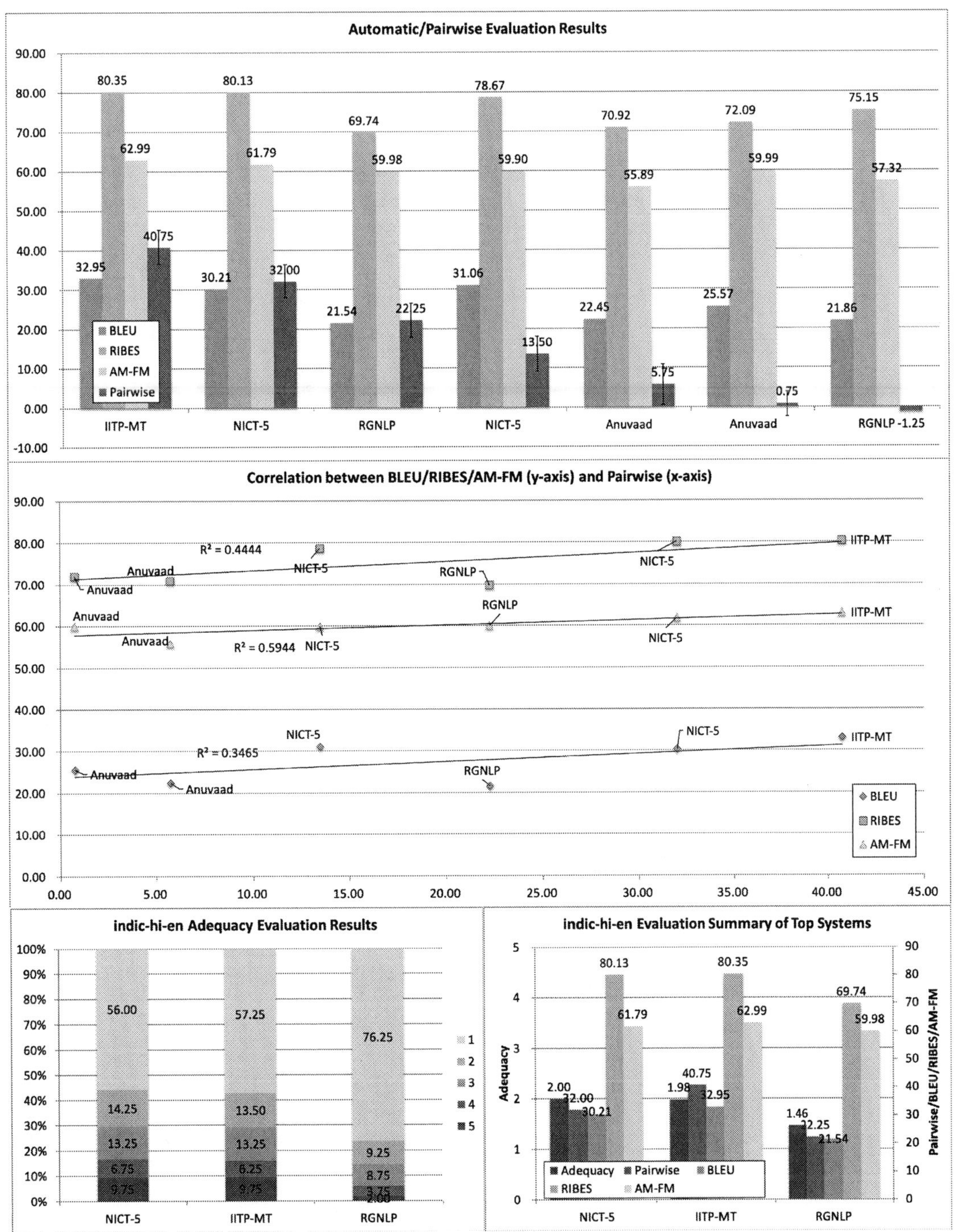

Figure 19: Official evaluation results of indic-hi-en.

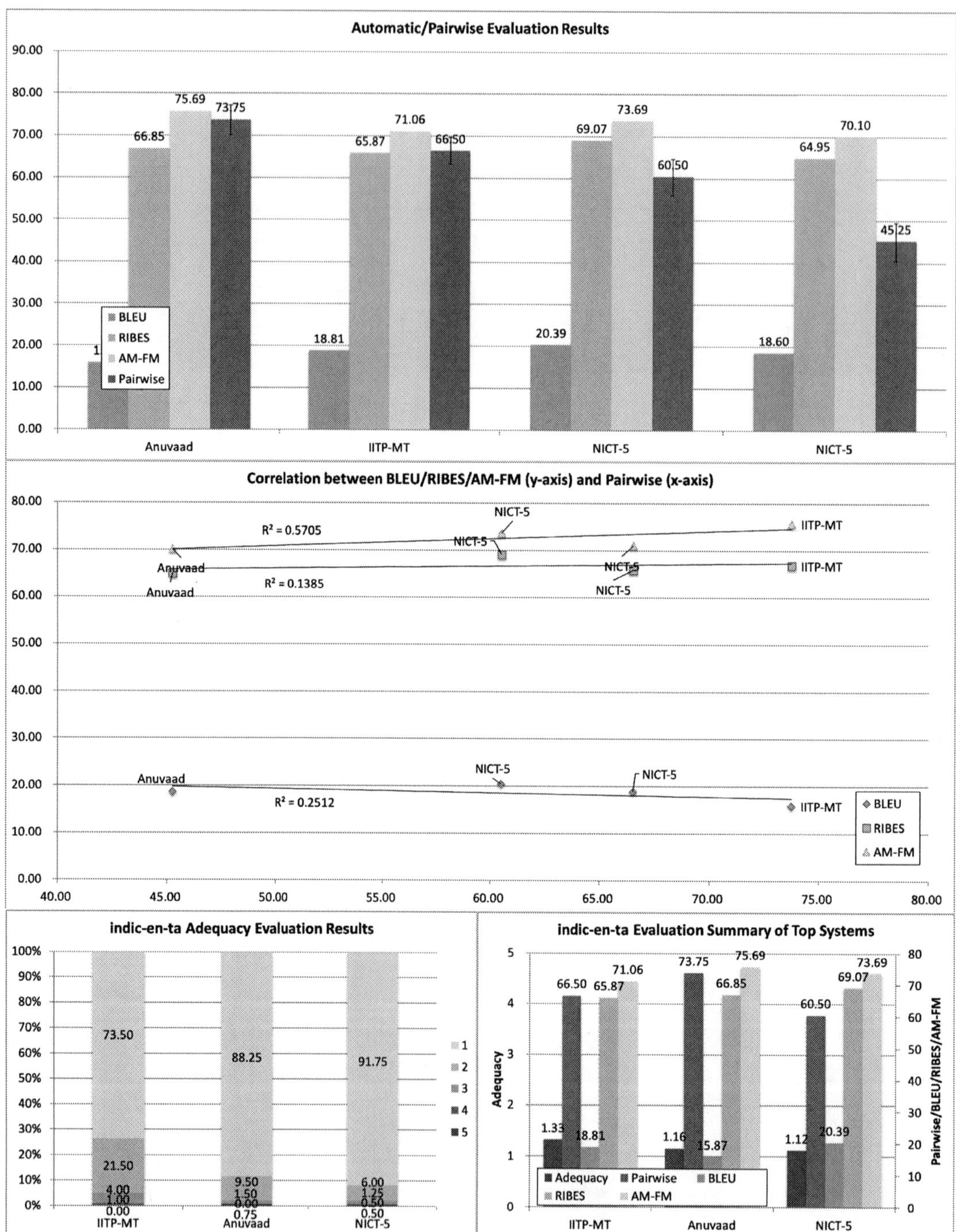

Figure 20: Official evaluation results of indic-en-ta.

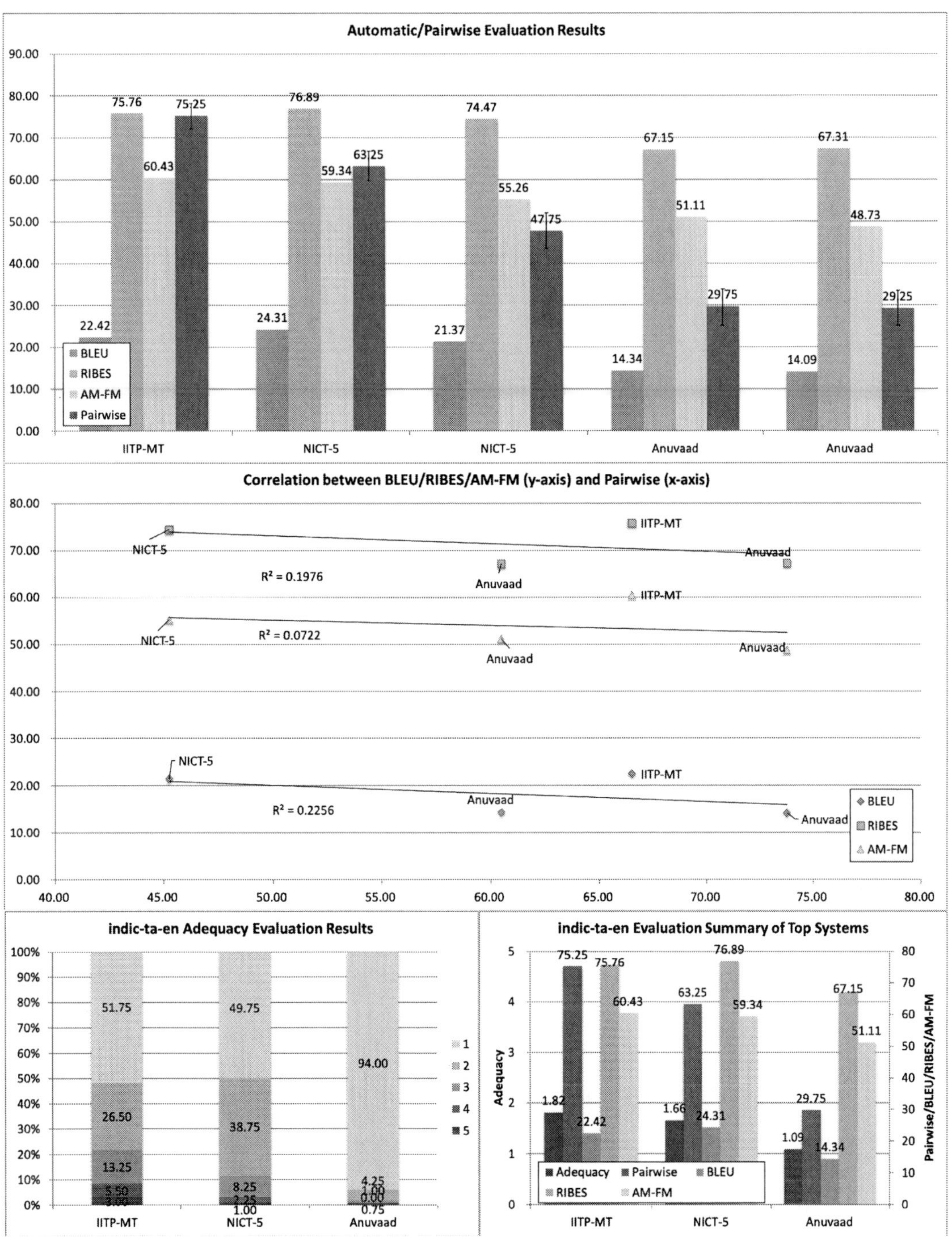

Figure 21: Official evaluation results of indic-ta-en.

Subtask	SYSTEM ID	DATA ID	Annotator A average	variance	Annotator B average	variance	all average	weighted κ	κ
aspec-ja-en	srcb	2474	4.37	0.49	4.63	0.44	4.50	0.15	0.25
	NICT-5	2174	4.37	0.61	4.60	0.51	4.49	0.26	0.32
	TMU	2464	3.94	0.91	3.92	1.41	3.94	0.34	0.48
	2017 best	1681	4.15	0.58	4.13	0.52	4.14	0.29	0.41
aspec-en-ja	NICT-5	2219	4.16	0.90	4.57	0.57	4.36	0.17	0.30
	srcb	2479	4.04	1.07	4.30	1.00	4.17	0.22	0.38
	Osaka-U	2439	3.74	1.34	4.17	0.88	3.95	0.25	0.42
	2017 best	1729	4.54	0.56	4.28	0.49	4.41	0.33	0.43
aspec-ja-zh	NICT-5	2266	4.67	0.32	4.27	0.90	4.47	0.28	0.36
	srcb	2473	4.69	0.30	4.16	0.98	4.42	0.19	0.24
	2017 best	1483	4.25	0.73	3.71	0.98	3.98	0.10	0.18
aspec-zh-ja	NICT-5	2267	4.78	0.26	4.48	0.67	4.63	0.31	0.33
	2017 best	1481	4.63	0.47	3.99	0.98	4.31	0.17	0.23
jpcn1-en-ja	EHR	2476	4.66	0.35	4.62	0.45	4.64	0.36	0.44
	2017 best	1454	4.74	0.45	4.76	0.38	4.75	0.32	0.48
jpcn1-ja-zh	USTC	2202	4.66	0.44	4.46	0.65	4.55	0.38	0.48
	2017 best	1465	3.99	1.12	4.19	0.94	4.09	0.22	0.32
jpcn1-zh-ja	USTC	2206	4.60	0.43	4.43	0.68	4.51	0.34	0.43
	EHR	2210	4.29	0.71	4.14	0.92	4.22	0.46	0.57
	2017 best	1484	4.41	0.68	4.51	0.64	4.46	0.26	0.34
jpcn1-ko-ja	EHR	2215	4.88	0.13	4.89	0.11	4.88	0.53	0.56
	2017 best	1448	4.82	0.24	4.87	0.11	4.84	0.55	0.55
jpcn2-en-ja	EHR	2477	4.32	0.72	4.40	0.73	4.36	0.35	0.50
jpcn2-ja-zh	USTC	2203	4.71	0.33	4.52	0.52	4.61	0.38	0.45
jpcn2-zh-ja	USTC	2207	4.54	0.48	4.38	0.82	4.46	0.42	0.56
	EHR	2211	4.37	0.65	4.08	1.07	4.22	0.33	0.46
jpcn2-ko-ja	EHR	2216	4.77	0.36	4.68	0.48	4.72	0.62	0.72
iitb-hi-en	CUNI	2381	2.96	2.55	2.96	2.52	2.96	0.48	0.76
	cvit-mt	2331	2.87	2.54	2.88	2.68	2.88	0.53	0.76
	2017 best	1511	3.43	1.64	3.60	1.74	3.51	0.22	0.45
iitb-en-hi	CUNI	2362	3.58	2.71	3.40	2.52	3.49	0.52	0.74
	cvit-mt	2254	3.21	2.58	3.18	2.56	3.20	0.64	0.81
	2017 best	1576	3.95	1.18	3.76	1.85	3.86	0.17	0.36
alt-en-my	NICT	2345	3.51	0.65	4.04	0.54	3.77	0.03	0.08
	NICT-4	2087	3.69	0.70	3.62	0.73	3.65	0.09	0.12
	UCSYNLP	2339	2.04	0.60	2.90	0.56	2.47	0.01	0.07
alt-my-en	NICT	2329	4.19	0.61	3.88	0.73	4.04	0.13	0.23
	NICT-4	2069	4.13	0.35	3.65	0.84	3.89	-0.00	0.07
	UCSYNLP	2332	2.09	0.66	2.71	0.71	2.40	0.06	0.18
indic-en-hi	IITP-MT	2354	1.92	1.35	1.63	1.03	1.77	0.27	0.48
	NICT-5	2128	1.88	1.23	1.57	1.02	1.73	0.29	0.57
	RGNLP	2417	1.46	0.82	1.44	0.86	1.45	0.48	0.67
indic-hi-en	NICT-5	2129	2.12	1.86	1.89	1.79	2.00	0.43	0.71
	IITP-MT	2347	2.02	1.91	1.94	1.75	1.98	0.43	0.67
	RGNLP	2367	1.46	0.92	1.47	0.86	1.46	0.54	0.75
indic-en-ta	IITP-MT	2356	1.36	0.42	1.28	0.29	1.32	0.33	0.43
	Anuvaad	2443	1.20	0.27	1.11	0.23	1.16	0.21	0.37
	NICT-5	2132	1.10	0.17	1.14	0.27	1.12	0.39	0.51
indic-ta-en	IITP-MT	2349	1.84	1.32	1.78	0.89	1.81	0.23	0.39
	NICT-5	2133	1.74	0.72	1.58	0.55	1.66	0.16	0.23
	Anuvaad	2400	1.15	0.33	1.03	0.05	1.09	0.10	0.14

Table 14: JPO adequacy evaluation results in detail.

	NICT-5 (2273)	srcb (2474)	TMU (2464)	Osaka-U (2440)	ORGANIZER (0006)	Osaka-U (2472)
NICT-5 (2174)	≫	≫	≫	≫	≫	≫
NICT-5 (2273)		≫	≫	≫	≫	≫
srcb (2474)			≫	≫	≫	≫
TMU (2464)				≫	≫	≫
Osaka-U (2440)					≫	≫
ORGANIZER (0006)						≫

	srcb (2479)	NICT-5 (2048)	Osaka-U (2439)	EHR (2245)	TMU (2469)	ORGANIZER (0005)	Osaka-U (2470)
NICT-5 (2219)	>	≫	≫	≫	≫	≫	≫
srcb (2479)		≫	≫	≫	≫	≫	≫
NICT-5 (2048)			≫	≫	≫	≫	≫
Osaka-U (2439)				≫	≫	≫	≫
EHR (2245)					≫	≫	≫
TMU (2469)						≫	≫
ORGANIZER (0005)							≫

Table 15: Statistical significance testing of the aspec-ja-en (left) and aspec-en-ja (right) Pairwise scores.

	NICT-5 (2266)	NICT-5 (2175)	ORGANIZER (0007)
srcb (2473)	≫	≫	≫
NICT-5 (2266)		-	≫
NICT-5 (2175)			≫

	NICT-5 (2052)	ORGANIZER (0008)
NICT-5 (2267)	≫	≫
NICT-5 (2052)		≫

Table 16: Statistical significance testing of the aspec-ja-zh (left) and aspec-zh-ja (right) Pairwise scores.

	cvit-mt (2254)	CUNI (2365)	cvit-mt (2251)
CUNI (2362)	≫	≫	≫
cvit-mt (2254)		≫	≫
CUNI (2365)			≫

	CUNI (2381)
cvit-mt (2331)	≫

Table 17: Statistical significance testing of the iitb-en-hi (left) and iitb-hi-en (right) Pairwise scores.

	NICT-4 (2087)	NICT (2282)	NICT-4 (2287)	UCSYNLP (2339)	kmust88 (2360)	Osaka-U (2437)	UCSYNLP (2340)	Osaka-U (2471)	UCSMNLP (2337)
NICT (2345)	>>>	>>>	>>>	>>>	>>>	>>>	>>>	>>>	>>>
NICT-4 (2087)		>>>	>>>	>>>	>>>	>>>	>>>	>>>	>>>
NICT (2282)			-	>>>	>>>	>>>	>>>	>>>	>>>
NICT-4 (2287)				>>>	>>>	>>>	>>>	>>>	>>>
UCSYNLP (2339)					-	>>>	>>>	>>>	>>>
kmust88 (2360)						>>>	>>>	>>>	>>>
Osaka-U (2437)							-	>>>	>>>
UCSYNLP (2340)								>>>	>>>
Osaka-U (2471)									>>>

	NICT (2329)	NICT-4 (2290)	NICT (2281)	NICT-5 (2056)	UCSYNLP (2332)	Osaka-U (2438)	Osaka-U (2463)	UCSMNLP (2338)
NICT-4 (2069)	-	>>	>>>	>>>	>>>	>>>	>>>	>>>
NICT (2329)		>	>>>	>>>	>>>	>>>	>>>	>>>
NICT-4 (2290)			>>>	>>>	>>>	>>>	>>>	>>>
NICT (2281)				>>>	>>>	>>>	>>>	>>>
NICT-5 (2056)					>>>	>>>	>>>	>>>
UCSYNLP (2332)						>>>	>>>	>>>
Osaka-U (2438)							>>	>>>
Osaka-U (2463)								>>>

Table 18: Statistical significance testing of the alt-en-my (left) and alt-my-en (right) Pairwise scores.

	IITP-MT (2354)	RGNLP (2417)	NICT-5 (2067)	Anuvaad (2445)	RGNLP (2422)
NICT-5 (2128)	>>>	>>>	>>>	>>>	>>>
IITP-MT (2354)		>>	>>>	>>>	>>>
RGNLP (2417)			-	>>	>>>
NICT-5 (2067)				>	>>>
Anuvaad (2445)					>>>

	NICT-5 (2129)	RGNLP (2367)	NICT-5 (2066)	Anuvaad (2406)	Anuvaad (2403)	RGNLP (2383)
IITP-MT (2347)	>>>	>>>	>>>	>>>	>>>	>>>
NICT-5 (2129)		>>>	>>>	>>>	>>>	>>>
RGNLP (2367)			>>>	>>>	>>>	>>>
NICT-5 (2066)				>>>	>>>	>>>
Anuvaad (2406)					>>	>>>
Anuvaad (2403)						-

Table 19: Statistical significance testing of the indic-en-hi (left) and indic-hi-en (right) Pairwise scores.

	IITP-MT (2356)	NICT-5 (2132)	NICT-5 (2109)
Anuvaad (2443)	>>>	>>>	>>>
IITP-MT (2356)		>>>	>>>
NICT-5 (2132)			>>>

	NICT-5 (2133)	NICT-5 (2111)	Anuvaad (2400)	Anuvaad (2408)
IITP-MT (2349)	>>>	>>>	>>>	>>>
NICT-5 (2133)		>>>	>>>	>>>
NICT-5 (2111)			>>>	>>>
Anuvaad (2400)				-

Table 20: Statistical significance testing of the indic-en-ta (left) and indic-ta-en (right) Pairwise scores.

aspec-ja-en

SYSTEM	DATA	κ
ORGANIZER	0006	0.216
TMU	2464	0.201
srcb	2474	0.183
Osaka-U	2440	0.128
Osaka-U	2472	0.130
NICT-5	2174	0.182
NICT-5	2273	0.145
ave.		0.169

aspec-en-ja

SYSTEM	DATA	κ
ORGANIZER	0005	0.394
TMU	2469	0.450
EHR	2245	0.314
srcb	2479	0.325
Osaka-U	2439	0.302
Osaka-U	2470	0.305
NICT-5	2048	0.324
NICT-5	2219	0.256
ave.		0.334

aspec-ja-zh

SYSTEM	DATA	κ
ORGANIZER	0007	0.254
srcb	2473	0.150
NICT-5	2175	0.162
NICT-5	2266	0.174
ave.		0.185

aspec-zh-ja

SYSTEM	DATA	κ
ORGANIZER	0008	0.389
NICT-5	2052	0.266
NICT-5	2267	0.282
ave.		0.312

iitb-en-hi

SYSTEM	DATA	κ
CUNI	2362	0.358
CUNI	2365	0.454
cvit-mt	2251	0.447
cvit-mt	2254	0.356
ave.		0.404

iitb-hi-en

SYSTEM	DATA	κ
CUNI	2381	0.404
cvit-mt	2331	0.381
ave.		0.393

alt-en-my

SYSTEM	DATA	κ
NICT	2282	0.181
NICT	2345	0.091
Osaka-U	2437	0.061
Osaka-U	2471	0.187
NICT-4	2087	0.205
NICT-4	2287	0.262
UCSYNLP	2339	0.268
UCSYNLP	2340	0.303
UCSMNLP	2337	0.212
kmust88	2360	0.275
ave.		0.205

alt-my-en

SYSTEM	DATA	κ
NICT	2281	0.107
NICT	2329	0.202
Osaka-U	2438	0.153
Osaka-U	2463	0.161
NICT-4	2069	0.284
NICT-4	2290	0.122
NICT-5	2056	0.072
UCSYNLP	2332	0.068
UCSMNLP	2338	0.087
ave.		0.140

indic-en-hi

SYSTEM	DATA	κ
IITP-MT	2354	0.330
RGNLP	2417	0.386
RGNLP	2422	0.417
NICT-5	2067	0.447
NICT-5	2128	0.341
Anuvaad	2445	0.437
ave.		0.393

indic-hi-en

SYSTEM	DATA	κ
IITP-MT	2347	0.204
RGNLP	2367	0.252
RGNLP	2383	0.411
NICT-5	2066	0.327
NICT-5	2129	0.263
Anuvaad	2403	0.441
Anuvaad	2406	0.281
ave.		0.311

indic-en-ta

SYSTEM	DATA	κ
IITP-MT	2356	0.209
NICT-5	2109	0.373
NICT-5	2132	0.443
Anuvaad	2443	0.308
ave.		0.333

indic-ta-en

SYSTEM	DATA	κ
IITP-MT	2349	0.299
NICT-5	2111	0.256
NICT-5	2133	0.185
Anuvaad	2400	0.159
Anuvaad	2408	0.139
ave.		0.208

Table 21: The Fleiss' kappa values for the pairwise evaluation results.

System	ID	Type	RSRC	BLEU			RIBES			AMFM			Pair	Adeq
				juman	kytea	mecab	juman	kytea	mecab	juman	kytea	mecab		
NMT	1900	NMT	NO	36.37	38.48	37.15	0.824985	0.831183	0.833207	0.759910	0.759910	0.759910	–	–
NICT-5 (1)	2219	NMT	NO	42.87	44.42	43.49	0.847134	0.849399	0.853634	0.779560	0.779560	0.779560	+28.50	4.36
srcb	2479	NMT	NO	42.49	44.11	43.20	0.850318	0.852209	0.857017	0.781000	0.781000	0.781000	+25.00	4.17
NICT-5 (2)	2048	NMT	NO	41.91	43.50	42.60	0.840776	0.845042	0.849326	0.771400	0.771400	0.771400	+20.25	–
Osaka-U (1)	2439	NMT	YES	38.01	40.00	39.10	0.825061	0.829328	0.833200	0.763140	0.763140	0.763140	+4.50	3.95
EHR	2245	NMT	NO	37.97	40.00	38.66	0.828746	0.833333	0.837806	0.758750	0.758750	0.758750	-0.50	–
TMU	2469	NMT	NO	35.08	37.69	36.14	0.823653	0.829156	0.831219	0.753040	0.753040	0.753040	-12.00	–
Osaka-U (2)	2470	SMT	NO	23.24	25.50	24.26	0.716889	0.726469	0.729323	0.705050	0.705050	0.705050	-82.25	–

Table 22: ASPEC en-ja submissions

System	ID	Type	RSRC	BLEU	RIBES	AMFM	Pair	Adeq
NMT	1901	NMT	NO	26.91	0.764968	0.595370	–	–
NICT-5 (1)	2174	NMT	NO	28.63	0.765933	0.608070	+15.75	4.49
NICT-5 (2)	2273	NMT	NO	29.65	0.774788	0.612060	+11.50	–
srcb	2474	NMT	NO	30.59	0.777896	0.619390	+5.75	4.50
TMU	2464	NMT	NO	25.85	0.761450	0.600730	-20.00	3.94
Osaka-U (1)	2440	NMT	YES	26.19	0.749825	0.588290	-37.00	–
Osaka-U (2)	2472	SMT	NO	13.97	0.665391	0.571400	-95.75	–

Table 23: ASPEC ja-en submissions

System	ID	Type	RSRC	BLEU			RIBES			AMFM			Pair	Adeq
				juman	kytea	mecab	juman	kytea	mecab	juman	kytea	mecab		
NMT	1902	NMT	NO	43.31	43.53	43.34	0.870734	0.866281	0.870886	0.782100	0.782100	0.782100	–	–
NICT-5 (1)	2267	NMT	NO	49.79	50.66	49.89	0.889674	0.886490	0.889853	0.804920	0.804920	0.804920	+22.75	4.63
NICT-5 (2)	2052	NMT	NO	48.43	48.78	48.52	0.884426	0.879456	0.884782	0.800670	0.800670	0.800670	+11.00	–

Table 24: ASPEC zh-ja submissions

System	ID	Type	RSRC	BLEU			RIBES			AMFM			Pair	Adeq
				kytea	stanford (ctb)	stanford (pku)	kytea	stanford (ctb)	stanford (pku)	kytea	stanford (ctb)	stanford (pku)		
NMT	1903	NMT	NO	33.26	33.33	33.14	0.844322	0.844572	0.844959	0.777600	0.777600	0.777600	–	–
srcb	2473	NMT	NO	37.60	37.34	37.35	0.859132	0.858042	0.858162	0.791120	0.791120	0.791120	+14.00	4.42
NICT-5 (1)	2266	NMT	NO	35.99	35.89	35.87	0.851382	0.851416	0.850944	0.781410	0.781410	0.781410	+7.00	4.47
NICT-5 (2)	2175	NMT	NO	35.71	35.67	35.55	0.851890	0.850699	0.850580	0.785440	0.785440	0.785440	+5.25	–

Table 25: ASPEC ja-zh submissions

Task	System	ID	Type	RSRC	BLEU			RIBES			AMFM			Adeq
					juman	kytea	mecab	juman	kytea	mecab	juman	kytea	mecab	
N1	NMT	1964	NMT	NO	43.84	45.28	43.70	0.860702	0.857422	0.859818	0.744270	0.744270	0.744270	–
	EHR	2476	NMT	YES	48.03	49.24	47.86	0.872828	0.870332	0.872442	0.759120	0.759120	0.759120	4.76
N2	NMT	1936	NMT	NO	38.51	40.60	38.47	0.825565	0.824420	0.824770	–	–	–	–
	EHR	2477	NMT	YES	42.12	43.76	42.06	0.840713	0.839052	0.841133	–	–	–	4.36

Table 26: JPC N1/N2 en-ja submissions

Task	System	ID	Type	RSRC	BLEU			RIBES			AMFM			Adeq
					juman	kytea	mecab	juman	kytea	mecab	juman	kytea	mecab	
N1	NMT	1966	NMT	NO	71.42	72.21	71.68	0.945593	0.944644	0.945126	0.868760	0.868760	0.868760	–
	EHR	2215	NMT	NO	71.45	72.35	71.74	0.945771	0.944284	0.945497	0.869540	0.869540	0.869540	4.89
N2	NMT	1947	NMT	NO	70.65	71.46	70.94	0.942943	0.942543	0.943101	–	–	–	–
	EHR	2216	NMT	NO	73.29	74.25	73.61	0.953524	0.952935	0.953640	–	–	–	4.73

Table 27: JPC N1/N2 ko-ja submissions

Task	System	ID	Type	RSRC	BLEU			RIBES			AMFM			Adeq
					juman	kytea	mecab	juman	kytea	mecab	juman	kytea	mecab	
N1	NMT	1963	NMT	NO	46.32	46.73	46.11	0.857318	0.855085	0.856442	0.761820	0.761820	0.761820	
	USTC	2206	NMT	NO	48.37	49.78	48.57	0.866232	0.864284	0.865423	0.771310	0.771310	0.771310	4.52
	EHR	2210	NMT	NO	48.10	48.51	47.96	0.858259	0.855649	0.858142	0.764670	0.764670	0.764670	4.22
N2	NMT	1941	NMT	NO	45.33	46.05	45.49	0.857120	0.854593	0.857052	–	–	–	–
	USTC	2207	NMT	NO	47.72	49.45	48.24	0.866873	0.865270	0.866705	–	–	–	4.46
	EHR	2211	NMT	NO	47.12	47.71	47.14	0.861697	0.859213	0.861437	–	–	–	4.22

Table 28: JPC N1/N2 zh-ja submissions

Task	System	ID	Type	RSRC	BLEU			RIBES			AMFM			Adeq
					kytea	stanford (ctb)	stanford (pku)	kytea	stanford (ctb)	stanford (pku)	kytea	stanford (ctb)	stanford (pku)	
N1	NMT	1960	NMT	NO	39.07	40.32	39.75	0.847112	0.850851	0.850913	0.752360	0.752360	0.752360	–
	USTC	2202	NMT	NO	39.71	40.54	40.05	0.846472	0.850750	0.849818	0.757690	0.757690	0.757690	4.56
N2	NMT	1961	NMT	NO	39.14	40.28	39.77	0.847486	0.852161	0.850707	–	–	–	–
	USTC	2203	NMT	NO	39.91	40.53	40.32	0.853978	0.859330	0.857456	–	–	–	4.61

Table 29: JPC N1/N2 ja-zh submissions

System	ID	Type	RSRC	BLEU	RIBES	AMFM	Pair	Adeq
NMT	2566	NMT	NO	13.76	0.710210	0.644860	–	–
CUNI (1)	2362	NMT	NO	17.63	0.753895	0.693830	+77.00	3.49
cvit-mt (1)	2254	NMT	YES	19.69	0.758365	0.699810	+69.50	3.20
CUNI (2)	2365	NMT	NO	20.07	0.761582	0.701300	+60.00	–
cvit-mt (2)	2251	NMT	NO	16.77	0.714197	0.664330	+50.50	–

Table 30: IITB en-hi submissions

System	ID	Type	RSRC	BLEU	RIBES	AMFM	Pair	Adeq
NMT	2567	NMT	NO	15.44	0.718751	0.586360	–	–
cvit-mt	2331	NMT	YES	20.63	0.751883	0.623240	+72.25	2.88
CUNI	2381	NMT	NO	17.80	0.731727	0.611090	+67.25	2.96

Table 31: IITB hi-en submissions

System	ID	Type	RSRC	BLEU	RIBES	AMFM	Pair	Adeq
Online-A	2142	Other	YES	20.31	0.678360	0.587120	–	–
Online-A (comma→0x104a)	2143	Other	YES	20.83	0.679968	0.594230	–	–
NMT	2227	NMT	NO	22.42	0.667437	0.745550	–	–
NICT (1)	2345	NMT	NO	29.89	0.726922	0.800230	+61.00	3.78
NICT-4 (1)	2087	NMT	NO	29.57	0.738538	0.803810	+53.00	3.65
NICT (2)	2282	NMT	NO	26.02	0.694652	0.785920	+42.50	–
NICT-4 (2)	2287	Other	NO	30.52	0.733501	0.809750	+39.75	–
UCSYNLP (1)	2339	NMT	NO	21.19	0.679800	0.756710	+10.50	2.47
kmust88	2360	NMT	NO	19.34	0.650796	0.721280	+9.75	–
Osaka-U (1)	2437	NMT	YES	22.33	0.668596	0.740760	+3.00	–
UCSYNLP (2)	2340	NMT	NO	19.19	0.671461	0.717480	+0.75	–
Osaka-U (2)	2471	SMT	NO	20.88	0.639517	0.774750	-23.50	–
UCSMNLP	2337	SMT	NO	8.16	0.470758	0.222510	-96.75	–

Table 32: ALT en-my submissions

System	ID	Type	RSRC	BLEU	RIBES	AMFM	Pair	Adeq
Online A	2141	Other	YES	14.24	0.598345	0.576780	–	–
NMT	2228	NMT	NO	14.44	0.696861	0.525950	–	–
NICT-4 (1)	2069	NMT	NO	21.97	0.753209	0.586770	+22.25	3.89
NICT (1)	2329	NMT	NO	20.82	0.740819	0.580690	+20.50	4.04
NICT-4 (2)	2290	Other	NO	22.53	0.753767	0.582230	+16.00	–
NICT (2)	2281	NMT	NO	16.31	0.710528	0.589020	+7.25	–
NICT-5	2056	NMT	NO	15.44	0.717430	0.579520	-6.50	–
UCSYNLP	2332	NMT	NO	9.56	0.642309	0.518990	-37.50	2.40
Osaka-U (1)	2438	NMT	YES	11.38	0.655643	0.510900	-57.00	–
Osaka-U (2)	2463	NMT	NO	9.99	0.648923	0.552040	-61.00	–
UCSMNLP	2338	SMT	NO	2.22	0.470280	0.354550	-99.50	–

Table 33: ALT my-en submissions

System	ID	Type	RSRC	BLEU	RIBES	AMFM	Pair	Adeq
NMT	2003	NMT	NO	20.78	0.682944	0.574960	–	–
NMT O2M	2146	NMT	NO	23.27	0.709586	0.601800	–	–
NMT M2M	2188	NMT	NO	22.24	0.705747	0.604040	–	–
NICT-5 (1)	2128	NMT	NO	26.59	0.734027	0.636900	+30.75	1.73
IITP-MT	2354	NMT	NO	26.60	0.722756	0.615620	+20.50	1.77
RGNLP (1)	2417	SMT	NO	44.08	0.751187	0.698550	+15.50	1.45
NICT-5 (2)	2067	NMT	NO	29.65	0.721379	0.636500	+13.75	–
Anuvaad	2445	SMT	NO	26.49	0.692385	0.657180	+11.00	–
RGNLP (2)	2422	NMT	NO	22.50	0.678207	0.584720	-0.25	–

Table 34: Indic en-hi submissions

System	ID	Type	RSRC	BLEU	RIBES	AMFM	Pair	Adeq
NMT	2004	NMT	NO	21.15	0.752783	0.559420	–	–
NMT M2O	2099	NMT	NO	26.71	0.787645	0.586760	–	–
NMT M2M	2189	NMT	NO	26.55	0.784968	0.577010	–	–
IITP-MT	2347	NMT	NO	32.95	0.803497	0.629890	+40.75	1.98
NICT-5 (1)	2129	NMT	NO	30.21	0.801291	0.617860	+32.00	2.00
RGNLP (1)	2367	SMT	NO	21.54	0.697379	0.599760	+22.25	1.46
NICT-5 (2)	2066	NMT	NO	31.06	0.786655	0.599000	+13.50	–
Anuvaad (1)	2406	SMT	NO	22.45	0.709235	0.558850	+5.75	–
Anuvaad (2)	2403	SMT	NO	25.57	0.720866	0.599880	+0.75	–
RGNLP (2)	2383	NMT	NO	21.86	0.751517	0.573160	-1.25	–

Table 35: Indic hi-en submissions

System	ID	Type	RSRC	BLEU	RIBES	AMFM	Pair	Adeq
NMT	2007	NMT	NO	7.12	0.457948	0.545370	–	–
NMT O2M	2148	NMT	NO	16.05	0.651935	0.706760	–	–
NMT M2M	2192	NMT	NO	15.41	0.664354	0.711080	–	–
Anuvaad	2443	SMT	NO	15.87	0.668548	0.756890	+73.75	1.16
IITP-MT	2356	NMT	NO	18.81	0.658740	0.710610	+66.50	1.33
NICT-5 (1)	2132	NMT	NO	20.39	0.690652	0.736930	+60.50	1.12
NICT-5 (2)	2109	NMT	NO	18.60	0.649454	0.700960	+45.25	–

Table 36: Indic en-ta submissions

System	ID	Type	RSRC	BLEU	RIBES	AMFM	Pair	Adeq
NMT	2008	NMT	NO	9.14	0.649417	0.488060	–	–
NMT M2O	2101	NMT	NO	19.71	0.751277	0.568020	–	–
NMT M2M	2193	NMT	NO	18.59	0.744884	0.561550	–	–
IITP-MT	2349	NMT	NO	22.42	0.757610	0.604300	+75.25	1.82
NICT-5 (1)	2133	NMT	NO	24.31	0.768865	0.593410	+63.25	1.66
NICT-5 (2)	2111	SMT	NO	21.37	0.744744	0.552630	+47.75	–
Anuvaad (1)	2400	SMT	NO	14.34	0.671535	0.511130	+29.75	1.09
Anuvaad (2)	2408	SMT	NO	14.09	0.673058	0.487250	+29.25	–

Table 37: Indic ta-en submissions

References

Rafael E. Banchs, Luis F. D'Haro, and Haizhou Li. 2015. Adequacy-fluency metrics: Evaluating mt in the continuous space model framework. *IEEE/ACM Trans. Audio, Speech and Lang. Proc.*, 23(3):472–482, March.

Tamali Banerjee, Anoop Kunchukuttan, and Pushpak Bhattacharyya. 2018. Multilingual Indian Language Translation System at WAT 2018: Many-to-one Phrase-based SMT. In *Proceedings of the 5th Workshop on Asian Translation (WAT2018)*, Hong Kong, China, December.

Jacob Cohen. 1968. Weighted kappa: Nominal scale agreement with provision for scaled disagreement or partial credit. *Psychological Bulletin*, 70(4):213 – 220.

Raj Dabre, Anoop Kunchukuttan, Atsushi Fujita, and Eiichiro Sumita. 2018. NICT's Participation in WAT 2018: Approaches Using Multilingualism and Recurrently. In *Proceedings of the 5th Workshop on Asian Translation (WAT2018)*, Hong Kong, China, December.

Terumasa Ehara. 2018. SMT reranked NMT (2). In *Proceedings of the 5th Workshop on Asian Translation (WAT2018)*, Hong Kong, China, December.

J.L. Fleiss et al. 1971. Measuring nominal scale agreement among many raters. *Psychological Bulletin*, 76(5):378–382.

Hideki Isozaki, Tsutomu Hirao, Kevin Duh, Katsuhito Sudoh, and Hajime Tsukada. 2010. Automatic evaluation of translation quality for distant language pairs. In *Proceedings of the 2010 Conference on Empirical Methods in Natural Language Processing*, EMNLP '10, pages 944–952, Stroudsburg, PA, USA. Association for Computational Linguistics.

Melvin Johnson, Mike Schuster, Quoc V. Le, Maxim Krikun, Yonghui Wu, Zhifeng Chen, Nikhil Thorat, Fernanda Viégas, Martin Wattenberg, Greg Corrado, Macduff Hughes, and Jeffrey Dean. 2017. Google's multilingual neural machine translation system: Enabling zero-shot translation. *Transactions of the Association for Computational Linguistics*, 5:339–351.

Yuki Kawara, Yuto Takebayashi, Chenhui Chu, and Yuki Arase. 2018. Osaka University MT Systems for WAT 2018: Rewarding, Preordering, and Domain Adaptation. In *Proceedings of the 5th Workshop on Asian Translation (WAT2018)*, Hong Kong, China, December.

Guillaume Klein, Yoon Kim, Yuntian Deng, Jean Senellart, and Alexander Rush. 2017. Opennmt: Opensource toolkit for neural machine translation. In *Proceedings of ACL 2017, System Demonstrations*, pages 67–72. Association for Computational Linguistics.

Tom Kocmi, Shantipriya Parida, and Ondrej Bojar. 2018. CUNI NMT System for WAT 2018 Translation Tasks. In *Proceedings of the 5th Workshop on Asian Translation (WAT2018)*, Hong Kong, China, December.

Philipp Koehn, Hieu Hoang, Alexandra Birch, Chris Callison-Burch, Marcello Federico, Nicola Bertoldi, Brooke Cowan, Wade Shen, Christine Moran, Richard Zens, Chris Dyer, Ondrej Bojar, Alexandra Constantin, and Evan Herbst. 2007. Moses: Open source toolkit for statistical machine translation. In *Annual Meeting of the Association for Computational Linguistics (ACL), demonstration session*.

Philipp Koehn. 2004. Statistical significance tests for machine translation evaluation. In Dekang Lin and Dekai Wu, editors, *Proceedings of EMNLP 2004*, pages 388–395, Barcelona, Spain, July. Association for Computational Linguistics.

T. Kudo. 2005. Mecab : Yet another part-of-speech and morphological analyzer. *http://mecab.sourceforge.net/*.

Sadao Kurohashi, Toshihisa Nakamura, Yuji Matsumoto, and Makoto Nagao. 1994. Improvements of Japanese morphological analyzer JUMAN. In *Proceedings of The International Workshop on Sharable Natural Language*, pages 22–28.

Yihan Li, Boyan Liu, Yixuan Tong, Shanshan Jiang, and Bin Dong. 2018. SRCB Neural Machine Translation Systems in WAT 2018. In *Proceedings of the 5th Workshop on Asian Translation (WAT2018)*, Hong Kong, China, December.

Benjamin Marie, Atsushi Fujita, and Eiichiro Sumita. 2018. Combination of Statistical and Neural Machine Translation for Myanmar-English. In *Proceedings of the 5th Workshop on Asian Translation (WAT2018)*, Hong Kong, China, December.

Yukio Matsumura, Satoru Katsumata, and Mamoru Komachi. 2018. TMU Japanese-English Neural Machine Translation System using Generative Adversarial Network for WAT 2018. In *Proceedings of the 5th Workshop on Asian Translation (WAT2018)*, Hong Kong, China, December.

Hsu Myat Mo, Yi Mon Shwe Sin, Thazin Myint Oo, Win Pa Pa, Khin Mar Soe, and Ye Kyaw Thu. 2018. UCSYNLP-Lab Machine Translation Systems for WAT 2018. In *Proceedings of the 5th Workshop on Asian Translation (WAT2018)*, Hong Kong, China, December.

Toshiaki Nakazawa, Hideya Mino, Isao Goto, Sadao Kurohashi, and Eiichiro Sumita. 2014. Overview of the 1st Workshop on Asian Translation. In *Proceedings of the 1st Workshop on Asian Translation (WAT2014)*, pages 1–19, Tokyo, Japan, October.

Toshiaki Nakazawa, Hideya Mino, Isao Goto, Graham Neubig, Sadao Kurohashi, and Eiichiro Sumita. 2015.

Overview of the 2nd Workshop on Asian Translation. In *Proceedings of the 2nd Workshop on Asian Translation (WAT2015)*, pages 1–28, Kyoto, Japan, October.

Toshiaki Nakazawa, Chenchen Ding, Hideya MINO, Isao Goto, Graham Neubig, and Sadao Kurohashi. 2016. Overview of the 3rd workshop on asian translation. In *Proceedings of the 3rd Workshop on Asian Translation (WAT2016)*, pages 1–46, Osaka, Japan, December. The COLING 2016 Organizing Committee.

Toshiaki Nakazawa, Shohei Higashiyama, Chenchen Ding, Hideya Mino, Isao Goto, Hideto Kazawa, Yusuke Oda, Graham Neubig, and Sadao Kurohashi. 2017. Overview of the 4th workshop on asian translation. In *Proceedings of the 4th Workshop on Asian Translation (WAT2017)*, pages 1–54. Asian Federation of Natural Language Processing.

Graham Neubig, Yosuke Nakata, and Shinsuke Mori. 2011. Pointwise prediction for robust, adaptable japanese morphological analysis. In *Proceedings of the 49th Annual Meeting of the Association for Computational Linguistics: Human Language Technologies: Short Papers - Volume 2*, HLT '11, pages 529–533, Stroudsburg, PA, USA. Association for Computational Linguistics.

Atul Kr. Ojha, Koel Dutta Chowdhury, Chao-Hong Liu, and Karan Saxena. 2018. The RGNLP Machine Translation Systems for WAT 2018. In *Proceedings of the 5th Workshop on Asian Translation (WAT2018)*, Hong Kong, China, December.

Kishore Papineni, Salim Roukos, Todd Ward, and Wei-Jing Zhu. 2002. Bleu: a method for automatic evaluation of machine translation. In *ACL*, pages 311–318.

Jerin Philip, Vinay P. Namboodiri, and C V Jawahar. 2018. CVIT-MT Systems for WAT-2018. In *Proceedings of the 5th Workshop on Asian Translation (WAT2018)*, Hong Kong, China, December.

Hammam Riza, Michael Purwoadi, Teduh Uliniansyah, Aw Ai Ti, Sharifah Mahani Aljunied, Luong Chi Mai, Vu Tat Thang, Nguyen Phuong Thai, Vichet Chea, Sethserey Sam, Sopheap Seng, Khin Mar Soe, Khin Thandar Nwet, Masao Utiyama, and Chenchen Ding. 2016. Introduction of the asian language treebank. In *In Proc. of O-COCOSDA*, pages 1–6.

Sukanta Sen, Kamal Kumar Gupta, Asif Ekbal, and Pushpak Bhattacharyya. 2018. IITP-MT at WAT2018: Transformer-based Multilingual Indic-English Neural Machine Translation System. In *Proceedings of the 5th Workshop on Asian Translation (WAT2018)*, Hong Kong, China, December.

Aye Thida, Nway Nway Han, and Sheinn Thawtar Oo. 2018. Statistical Machine Translation Using 5-grams Word Segmentation in Decoding. In *Proceedings of the 5th Workshop on Asian Translation (WAT2018)*, Hong Kong, China, December.

Huihsin Tseng. 2005. A conditional random field word segmenter. In *In Fourth SIGHAN Workshop on Chinese Language Processing*.

Masao Utiyama and Hitoshi Isahara. 2007. A japanese-english patent parallel corpus. In *MT summit XI*, pages 475–482.

Boli Wang, Jinming Hu, Yidong Chen, and Xiaodong Shi. 2018a. XMU Neural Machine Translation Systems for WAT2018 Myanmar-English Translation Task. In *Proceedings of the 5th Workshop on Asian Translation (WAT2018)*, Hong Kong, China, December.

Rui Wang, Chenchen Ding, Masao Utiyama, and Eiichiro Sumita. 2018b. English-Myanmar NMT and SMT with Pre-ordering: NICT's machine translation systems at WAT-2018. In *Proceedings of the 5th Workshop on Asian Translation (WAT2018)*, Hong Kong, China, December.

Yi Mon Shwe Sin and Khin Mar Soe. 2018. Syllable-based myanmar-english neural machine translation. In *In Proc. of ICCA*, pages 228–233.

Longtu Zhang, Yuting Zhao, and Mamoru Komachi. 2018. TMU Japanese-Chinese Unsupervised NMT System for WAT 2018 Translation Task. In *Proceedings of the 5th Workshop on Asian Translation (WAT2018)*, Hong Kong, China, December.

CUNI NMT System for WAT 2018 Translation Tasks

Tom Kocmi   **Shantipriya Parida**   **Ondřej Bojar**
Charles University, Faculty of Mathematics and Physics
Institute of Formal and Applied Linguistics
Malostranské náměstí 25, 118 00 Prague, Czech Republic
{kocmi,parida,bojar}@ufal.mff.cuni.cz

Abstract

This paper describes the CUNI submission to WAT 2018 for the English-Hindi translation task using a transfer learning techniques which has proven effective under low resource conditions. We have used the Transformer model and utilized an English-Czech parallel corpus as additional data source. Our simple transfer learning approach first trains a "parent" model for a high-resource language pair (English-Czech) and then continues the training on the low-resource (English-Hindi) pair by replacing the training corpus. This setup improves the performance compared with the baseline and in combination with back-translation of Hindi monolingual data, it allowed us to win the English-Hindi task. The automatic scoring by BLEU did not correlate well with human judgments.

1   Introduction

Neural Machine Translation (NMT) systems are superior to Phrase-Based Statistical Machine Translation (PBMT) in large data conditions but they suffer when parallel resources are limited (Bojar et al., 2017; Koehn and Knowles, 2017; Lakew et al., 2017). In the current situation, only few language pairs have such high quality parallel corpora of sufficient size (Chu and Wang, 2018).

Many approaches were proposed in the past few years to utilize additional data to improve machine translation for low-resource languages. Currey et al. (2017) copied the target side of monolingual data to the source to forge a parallel corpus creating a "copied corpus". After mixing with the bilingual

corpus and training NMT systems, they got accuracy improvements. Zoph et al. (2016) proposed transfer learning which uses an additional large corpus of another language pair (parent model) for training and then transfer the learned parameters to the low resource pair (child model) to initialize and constrain training, resulting an increase of BLEU scores. Nguyen and Chiang (2017) proposed transfer learning for low resource language pairs starting from a low resource parent pair. They used sub-word units (BPE, Sennrich et al. (2016a); Shibata et al. (1999)) and focused on increasing vocabulary overlap during transfer of model parameter from the parent language pair to the child one. Closely related to the transfer learning is also curriculum learning (Bengio et al., 2009; Kocmi and Bojar, 2017), where the training data can be ordered from parent out-of-domain to the child in-domain training examples.

In this system description paper, we explain our approach of using Hindi monolingual data and applying transfer learning using additional English-Czech parallel corpus. Section 1 describes related work carried out by different researchers using domain adaptation techniques. Section 2 explains the techniques which we followed in our work. Section 3 describes the datasets used in our experiment. Section 4 presents the model and experimental setups used in our approach. Section 5 provides the official evaluation results of WAT 2018 followed by the conclusion in Section 6.

2   Method Description

We utilize transfer learning based on the work of Kocmi and Bojar (2018). The method of training is

| | | #Tokens | | |
Set	#Sentences	EN	CS	HI
Train (EN-CS)	40.1M	563.4M	490.5M	-
Train (EN-HI)	1.4M	20.6M	-	22.1M
TrainBack (EN-HI)	8.8M	161M	-	167M
Dev (EN-HI)	520	10656	-	10174
Test (EN-HI)	2507	49394	-	57037

Table 1: Statistics of our data.

similar to domain adaptation, where we first train a more general model later followed by training on a more domain-specific dataset. The domain in our case is the actual language pair. The method by Kocmi and Bojar (2018) does not require any of the languages to be linguistically related.

The method has only one constrain and that is a shared vocabulary between language pairs of parent and child. This is solved by generating word-piece segmentation (Johnson et al., 2017) from the concatenated source and target sides of both the parent and the child language pair. To avoid bias in the vocabulary towards the high-resource language pair, Kocmi et al. (2018b) showed that best performance is obtained by using a "balanced vocabulary" approach which uses only as many sentence pairs from the high-resource pair as there are available for the low-resource pair.

We start with the parent model, in our case English to Czech translation, and keep training as long as it improves the results on the development set. Then the training corpus is switched to the child parallel corpus and the training continues without any hyperparameter modifications. We do not even reset the learning rate.

This transfer learning method does not need any modifications of existing NMT frameworks.

We have observed that a small number of outputs of some of our systems were not translated into the target language. For those cases identified by the Python language detection library "langdetect" (Thoma, 2018), we use the output with the output of another model with different settings instead.

3 Dataset

This section describes the dataset provided by WAT 2018 for the translation task and the dataset used for domain adaptation. We have used two language pairs: one as the high-resource one (parent model) and another as the low-resource one (child model).

Kocmi and Bojar (2018) showed, that relatedness of parent and child language is not the main criterion for better performance, but it is the sheer volume of parent training size. Therefore we have decided to use Czech-English as the parent model, since it is one of the most resourceful language pairs available and allowed for the WAT 2018 shared task. And it is reasonably clean since it does not contain dirty crawled data.

We use CzEng 1.7 (Bojar et al., 2016) as the parent language pair training set. We preprocessed the data in the same manner as in the work of Kocmi et al. (2018a) by dropping sentences shorter than 4 words and longer than 75 words. We use IITB English-Hindi parallel corpus[1] (Kunchukuttan et al., 2018) provided by WAT 2018 for the English-Hindi translation task as the child language pair. This is supposedly the largest publicly available English-Hindi parallel corpus. This corpus contain 1.49 million parallel segments and 45 million monolingual segments and it was found very effective for English-Hindi translation task (Parida and Bojar, 2018). Apart from the above language pairs, we have also used the Hindi monolingual dataset for generating synthetic data using back translation. Recently many researchers have shown that back translating monolingual data can be used to create synthetic parallel corpora which in combination with authentic parallel data helps to train a high quality MT system (Bojar and Tamchyna, 2011; Sennrich et al., 2016b; Poncelas et al., 2018; Popel, 2018). The usage of monolingual data in the target language provides the NMT system with more evidence on which words are more common and which are not (Koehn, 2017). We com-

---

[1] http://www.cfilt.iitb.ac.in/iitb_parallel/

Setting	Direction	Use synthetic	Use genuine	Transfer Learning	Avg (8 Last Models)
S1	EN-HI	✓	✗	✗	✓
S2	EN-HI	✓	✗	1M steps of EN-CS	✓
S3	EN-HI	✓	✓	1M steps of EN-CS	✓
S4	EN-HI	✗	✓	1M steps of EN-CS	✓
S5	EN-HI	✗	✓	1M steps of EN-CS	✓
S6	HI-EN	✗	✓	1M steps of CS-EN	✓

Table 2: Main differences between model settings.

bine transfer learning with back translation. We first train a CS-EN system, continue its training with HI-EN and then apply it to Hindi monolingual data to obtain a synthetic EN-HI corpus. The statistics of all the datasets are shown in Table 1.

4 Experiments

This section describes our experiments conducted for the translation task.

4.1 Tokenization and Vocabulary

We have used shared vocabulary of subword units, word pieces (Johnson et al., 2017), across both language pairs, where the word pieces handle tokenization automatically.

Our approach requires a shared vocabulary across the parent model (English to Czech) and the child model (English to Hindi). Our generated vocabulary contains 32k sub-word types.

4.2 NMT Model Description

In our approach, we train the parent language pair until the BLEU scores on the development set seem more or less stable and switch the training corpus to the child language pair without any hyper-parameter change.

We use the Transformer model as implemented in Tensor2Tensor (Vaswani et al., 2018) version 1.4.2. We have used the "Big Single GPU" configuration for our experiments. To fit the model to our GPUs (NVIDIA GeForce GTX 1080 Ti with 11 GB RAM), we set the batch size to 2300 and limit sentence length to 100 wordpieces. We use Noam learning rate decay[2] (Vaswani et al., 2017; Popel and Bojar, 2018) with the starting learning rate of 0.2 and 32000

warm up steps. In our experiments, we find that it is undesirable to reset the learning rate when switching to the child language pair as it leads to the loss of the performance gained in the parent model. Decoding uses the beam size of 8 and length normalization penalty is set to 1. The parent model was trained for 1M steps (approximately 6 days), the child models were trained for approximately 500k steps, which was sufficient for models to converge to the best performance. We selected the model with the best performance on the development test for the final evaluation on the test set. We also use checkpoint averaging which we confirmed to be effective for Transformer model (Popel and Bojar, 2018). We average the last 8 models.

4.3 Model Setups

We have used 6 settings for our English-to-Hindi and Hindi-to-English Translation Task as shown in Table 2 and described as follows:

1. *S1: TransBig (Back Translation, Averaging)*
   Transformer big, only back translation EN-HI. We have not used any parallel data for EN-HI, only the back translated EN-HI data, beam=8; alpha=0.8; averaging of last 8 models; stopped after 1300k steps.

   Here, we have applied the output correction by identifying the source language (English) texts in the S1 model's output and replacing them with the corresponding target language (Hindi) output generated from the model S2. This ensures that less English language text appears in the S1 model output. English segments which still remained untranslated in the output were substituted by outputs of the model S3.

2. *S2: TransBig (1M EN-CS Transfer Learning, Averaging)*

---

[2]`https://nvidia.github.io/OpenSeq2Seq/html/`
`api-docs/optimizers.html`

Corpus	Task	Setting	BLEU
IITB	EN-HI	S1: Back Translation (EN-HI)	**20.28**
IITB	EN-HI	S2: 1M EN-CS Transfer Learning, Back Translation (EN-HI)	20.07
IITB	EN-HI	S3: 1M EN-CS Transfer Learning, Back Translation (EN-HI), Genuine (EN-HI)	17.63
IITB	EN-HI	S4: 1M EN-CS Transfer Learning, Genuine (EN-HI)	16.49
IITB	EN-HI	S5: 1M EN-CS Transfer Learning, Genuine (EN-HI)	14.20
IITB	HI-EN	S6: 1M CS-EN Transfer Learning, Genuine (HI-EN)	17.80

Table 3: WAT 2018 Official Automatic Evaluation Results of our Models. All setups use "Transformer-Big" and checkpoint averaging.

Transformer big, transfer learning from EN-CS 1M steps. We have not used any parallel data for EN-HI, we only used the back translated EN-HI data, beam=8; alpha=0.8; averaging of last 8 models; stopped after 700k steps.

We also applied a similar output correction as in S1. We resorted to outputs of the model S1 or eventually S3 if English was produced instead of Hindi.

3. *S3: TransBig (1M EN-CS Transfer Learning, Back Translation (EN-HI Back + EN-HI Genuine, Averaging)*
Transformer big, transfer learning from EN-CS 1M steps, followed by only back translation EN-HI for 300k steps, followed by genuine EN-HI for 500k steps, beam=8; alpha=0.8; averaging of last 8 models.

4. *S4: TransBig (1M EN-CS Transfer Learning, Averaging)*
Transformer big, transfer learning from EN-CS 1M steps, only genuine EN-HI, beam=8; alpha=0.8; averaging of last 8 models; stopped after 230k steps.

5. *S5: TransBig (1M EN-CS Transfer Learning, Averaging)*
Baseline, transformer big only EN-HI, beam=8, alpha=0.8, averaging 8 steps; stopped after 330k steps.

6. *S6: TransBig (1M CS-EN Transfer Learning, Averaging)*
Transformer big, transfer learning from CS-EN 1M steps, only genuine HI-EN, beam=8; alpha=0.8; averaging of last 8 models; stopped after 230k steps. This model used primarily in back translation but we also submitted it to the HI-EN task.

5 Official Results

This section shows the official results of our models as published by WAT 2018 using automatic and manual evaluation. Further details on the evaluation can be found in Nakazawa et al. (2018) and all scores are available on the WAT 2018 website.[3]

We report the official automatic evaluation results of all our models for the test dataset here in Table 3. We see that the model S1 performed best in automatic evaluation. We observed similarly high BLEU scores on the development set but a small manual validation revealed that the translation quality is actually better in model S2 and S3, esp. due to Hindi grammar and word selection. Figure 1 provides an illustration. The output by S1 is a little shorter, so it risks fewer incorrect n-grams in BLEU evaluation (and the brevity penalty still does not strike too hard).

Based on this small manual analysis, we decided to submit models S2 and S3 and not model S1 for manual evaluation. (Participants could submit up to two models for manual evaluation.) The WAT2018 official manual scores for our systems and a competitor are shown in Table 4. This larger evaluation confirms our observation that BLEU does not correlate well with human judgment in this setting. We see that the model S3 outperformed S2 and also the competing system from another team by a large margin. In sum, it was S3, our third setup in terms of BLEU, that topped among all submission for EN-HI task in WAT2018.

---

[3] `http://lotus.kuee.kyoto-u.ac.jp/WAT/evaluation/`

English Input:
Politicians are loath to raise the tax even one penny when gas prices are high.
S1 Translated Output:
जब गैस की कीमतें ऊंची होती हैं तो राजनीतिज्ञ कर एक पैसा भी बढ़ा देते हैं .
Gloss: When gas prices are high then politician tax one penny high
S2 Translated Output:
गैस की कीमतें ज्यादा होने पर एक पैसा भी टैक्स बढ़ाने के लिए राजनीतिज्ञ लोन ले रहे हैं ।
Gloss: In case of gas prices are high politicians take loan even to increase one penny of tax
S3 Translated Output:
राजनीतिज्ञों को गैस की कीमतें ऊंची होने पर भी एक पैसे का कर बढ़ाने की घृणा है ।
Gloss: Politicians are hate to increase one penny of tax even though gas prices are high

Figure 1: Sample Hindi Output Generated by the Settings S1, S2, and S3.

Team	Task	System	BLEU	Human	Note
CUNI	EN-HI	S3	17.63	**77.00**	
competitor	EN-HI	ConvS2S	19.69	69.50	Used external data
CUNI	EN-HI	S2	**20.07**	60.00	
competitor	EN-HI	ConvS2S	16.77	50.50	
competitor	HI-EN	ConvS2S	**20.63**	**72.25**	Used external data
CUNI	HI-EN	S6	17.80	67.25	

Table 4: WAT2018 Official Automatic and Manual Evaluation Results for IITB corpora.

6   Conclusion and Future Plans

In this system description paper, we presented our English-Hindi NMT system. We have highlighted the benefits of synthetic data and transfer learning. Our model that used all our components (synthetic data, genuine data and transfer learning from an unrelated English-Czech dataset) performed best in the official manual evaluation. We observed a clear mismatch of BLEU and manual evaluation.

As the next step, we plan to investigate corpus filtering, and iterative augmentation for performance improvement. Further exploration of the poor BLEU performance in this setting is also highly desirable.

Acknowledgments

This study was supported in parts by the grants SVV 260 453, GAUK 8502/2016, and 18-24210S of the Czech Science Foundation. This work has been using language resources and tools stored and distributed by the LINDAT/CLARIN project of the Ministry of Education, Youth and Sports of the Czech Republic (projects LM2015071 and OP VVV VI CZ.02.1.01/0.0/0.0/16 013/0001781).

References

Yoshua Bengio, Jérôme Louradour, Ronan Collobert, and Jason Weston. Curriculum learning. In *Proceedings of the 26th annual international conference on machine learning*, pages 41–48. ACM, 2009.

Ondřej Bojar and Aleš Tamchyna. Improving translation model by monolingual data. In *Proceedings of the Sixth Workshop on Statistical Machine Translation, WMT@EMNLP 2011, Edinburgh, Scotland, UK, July 30-31, 2011*, pages 330–336, 2011. URL https://aclanthology.info/papers/W11-2138/w11-2138.

Ondřej Bojar, Ondřej Dušek, Tom Kocmi, Jindřich Libovický, Michal Novák, Martin Popel, Roman Sudarikov, and Dušan Variš. CzEng 1.6: Enlarged Czech-English parallel corpus with processing tools dockered. In *International Conference on Text, Speech, and Dialogue*, pages 231–238. Springer, 2016.

Ondřej Bojar, Rajen Chatterjee, Christian Federmann, Yvette Graham, Barry Haddow, Shujian Huang, Matthias Huck, Philipp Koehn, Qun Liu,

Varvara Logacheva, et al. Findings of the 2017 conference on machine translation (wmt17). In *Proceedings of the Second Conference on Machine Translation*, pages 169–214, 2017.

Chenhui Chu and Rui Wang. A Survey of Domain Adaptation for Neural Machine Translation. *arXiv preprint arXiv:1806.00258*, 2018.

Anna Currey, Antonio Valerio Miceli Barone, and Kenneth Heafield. Copied monolingual data improves low-resource neural machine translation. In *Proceedings of the Second Conference on Machine Translation*, pages 148–156, 2017.

Melvin Johnson, Mike Schuster, Quoc V. Le, Maxim Krikun, Yonghui Wu, Zhifeng Chen, Nikhil Thorat, Fernanda Viégas, Martin Wattenberg, Greg Corrado, Macduff Hughes, and Jeffrey Dean. Google's multilingual neural machine translation system: Enabling zero-shot translation. *Transactions of the Association for Computational Linguistics*, 5:339–351, 2017. URL `http://aclweb.org/anthology/Q17-1024`.

Tom Kocmi and Ondřej Bojar. Curriculum Learning and Minibatch Bucketing in Neural Machine Translation. In *Recent Advances in Natural Language Processing 2017*, September 2017.

Tom Kocmi and Ondřej Bojar. Trivial Transfer Learning for Low-Resource Neural Machine Translation. In *Proceedings of the 3rd Conference on Machine Translation (WMT)*, Brussels, Belgium, November 2018.

Tom Kocmi, Roman Sudarikov, and Ondřej Bojar. CUNI Submissions in WMT18. In *Proceedings of the 3rd Conference on Machine Translation (WMT)*, Brussels, Belgium, November 2018a.

Tom Kocmi, Dušan Variš, and Ondřej Bojar. CUNI Basque-to-English Submission in IWSLT18. *IWSLT. Bruges, Belgium*, 2018b.

Philipp Koehn. Neural machine translation. *arXiv preprint arXiv:1709.07809*, 2017.

Philipp Koehn and Rebecca Knowles. Six challenges for neural machine translation. In *Proceedings of the First Workshop on Neural Machine Translation*, pages 28–39, 2017.

Anoop Kunchukuttan, Pratik Mehta, and Pushpak Bhattacharyya. The IIT Bombay English-Hindi Parallel Corpus. In Nicoletta Calzolari (Conference chair), Khalid Choukri, Christopher Cieri, Thierry Declerck, Sara Goggi, Koiti Hasida, Hitoshi Isahara, Bente Maegaard, Joseph Mariani, Hélène Mazo, Asuncion Moreno, Jan Odijk, Stelios Piperidis, and Takenobu Tokunaga, editors, *Proceedings of the Eleventh International Conference on Language Resources and Evaluation (LREC 2018)*, Miyazaki, Japan, May 7-12, 2018 2018. European Language Resources Association (ELRA). ISBN 979-10-95546-00-9.

Surafel Melaku Lakew, Mattia Antonino Di Gangi, and Marcello Federico. Multilingual Neural Machine Translation for Low Resource Languages. In *CLiC-it*, 2017.

Toshiaki Nakazawa, Shohei Higashiyama, Chenchen Ding, Raj Dabre, Anoop Kunchukuttan, Win Pa Pa, Isao Goto, Hideya Mino, Katsuhito Sudoh, and Sadao Kurohashi. Overview of the 5th Workshop on Asian Translation. In *Proceedings of the 5th Workshop on Asian Translation (WAT2018)*, Hong Kong, China, December 2018.

Toan Q. Nguyen and David Chiang. Transfer learning across low-resource, related languages for neural machine translation. In *Proceedings of the Eighth International Joint Conference on Natural Language Processing (Volume 2: Short Papers)*, pages 296–301. Asian Federation of Natural Language Processing, 2017. URL `http://aclweb.org/anthology/I17-2050`.

Shantipriya Parida and Ondřej Bojar. Translating short segments with nmt: A case study in english-to-hindi. In *21st Annual Conference of the European Association for Machine Translation*, page 229, 2018.

Alberto Poncelas, Dimitar Shterionov, Andy Way, Gideon Maillette de Buy Wenniger, and Peyman Passban. Investigating backtranslation in neural machine translation. 2018.

Martin Popel. Cuni transformer neural mt system for wmt18. In *Proceedings of the Third Conference on Machine Translation*, pages 486–491, Belgium, Brussels, October 2018. Association for Computational Linguistics. URL `http://www.aclweb.org/anthology/W18-64051`.

Martin Popel and Ondřej Bojar. Training tips for the

transformer model. *The Prague Bulletin of Mathematical Linguistics*, 110(1):43–70, 2018.

Rico Sennrich, Barry Haddow, and Alexandra Birch. Neural machine translation of rare words with subword units. In *Proceedings of the 54th Annual Meeting of the Association for Computational Linguistics (Volume 1: Long Papers)*, pages 1715–1725, Berlin, Germany, August 2016a. Association for Computational Linguistics. URL `http://www.aclweb.org/anthology/P16-1162`.

Rico Sennrich, Barry Haddow, and Alexandra Birch. Improving neural machine translation models with monolingual data. In *Proceedings of the 54th Annual Meeting of the Association for Computational Linguistics (Volume 1: Long Papers)*, volume 1, pages 86–96, 2016b.

Yusuxke Shibata, Takuya Kida, Shuichi Fukamachi, Masayuki Takeda, Ayumi Shinohara, Takeshi Shinohara, and Setsuo Arikawa. Byte pair encoding: A text compression scheme that accelerates pattern matching. Technical report, Technical Report DOI-TR-161, Department of Informatics, Kyushu University, 1999.

Martin Thoma. The wili benchmark dataset for written language identification. *arXiv preprint arXiv:1801.07779*, 2018.

Ashish Vaswani, Noam Shazeer, Niki Parmar, Jakob Uszkoreit, Llion Jones, Aidan N Gomez, Łukasz Kaiser, and Illia Polosukhin. Attention is all you need. In *Advances in Neural Information Processing Systems*, pages 5998–6008, 2017.

Ashish Vaswani, Samy Bengio, Eugene Brevdo, Francois Chollet, Aidan Gomez, Stephan Gouws, Llion Jones, Łukasz Kaiser, Nal Kalchbrenner, Niki Parmar, Ryan Sepassi, Noam Shazeer, and Jakob Uszkoreit. Tensor2tensor for neural machine translation. In *Proceedings of the 13th Conference of the Association for Machine Translation in the Americas (Volume 1: Research Papers)*, pages 193–199. Association for Machine Translation in the Americas, 2018. URL `http://aclweb.org/anthology/W18-1819`.

Barret Zoph, Deniz Yuret, Jonathan May, and Kevin Knight. Transfer learning for low-resource neural machine translation. In *Proceedings of the 2016 Conference on Empirical Methods in Natural Language Processing*, pages 1568–1575. Association for Computational Linguistics, 2016. doi: 10.18653/v1/D16-1163. URL `http://www.aclweb.org/anthology/D16-1163`.

NICT's Participation in WAT 2018:
Approaches Using Multilingualism and Recurrently Stacked Layers

Raj Dabre
NICT,
3-5 Hikaridai, Seika-cho, Soraku-gun,
Kyoto 619-0289, Japan
`raj.dabre@nict.go.jp`

Anoop Kunchukuttan
Microsoft AI and Research, India
`ankunchu@microsoft.com`

Atsushi Fujita
NICT,
3-5 Hikaridai, Seika-cho, Soraku-gun,
Kyoto 619-0289, Japan
`atsushi.fujita@nict.go.jp`

Eiichiro Sumita
NICT,
3-5 Hikaridai, Seika-cho, Soraku-gun,
Kyoto 619-0289, Japan
`eiichiro.sumita@nict.go.jp`

Abstract

In this paper we describe all our NMT systems for the following translation tasks we participated in: ASPEC (all tasks), Indic Languages (multilingual tasks) and the Myanmar-English task. Our team, "NICT-5", focused on the utility of bidirectional, recurrently stacked layered and multilingual models for AS-PEC, simple domain adaptation approaches for Myanmar-English and multilingual models for Indic Languages. In the case of AS-PEC translation, we noted that a single multilingual/bidirectional model (without ensembling) has the potential to achieve (near) state-of-the-art results for all the language pairs. We also noted that models that use recurrently stacking layers do not experience a large loss in translation quality despite having significantly fewer parameters compared to the vanilla NMT models. An interesting observation is that systems with the best BLEU might not be the best in terms of human evaluation.

1 Introduction

Neural machine translation (NMT) (Cho et al., 2014; Sutskever et al., 2014; Bahdanau et al., 2015) has enabled end-to-end training of a translation system without needing to deal with word alignments, translation rules, and complicated decoding algorithms, which are the characteristics of phrase-based statistical machine translation (PBSMT) (Koehn et al., 2007). Although vanilla NMT is significantly better than PBSMT in resource-rich scenarios, PBSMT performs better in resource-poor scenarios (Zoph et al., 2016). By exploiting transfer learning techniques, the performance of NMT approaches can be improved substantially.

For WAT 2018, we participated as team "NICT-5" and worked on ASPEC Chinese-Japanese and English-Japanese translation, UCSY Myanmar-English translation and Indic multilingual translation directions. The techniques we focused on for each translation task can be summarized as below:

- For the ASPEC translation tasks, we mostly relied on multilingual Transformer (Vaswani et al., 2017) models and experimented with Recurrently Stacked NMT (RS-NMT) (Dabre and Fujita, 2018) models in order to determine the trade-off between compactness of models and the loss in their performance.

- For the UCSY Myanmar-English translation task, we tried domain adaptation techniques such as Mixed Fine Tuning (Chu et al., 2017) since the the final objective was to achieve high quality translation for a low-resource domain (ALT).

- For the Indic multilingual task, we explored the feasibility of bilingual, N-to-1, 1-to-N and N-to-N way translation models. We also tried an approach where we mapped the scripts of all Indic languages to a common script (Devanagari) to see if it helps improve the performance of a multilingual model.

For additional details of how our submissions are ranked relative to the submissions of other WAT participants, kindly refer to the overview paper (Nakazawa et al., 2018).

2 NMT Models and Approaches

We will first describe the Transformer which is the state-of-the-art NMT model we used for our experiments.

2.1 The Transformer

The Transformer (Vaswani et al., 2017) is the current state-of-the-art model for NMT. It is a sequence-to-sequence neural model that consists of two components, the *encoder* and the *decoder*. The encoder converts the input word sequence into a sequence of vectors of high dimensionality. The decoder, on the other hand, produces the target word sequence by predicting the words using a combination of the previously predicted word and relevant parts of the input sequence representations. Due to lack of space, we briefly describe the encoder and decoder as follows. The reader is encouraged to read the Transformer paper (Vaswani et al., 2017) for a deeper understanding.

Suppose that X and Y are the input and output word sequences where $X = [x_0, x_1, ..., x_n]$ and $Y = [y_0, y_1, ..., y_m]$. The objective is to predict the best word sequence:

$$\hat{Y} = \arg\max_Y P(Y|X).$$

The first step is to compute initial high dimensional vector space representations E_X for the input word sequence X by using its word embeddings where:

$$E_X^{encoder} = embedding_{encoder}(X).$$

Positional information is also incorporated into the word embeddings, which has been shown to be important for good performance. The embeddings, computed by an embedding layer, are stored in an embedding matrix in which the number of rows is equal to the size of the vocabulary of the input sequence. These word embeddings are then processed by N neural network layers composed of self attention, feed-forward layers and normalization sublayers which help produce a high-level representation of the input sequence denoted by S_X^N where:

$$S_X^i = Layer_{encoder}(S_X^{i-1}),$$

and $S_X^0 = E_X^{encoder}$. These processing steps describe the Encoder.

Due to the use of self-attention layer instead of the traditional recurrent layer, the input sequence can be processed in parallel, the result of which is significantly faster processing because of parallel computation.

The decoder, on the other hand, predicts one word at a time by taking into account the previously predicted words. At each time step i, the decoder takes the previously predicted word y_{i-1}, computes its embedding as:

$$E_{y_{i-1}}^{decoder} = embedding_{decoder}(y_{i-1}),$$

processes this embedding through N layers of self-attention, cross-attention (to access the relevant information from the source hidden-state representations) to give the decoder hidden-state s_i. s_i is then converted into a probability distribution to predict y_i:

$$y_i = argmax_{y_i} P(y_i|X, y_{i-1}, y_{i-2}, ..., y_0).$$

The distribution is obtained using a softmax layer as follows:

$$P(y_i|X, y_{i-1}, y_{i-2}, ..., y_0) = softmax(W^T \times s_i),$$

where W is a matrix which maps s_i to a vector of the size of the vocabulary of the target sequence. $W^T \times s_i$ is also known as the logit vector for the ith word to be predicted, denoted as L_i.

2.2 Multilingualism in NMT

In order to train multilingual models using the Transformer, we used the artificial token based approach (Johnson et al., 2017) which is also useful for zero-shot translation. We simply concatenate the corpora for all translation directions after inserting a token like "XX" at the beginning of the source sentence, where "XX" is a special token that indicates the target language such as JA (for Japanese) or EN (for English). "XX" should be a token which is not already present in the corpus. We also over-sample the smaller corpora to match the size of the larger corpora.

2.3 Domain Adaptation in NMT

The primary domain adaptation technique we explored was Mixed Fine Tuning (MFT) (Chu et al., 2017) since it can be used without any modification to the model architecture. The approach can be summarized as follows:

- Learn a joint vocabulary for the out-of-domain and in-domain corpora.

- Train the NMT model on the out-of-domain corpus only until convergence.

- Resume training the same NMT model on the combination of out-of-domain and in-domain corpora[1] till convergence.

This method is extremely easy to use.

2.4 Recurrently Stacked Layers in NMT

Recurrently Stacked Layers for NMT (RS-NMT) (Dabre and Fujita, 2018) proposes to reuse share the parameters of among all layers of the encoder or the decoder. A N-layer (encoder-decoder) RS-NMT has the same number of parameters as a 1-layer vanilla NMT model. The only major difference is that the same layer is recurrently stacked N times for each of the encoder and the decoder. As a result of recurrently stacking layers, the NMT model learns to refine the representations of sentences leading to significantly better performance than a vanilla 1-layer model. A generalized version of this approach is proposed in the work on the Universal Transformer (Dehghani et al., 2018). In this work a 6-layer transformer is recurrently stacked M times where M is dynamically decided. The major difference between RS-NMT and Universal Transformers is that the former seeks to reduce the number of model parameters with minimal loss in performance whereas the latter seeks to improve the model performance over its vanilla counterpart without increasing the number of parameters.

In this paper, we choose an intermediate approach where we consider a 3-layer transformer and recurrently stack it 4 times. We do not opt for the dynamic recurrent stacking approach for simplicity.

---

[1] The in-domain data will be oversampled so that the training phase sees equal amounts of data from both domains.

Split	ASPEC JC	ASPEC JE
Train	672,315	3,008,500
Dev	2,090	1,790
Test	2,107	1,812

Table 1: ASPEC dataset splits. The number indicates the number of lines in the split.

3 Model Training Details

Since we pre-processed all our data according to the organizer's guidelines, we do not mention them here. For all our experiments, we used the tensor2tensor[2] version 1.6 implementation of the Transformer (Vaswani et al., 2017) model. We chose this implementation because it is known to give the state-of-the-art results for NMT. In order to train multilingual models we used the artificial token trick used for zero-shot NMT (Johnson et al., 2017). We always oversample the smaller datasets to ensure that the training phase sees equal amounts of data from all datasets. We also modified the tensor2tensor implementation to train Recurrently Stacked NMT (RS-NMT) models (Dabre and Fujita, 2018). We used the default hyperparameters in tensor2tensor for all our models with the exception of the number of training iterations. Unless mentioned otherwise we use the "base" transformer model hyperparameter settings with a 32000 subword vocabulary which is learned using tensor2tensor's default subword segmentation mechanism. During training, a model checkpoint is saved every 1000 iterations. We averaged the last 10 model checkpoints and used it for decoding the test sets.

4 ASPEC Task

4.1 Datasets

For the ASPEC (Nakazawa et al., 2016) tasks we used the official data provided by the organizers. The objective of the ASPEC task is to push the state-of-the-art for scientific domain machine translation for Japanese-English and Japanese-Chinese. The parallel corpora available, belong to the scientific domain and are sufficiently large in size. Refer to Table 1 for an overview of the data splits. For our ex-

---

[2] https://github.com/tensorflow/tensor2tensor

Task	Model	Our BLEU	Top BLEU	BLEU Ranking	Human Ranking
English-Japanese	Bidirectional	42.87	43.43	2/6	1/5
English-Japanese	RS-NMT*	41.91	43.43	-	-
Japanese-English	Multilingual	29.65	30.59	2/4	1/4
Japanese-English	Unidirectional*	28.63	30.59	-	-
Chinese-Japanese	Multilingual	49.79	49.79	1/2	1/1
Chinese-Japanese	MFT*	49.67	49.79	-	-
Japanese-Chinese	Multilingual	35.99	37.60	2/3	2/2
Japanese-Chinese	Vanilla*	35.71	37.60	-	-

Table 2: ASPEC task results. Entries with an asterisk mark are the comparative submissions and hence are not considered in the overall ranking.

Split	UCSY	ALT
Train	208,638	17,965
Dev	-	993
Test	-	1,007

Table 3: Myanmar-English dataset splits. The number indicates the number of lines in the split.

periments we used all the data for ASPEC Japanese-Chinese but for Japanese-English we used only the top 1.5 million lines since the bottom half of the corpus is of poorer quality and contains many badly aligned segments.

4.2 Models Trained

For the ASPEC task we trained vanilla and recurrently stacked NMT models for unidirectional translation. We used shared encoder-decoder vocabularies for multilingual (including bidirectional) models and for Chinese-Japanese models in order to enable cognate sharing. Kindly note that in this paper, unidirectional models can only translate in one direction and bidirectional models can translate in both directions. Our usage of the words uni and bidirectional are not related to the bidirectional RNNs used in the traditional seq2seq models. For vanilla English-Japanese models we use separate vocabularies because there is no scope for cognate sharing. For each translation direction we submitted two types of models which are as follows:

- English to Japanese: a. A bidirectional transformer using the top 1.5M lines of the English-Japanese corpus. This model uses the "big" model hyperparameter setting as defined in the

original paper. b. A RS-NMT model in which a 3 layer transformer was recurrently stacked 4 times.[3] This model was trained using the whole corpus of 3M lines. Both models were trained for 300k iterations.

- Japanese to English: a. A multilingual transformer that uses 1.5M lines of English-Japanese and the whole Japanese-Chinese corpus. This single transformer model can translate both two and from English and Japanese as well as Japanese and Chinese. This transformer also uses the "big" model hyperparameter settings. b. A unidirectional Japanese to English transformer using the full 3M lines corpus.

- Chinese to Japanese: a. The same multilingual model used for Japanese to English translation. b. A model that uses mixed fine tuning by first training on 3M lines of En-Ja for 200k iterations followed by an additional 100k iterations on a combined dataset of 3M lines of En-Ja.

- Japanese to Chinese: a. The same multilingual model used for Japanese to English translation. b. The vanilla transformer model.

4.3 Results

Refer to Table 2 for an overview of the ASPEC task results. In general our submissions secured second rank in terms of BLEU for 3/4 tasks and first rank

---

[3]In the original RS-NMT model (Dabre and Fujita, 2018) a single layer is recurrently stacked N times. As such the number of parameters is the same as a 1-layer transformer. However in our case the number of parameters is the same as a 3-layer transformer.

Split	Bengali	Hindi	Malayalam	Tamil	Telugu	Urdu	Sinhalese
Train	337,428	337,428	359,423	26,217	22,165	26,619	521,726
Dev	500	500	500	500	500	500	500
Test	1,000	1,000	1,000	1,000	1,000	1,000	1,000

Table 4: Indic languages dataset splits. The number indicates the number of lines in the split.

in terms of human evaluation for 3/4 tasks. It is important to note that the best performing submission (in terms of BLEU) for 3/4 tasks used ensembling (possibly on top of checkpoint averaging) for decoding whereas our submissions used only checkpoint averaging. In the case of Japanese-Chinese, the submission with the best BLEU used an ensemble of 10 models. In comparison our submissions involve only one model and hence we believe that our models are better suited for deployment in a practical scenario. It is also important to note that our English-Japanese RS-NMT model is within 1 BLEU point of our best submission. This shows that recurrent stacking of layers is quite formidable and deserves plenty of exploration in the future. For reference, the number of parameters in the 6-layer English-Japanese model is 283,313,671 (BLEU 41.31) whereas for the RS-NMT model this number drops to 217,171,975 (BLEU 41.31). It is clear that RS-NMT can help create compact models without loss in translation quality.

5 Myanmar to English Translation Task

5.1 Datasets

The Myanmar-English datasets consist of parallel corpora from two different domains. The objective of the Myanmar-English translation task is to improve the translation quality for the ALT (Asian Language Treebank) (Riza et al., 2016) which consists of relatively low-resource language pairs. For this domain the parallel corpus is extremely small. As such, a larger out-of-domain corpus for the same language pair also known as the UCSY[4] corpus is provided. Refer to Table 3 for the corpora splits.

5.2 Models Trained

For Myanmar to English translation, we submitted only one model which was trained using mixed fine tuning (MFT). We first trained a model on the

out-of-domain UCSY data for 100000 iterations followed by training for a further 20000 iterations on a combination of UCSY and ALT data. Since this is a low-resource setting we used separate encoder-decoder vocabularies of 16k subwords.

5.3 Results

For Myanmar-English the best BLEU score we obtained was 15.44 using only UCSY and ALT data by training the model using mixed fine tuning (MFT). In comparison the best performing submission had a BLEU of 29.14. It should be noted that this system used additional monolingual data. Our BLEU based ranking is 3/6 and our human evaluation based ranking is 3/5. In the future we will explore more sophisticated mechanisms for this language pair and adopt the use of monolingual corpora which is shown to be highly effective.

6 Indic Languages Task

6.1 Datasets

The Indic language dataset spans 8 languages, 7 of which are Indic languages and one of them being English. The objective of the Indic shared task is to test the feasibility of multilingualism for low-resource machine translation for related languages. The Indic languages involved are Bengali, Hindi, Malayalam, Tamil, Telugu, Sinhalese and Urdu. The corpus belongs to the OpenSubtitles domain. Refer to Table 4 for the corpora splits. Although monolingual corpora were provided, we did not use them.

6.2 Models Trained

We trained the following five types of models:

- Unidirectional models: We trained separate vocabulary models for translating from English to the Indic languages and from the Indic languages to English. The vocabulary size was 8k and separate encoder-decoder vocabularies

---

[4]`http://www.nlpresearch-ucsy.edu.mm/`

Task	Model	Our BLEU	Top BLEU	BLEU Ranking	Human Ranking
English-Bengali	uni	14.55	18.81	-	-
English-Bengali	En-XX	10.45	18.81	-	-
English-Bengali	XX-YY	10.39	18.81	-	-
English-Hindi	uni	26.35	44.08	-	-
English-Hindi	En-XX	29.65	44.08	2/4	-
English-Hindi	XX-YY	26.59	44.08	-	1/4
English-Malayalam	uni	16.56	16.56	-	-
English-Malayalam	En-XX	7.29	16.56	-	-
English-Malayalam	XX-YY	4.87	16.56	-	-
English-Tamil	uni	8.74	30.53	-	-
English-Tamil	En-XX	18.60	30.53	-	-
English-Tamil	XX-YY	20.39	30.53	2/4	3/3
English-Telugu	uni	10.74	41.89	-	-
English-Telugu	En-XX	25.64	41.89	-	-
English-Telugu	XX-YY	29.17	41.89	-	-
English-Urdu	uni	20.21	32.86	-	-
English-Urdu	En-XX	27.05	32.86	-	-
English-Urdu	XX-YY	29.05	32.86	-	-
English-Sinhalese	uni	9.78	18.09	-	-
English-Sinhalese	En-XX	8.35	18.09	-	-
English-Sinhalese	XX-YY	7.51	18.09	-	-

Table 5: Indic task results for translation from English to Indic Languages. We only consider the ranking of our submissions with the highest BLEU/human scores. As such, some submissions have a BLEU ranking but not a human ranking and vice versa. Note that, only English-Hindi, Hindi-English, English-Tamil and Tamil-English translation directions were submitted for human evaluation.

were used. Due to lack of time required for hyperparameter tuning, we trained the models for 100k iterations on the default model setting.

- Multilingual XX-En model: We trained a single model to translate from all the Indic languages to English by combining all the training data. Since the target language is the same, this is the only multilingual model that does not need artificial tokens to indicate the target language. We trained this model for 500k iterations.

- Multilingual En-XX model: We trained a single model to translate from English to all the Indic languages. This is essentially the reverse of the XX-En model. We also trained this model for 500k iterations.

- Multilingual XX-YY model: We trained a single model to translate from all the Indic languages to English and vice versa. Unlike the previous multilingual models, we trained this model only for 180k iterations due to lack of time.

- Multilingual Shared Indic Script XX-En model: This model is similar to the XX-En model except that the scripts for all the Indic languages are mapped to a common script. We used Devanagari as the common script, and used the *Indic NLP Library*[5] (Kunchukuttan et al., 2015) for script conversion. As such, this increases the chance of vocabulary sharing. Because the training corpus diversity is significantly reduced we trained this model for 100k iterations because it is technically equivalent

---

[5]https://github.com/anoopkunchukuttan/indic_nlp_library/

Task	Model	Our BLEU	Top BLEU	BLEU Ranking	Human Ranking
Bengali-English	uni	19.17	20.05	-	-
Bengali-English	XX-En	18.03	20.05	-	-
Bengali-English	UXX-En	18.82	20.05	-	-
Bengali-English	XX-YY	16.68	20.05	-	-
Hindi-English	uni	26.05	32.95	2/4	-
Hindi-English	XX-En	31.06	32.95	-	-
Hindi-English	UXX-En	31.51	32.95	-	-
Hindi-English	XX-YY	30.21	32.95	-	2/4
Malayalam-English	uni	22.87	22.87	-	-
Malayalam-English	XX-En	14.06	22.87	-	-
Malayalam-English	UXX-En	15.91	22.87	-	-
Malayalam-English	XX-YY	10.90	22.87	-	-
Tamil-English	uni	11.09	24.31	-	-
Tamil-English	XX-En	21.37	24.31	-	-
Tamil-English	UXX-En	21.27	24.31	-	-
Tamil-English	XX-YY	24.31	24.31	1/4	2/4
Telugu-English	uni	15.76	33.23	-	-
Telugu-English	XX-En	29.85	33.23	-	-
Telugu-English	UXX-En	30.23	33.23	-	-
Telugu-English	XX-YY	33.23	33.23	-	-
Urdu-English	uni	20.65	30.84	-	-
Urdu-English	XX-En	27.88	30.84	-	-
Urdu-English	UXX-En	26.73	30.84	-	-
Urdu-English	XX-YY	30.84	30.84	-	-
Sinhalese-English	uni	21.85	21.85	-	-
Sinhalese-English	XX-En	18.73	21.85	-	-
Sinhalese-English	UXX-En	19.19	21.85	-	-
Sinhalese-English	XX-YY	17.25	21.85	-	-

Table 6: Indic task results for translation from Indic Languages to English. We only consider the ranking of our submissions with the highest BLEU/human scores. As such, some submissions have a BLEU ranking but not a human ranking and vice versa. Note that, only English-Hindi, Hindi-English, English-Tamil and Tamil-English translation directions were submitted for human evaluation.

to a unidirectional translation model.

6.3 Results

Refer to Tables 5 and 6 for the results for the Indic Languages translation task. We give the results for the unidirectional (uni), multitarget (En-XX), multisource (XX-En), multilingual shared Indic script (UXX-En) and multisource multitarget (XX-YY) models. In case of translation to the Indic languages, our best submissions was able to secure 2nd rank (BLEU) for most language pairs. On the other hand, for translation from the Indic languages, our best

submissions were able to secure 1st rank (BLEU) for most language pairs. In terms of human evaluation we also managed to secure 2nd rank most of the times for the language pairs that were submitted.

From our results it is clear that multilingual models do not work perfectly well for all translation directions but they do help in improving translation quality for the low-resource languages (Hindi, Tamil, Urdu and Telugu). Multilingual models led to poor performance for the resource rich translation directions. As expected, vocabulary unification did lead to slight improvements in translation quality and we believe that such approaches deserve further exploration. Due to lack of time we did not try advanced multilingual models and training approaches which we expect will lead to a single multilingual model that will perform well for all translation directions.

7 Conclusion

In this paper we have described our submissions to WAT 2018. We managed to obtain near state-of-the-art results for ASPEC and showed the effectiveness of multilingual transformers. We also showed that recurrently stacked NMT models can lead to high quality models while significantly reducing the number of model parameters. We explored the utility of mixed fine tuning for Myanmar-English translation. We also studied the impact of multilingualism in the case of Indic languages translation.

Overall we have observed that multilingualism leads to significant improvements in translation quality and reduce the need to train multiple translation models effectively leading to parameter reduction. We have also observed that BLEU score based ranking is mostly inconsistent with human evaluation based ranking, especially for the ASPEC task. We believe that this calls for innovation into newer automatic evaluation metrics that correlate well with human evaluations. In the future we plan to explore more sophisticated multilingual models which should help push the state-of-the-art even further.

Acknowledgments

We would like to thank the reviewers for their comments which helped improve the quality of this paper.

References

Dzmitry Bahdanau, Kyunghyun Cho, and Yoshua Bengio. 2015. Neural machine translation by jointly learning to align and translate. In *Proceedings of the 3rd International Conference on Learning Representations (ICLR 2015)*, San Diego, USA, May. International Conference on Learning Representations.

Kyunghyun Cho, Bart van Merriënboer, Çalar Gülçehre, Dzmitry Bahdanau, Fethi Bougares, Holger Schwenk, and Yoshua Bengio. 2014. Learning phrase representations using rnn encoder–decoder for statistical machine translation. In *Proceedings of the 2014 Conference on Empirical Methods in Natural Language Processing (EMNLP)*, pages 1724–1734, Doha, Qatar, October. Association for Computational Linguistics.

Chenhui Chu, Raj Dabre, and Sadao Kurohashi. 2017. An empirical comparison of domain adaptation methods for neural machine translation. In *Proceedings of the 55th Annual Meeting of the Association for Computational Linguistics*, Vancouver, Canada, July. Association for Computational Linguistics.

Raj Dabre and Atsushi Fujita. 2018. Recurrent stacking of layers for compact neural machine translation models. *CoRR*, abs/1807.05353.

Mostafa Dehghani, Stephan Gouws, Oriol Vinyals, Jakob Uszkoreit, and Łukasz Kaiser. 2018. Universal transformers. *CoRR*, abs/1807.03819.

Melvin Johnson, Mike Schuster, Quoc V. Le, Maxim Krikun, Yonghui Wu, Zhifeng Chen, Nikhil Thorat, Fernanda Viégas, Martin Wattenberg, Greg Corrado, Macduff Hughes, and Jeffrey Dean. 2017. Google's multilingual neural machine translation system: Enabling zero-shot translation. *Transactions of the Association for Computational Linguistics*, 5:339–351.

Philipp Koehn, Hieu Hoang, Alexandra Birch, Chris Callison-Burch, Marcello Federico, Nicola Bertoldi, Brooke Cowan, Wade Shen, Christine Moran, Richard Zens, Chris Dyer, Ondrej Bojar, Alexandra Constantin, and Evan Herbst. 2007. Moses: Open source toolkit for statistical machine translation. In *Proceedings of the 45th Annual Meeting of the Association for Computational Linguistics Companion Volume Proceedings of the Demo and Poster Sessions*, pages 177–180, Prague, Czech Republic, June. Association for Computational Linguistics.

Anoop Kunchukuttan, Ratish Puduppully, and Pushpak Bhattacharyya. 2015. Brahmi-Net: A transliteration and script conversion system for languages of the Indian subcontinent. In *Conference of the North American Chapter of the Association for Computational Linguistics - Human Language Technologies: System Demonstrations*.

Toshiaki Nakazawa, Manabu Yaguchi, Kiyotaka Uchimoto, Masao Utiyama, Eiichiro Sumita, Sadao Kurohashi, and Hitoshi Isahara. 2016. Aspec: Asian scientific paper excerpt corpus. In *Proceedings of the Tenth International Conference on Language Resources and Evaluation (LREC 2016)*, Paris, France, May. European Language Resources Association (ELRA).

Toshiaki Nakazawa, Shohei Higashiyama, Chenchen Ding, Raj Dabre, Anoop Kunchukuttan, Win Pa Pa, Isao Goto, Hideya Mino, Katsuhito Sudoh, and Sadao Kurohashi. 2018. Overview of the 5th workshop on asian translation. In *Proceedings of the 5th Workshop on Asian Translation (WAT2018)*, Hong Kong, China, December.

H. Riza, M. Purwoadi, Gunarso, T. Uliniansyah, A. A. Ti, S. M. Aljunied, L. C. Mai, V. T. Thang, N. P. Thai, V. Chea, R. Sun, S. Sam, S. Seng, K. M. Soe, K. T. Nwet, M. Utiyama, and C. Ding. 2016. Introduction of the asian language treebank. In *2016 Conference of The Oriental Chapter of International Committee for Coordination and Standardization of Speech Databases and Assessment Techniques (O-COCOSDA)*, pages 1–6, Oct.

Ilya Sutskever, Oriol Vinyals, and Quoc V. Le. 2014. Sequence to sequence learning with neural networks. In *Proceedings of the 27th International Conference on Neural Information Processing Systems*, NIPS'14, pages 3104–3112, Cambridge, MA, USA. MIT Press.

Ashish Vaswani, Noam Shazeer, Niki Parmar, Jakob Uszkoreit, Llion Jones, Aidan N Gomez, Łukasz Kaiser, and Illia Polosukhin. 2017. Attention is all you need. In I. Guyon, U. V. Luxburg, S. Bengio, H. Wallach, R. Fergus, S. Vishwanathan, and R. Garnett, editors, *Advances in Neural Information Processing Systems 30*, pages 5998–6008. Curran Associates, Inc.

Barret Zoph, Deniz Yuret, Jonathan May, and Kevin Knight. 2016. Transfer learning for low-resource neural machine translation. In *Proceedings of the 2016 Conference on Empirical Methods in Natural Language Processing, EMNLP 2016, Austin, Texas, USA, November 1-4, 2016*, pages 1568–1575.

32nd Pacific Asia Conference on Language, Information and Computation
The 5th Workshop on Asian Translation
Hong Kong, 1-3 December 2018

SRCB Neural Machine Translation Systems in WAT 2018

Yihan Li   Boyan Liu   Yixuan Tong   Shanshan Jiang   Bin Dong

Ricoh Software Research Center Beijing Co., Ltd.

{yihan.li, boyan.liu, yixuan.tong, shanshan.jiang, bin.dong}@srcb.ricoh.com

Abstract

This is the first time SRCB participates in WAT. This paper describes the Neural Machine Translation systems for the shared translation tasks of WAT 2018. We participated in ASPEC tasks, and submitted results on English-Japanese, Japanese-English and Japanese-Chinese three language pairs. We employed Transformer as baseline model, and experimented subword segmentation, relative position representation and model ensembling. Experiments show that all these methods can yield substantial improvements.

1   Introduction

The advent of neural networks in machine translation has brought great improvement on translation quality over traditional statistical machine translation (SMT) in recent years (Kalchbrenner and Blunsom, 2013; Sutskever et al., 2014; Cho et al., 2014; Bahdanau et al., 2014). A lot of research efforts have been attracted to investigate neural networks in machine translation. This paper describes the Neural Machine Translation systems of Ricoh Software Research Center Beijing (SRCB) for the shared translation tasks of WAT 2018 (Nakazawa et al., 2018). We participated in ASPEC tasks, and submitted results on three language pairs, including English-Japanese, Japanese-English and Japanese-Chinese.

In the ASPEC tasks, we employed Transformer (Vaswani et al., 2017) as our baseline model and built our translation system based on OpenNMT (Klein et al., 2017) open source toolkit [1]. To enhance the performance of the model, we made the following changes: 1) To deal with out of vocabulary (OOV) and rare words problem in

[1] http://opennmt.net/

translation, we used subword unit, that is Joint Byte Pair Encoding (BPE) (Sennrich et al., 2016c) scheme, to encoder vocabulary for both source and target language. 2) We proposed a synthetic data augmentation method and it was observed to be useful in Japanese-English corpus. 3) We incorporated relative position representation (Shaw et al., 2018) into Transformer model. 4) We used two ensemble techniques to further improve translation quality.

The remainder of this paper is organized as follows: Section 2 describes our NMT system. Section 3 describes the processing of the data and all experimental results and analysis. Finally, we conclude in section 4.

2   Systems

2.1   Base Model

Our NMT system is built upon Transformer (Vaswani et al., 2018) model. We used open source OpenNMT[1] and imported some changes and new features such as relative position embedding (Shaw et al., 2018) and ensembling.

The Transformer (Vaswani et al., 2017) also adopts sequence to sequence architecture and it consists of an encoder layer and a decoder layer. Different from traditional Seq2Seq model (Bahdanau et al., 2014), the encoder layer consists of two sublayers: a multi-head self-attention layer and a position-wise fully connected feed-forward layer. Instead of employing a single attention function mechanism (Luong et al., 2015), the multi-head self-attention adopts several different learnt linear projections to queries, keys and values respectively. This mechanism allows model to jointly attend to information from different representation subspaces at different positions. The decoder layer consists of three sublayers: a masked multi-head self-attention, followed by encoder-decoder attention and a position-wise feed-forward layer. Residual connections (He et al., 2016) followed by layer normalization (Ba et al., 2016) are used between each sublayer, which can prevent gradient vanishing (Hochreiter et al., 1998) and propagate information to higher layers. The masked multi-head self-attention uses masking in its self-attention to prevent a given output position from incorporating information about future output positions during training.

To make use of the order of the sequence, the Transformer models add positional encodings to capture information about the absolute position of the tokens in the sequence. The positional encodings are based on sinusoids of varying frequency and are added to the input embeddings at the bottoms of the encoder and decoder stacks. The absolute position representations hypothesized that sinusoidal position encodings would help the model to generalize to sequence lengths unseen during training.

2.2 Relative Position Representation

Instead of using absolute position encodings, Shaw et al. (2018) presented an alternative approach, extending the self-attention mechanism to efficiently consider representations of the relative positions, or distance between sequence elements. The approach can be cast as a special case of considering arbitrary relations between any two elements of the inputs.

The approach learns two relative position representations. The first representation is to propagate edge information to the sublayer output when computing weighted sum of a linearly transformed input elements. Similarly, the second representation is to consider edges when computing a compatibility function that compares two input elements.

In their experiments, they observed significant improvement over absolute position representations. Furthermore, they observed that combing relative and absolute position representations yields no further improvement in translation quality. Thus, in our translation system, we incorporated relative position representation and removed absolute position encodings from encoder layers.

2.3 Ensembling

It has been investigated that ensembling different model can yield significant improvement in translation quality (Denkowski and Neubig, 2017). In our systems, we adopted two ensembling schemes. For one configured translation model, once the model finishes training, the last 8 checkpoints of the model are averaged to get one trained model. Then, we make different configurations and train several models independently. After averaging checkpoints for each model, we do step-wise ensembling. Specifically, these models are run at each time step and an arithmetic mean of predicted probability is obtained, which is used to determine the next word.

2.4 Data Augmentation

For ASPEC dataset (Nakazawa et al., 2014), the quality of first 1M data is better than other 2M data. Thus, first 1M data are included in our training data. Furthermore, in order to use more data, we proposed an approach to select pairs from the second 1M data. Specifically, we first train a translation model using first 1M data, and then for each source sentence in the second 1M data, we generate a predicted sentence based on trained model. A BLEU score is calculated by comparing predicted sentence with target sentence. If the BLEU score is zero, then the source sentence and corresponding target sentence is added to training dataset. Finally, we train a new model based on augmented dataset. The intuition is that predicted sentences with zero BLEU scores are supposed to be not fully understood by trained model, so these sentences are added to training dataset and translation model is expected to learn more pattern from these data.

3 Experiments

We experimented our NMT system on Japanese-English, English-Japanese, and Japanese-Chinese scientific paper translation subtasks.

3.1 Datasets

We used Asian Scientific Paper Excerpt Corpus (ASPEC) (Nakazawa et al., 2014) as parallel corpora for all language pairs. For Japanese-Chinese subtask, all the sentences in ASPEC corpora are used as training data. For Japanese-

English and English-Japanese subtasks, we used only the first 1 million sentences sorted by sentence-alignment similarity. Furthermore, for Japanese-English subtask, we augmented training data to nearly 2 million by our proposed method. And, for all corpora, Japanese sentences were segmented by the morphological analyzer Juman[2] and English sentences were tokenized by tokenizer.perl of Moses (Koehn et al., 2007). Sentences with more than 60 words were excluded. We used subword unit, that is Joint Byte Pair Encoding (BPE) (Sennrich et al., 2016c) scheme, to encoder vocabulary for both source and target sentences. Table 1 shows the numbers of the sentences in each parallel corpus.

	Ja-En	En-Ja	Ja-Ch
Train	1,770,818	1,000,000	672,315
Dev	1,790	1,790	2,741
test	1,812	1,812	2,300

Table 1: Number of parallel sentences

3.2 Results

Table 2 lists our final results for three languages subtasks. According to evaluation systems, for all these subtask, we got best performance in BLEU measure. We described experimental results in detail in the following subsections.

	Ja-En	En-Ja	Ja-Zh
BLEU	30.59	43.43	37.60

Table 2: Results of Subtasks

Japanese-English subtask:
The Japanese-English subtask is the main subtask that we participated in and all the technical points mentioned in section 2 have been used. All the useful ones with corresponding contributions are listed in Table 3.

System	BLEU
Baseline	26.27
BPE Subword 1M	28.34
Data Augmentation	29.41
Relative Position	29.77
Average checkpoint	30.18
Step-wise	30.59

Table 3: Technical point contributions

[2] http://nlp.ist.i.kyoto-u.ac.jp/EN/index.php?JUMAN

The baseline model is the transformer model with 3M parallel sentences. There can be more than 2 BLEU scores improvement only by using the first 1M parallel sentences with BPE subword. In relation to data augmentation, if the second 1M data are all added to the first 1M training data, the BLEU score decreases to 28.28. On the other hand, if only the sentences with zero BLEU scores are added, the BLEU score for the model increases by more than 1 point. According to the BLEU measurement, the zero score indicates that there is no matched 4-gram between predictions and references, which means these sentences have not been trained well. Relative position can also yield more than 1 score improvement based on the baseline system. As for the ensemble part, both average checkpoint and step-wise can increase almost 0.5 BLEU score. And the ensemble turn is using average checkpoint first followed by step-wise.

The results show each technical points has an obvious contribution, however, they are not precisely superimposed, adding the contributions together is an important part in our real work.

English-Japanese subtask:

	Baseline	3 models	4 models
BLEU	41.98	42.49	43.43

Table 4: Results of step-wise Ensemble

The English-Japanese subtask is the opposite direction of the Japanese-English subtask, so the language characteristics are almost the same. Thus we used the same technical points as Japanese-English subtask except that turn over the training dataset. In addition, due to the limited time, we don't use data augmentation in this subtask. The results are shown in table 4. As we can figure out the BLEU score of 4 models is higher nearly 1 score than 3 models, so there is potential to get higher scores with more models.

Japanese-Chinese subtask:

	2 models	4 models	10 models
BLEU	36.31	37.03	37.53

Table 5: Results of step-wise ensembling

The results of step-wise ensembling for Japanese-Chinese are showed in table 5. To introduce variation, models are trained with different hyperparameters. Due to the resource limitation, only 10 models with BLEU score between 35.93 and 36.33 are selected to perform the final ensemble. It can be observed that the BLEU score goes up as the number of models increases. Based on the translation candidates generated by the model with BLEU score 37.53, we apply rerank method to achieve the final result shown in table 2.

4 Conclusion

In this paper, we described our NMT system, which is based on Transformer model. We made several changes to original Transformer model, including relative position representation and ensembling. We evaluated our Transformer system on Japanese-English, English-Japanese and Japanese-Chinese scientific paper translation subtasks at WAT 2018. The experimental results show that the implementation of relative position representation and ensembling decoding can effectively improve the translation quality.

In our future work, we plan to explore more vocabulary encoding schemes and compare with byte pair encoding (BPE) (Sennrich et al., 2016). In addition, we will attempt to implement the weighted transformer (Ahmed et al., 2017), which replaces the multi-head attention by multiple self-attention branches that the model learns to combine during training process. We also plan to investigate the impact of parameters, such as batch size and learning rate, on translation quality in future.

References

Nal Kalchbrenner and Phil Blunsom. 2013. Recurrent continuous translation models. In Proceeding of the ACL Conference on Empirical Methods in Natural Language Processing (EMNLP), 1700-1709.

Ilya Sutskever, Oriol Vinyals,and Quoc Le. 2014. Sequence to sequence learning with neural networks. In Advances in Neural Information Processing Systems (NIPS 2014), December.

Kyunghyun Cho, Bart Van and et al. 2014. Learning phrase representations using RNN encoder-decoder for statistical machine translation. In Proceedings of the Empirical Methods in Natural Language Processing (EMNLP 2014), October.

Dzmitry Bahdanau, Kyunghyun Cho, and Yoshua Bengio. 2014. Neural machine translation by jointly learning to align and translate. arXiv preprint arXiv:1409.0473.

Vaswani A, Shazeer N, Parmar N, et al. 2017 Attention is all you need. Advances in Neural Information Processing Systems, 5998-6008.

Rico Sennrich, Barry Haddow, and Alexandra Birch. 2016c. Neural machine translation of rare words with subword units. In Proceedings of ACL, pages 1715–1725.

Shaw P, Uszkoreit J, Vaswani A. 2018. Self-Attention with Relative Position Representations. arXiv preprint arXiv:1803.02155.

Jimmy Lei Ba, Jamie Ryan Kiros, and Geoffrey E Hinton. 2016. Layer normalization. arXiv preprint arXiv:1607.06450 .

Toshiaki Nakazawa, Manabu Yaguchi, Kiyotaka Uchimoto, Masao Utiyama, Eiichiro Sumita, Sadao Kurohashi, and Hitoshi Isahara. 2014. ASPEC : Asian Scientific Paper Excerpt Corpus. In Proceedings of the Tenth International Conference on Language Resources and Evaluation (LREC), pages 2204–2208.

Toshiaki Nakazawa and Shohei Higashiyama and Chenchen Ding and Raj Dabre and Anoop Kunchukuttan and Win Pa Pa and Isao Goto and Hideya Mino and Katsuhito Sudoh and Sadao Kurohashi. 2018. Overview of the 5th Workshop on Asian Translation. In Proceedings of the 5th Workshop on Asian Translation (WAT2018).

Ahmed K, Keskar N S, Socher R. 2017. Weighted Transformer Network for Machine Translation. arXiv preprint arXiv:1711.02132.

Thang Luong, Hieu Pham, and Christopher D. Manning. 2015. Effective approaches to attention-based neural machine translation. In Proceedings of the 2015 Conference on Empirical Methods in Natural Language Processing, pages 1412–1421, Lisbon, Portugal. Association for Computational Linguistics.

He K, Zhang X, Ren S, et al. 2016 Deep residual learning for image recognition. Proceedings of the IEEE conference on computer vision and pattern recognition, pages 770-778.

Hochreiter S. The vanishing gradient problem during learning recurrent neural nets and problem solutions. 1998. International Journal of Uncertainty, Fuzziness and Knowledge-Based Systems, 6(02): 107-116.

Michael Denkowski and Graham Neubig. 2017. Stronger baselines for trustable results in neural machine translation. In Proceedings of the First

Workshop on Neural Machine Translation (WNMT), pages 18–27.

Guillaume Klein, Yoon Kim, Yuntian Deng, Jean Senellart, and Alexander M. Rush. 2017. Open-NMT: Open-Source Toolkit for Neural Machine Translation. arXiv preprint arXiv:1701.02810.

Philipp Koehn, Hieu Hoang, and et al. 2007. Moses: Open source toolkit for statistical machine translation. In Proceedings of the ACL-2007.

SMT reranked NMT (2)

Terumasa Ehara
Ehara NLP Research Laboratory
Seijo, Setagaya, Tokyo Japan
http://www.ne.jp/asahi/eharate/eharate/

Abstract

System architecture, experimental settings and experimental results of the EHR team for the WAT2018 tasks are described. System architecture is same as the WAT2017 submission. We participate four tasks this time. We can improve 1.5 to 3.0 BLEU score compared with the baseline scores. On the other hand, the pairwise evaluation score of our system to the baseline is negative in ASPEC en-ja task. Our technique also decreases the number of under-translation that is frequently appears in a NMT output.

1 Introduction

Although the NMT provides high quality and fluent translations, it has several drawbacks. One of them is under- and over-translation which is infrequent in a SMT output. We have proposed a reranking method for n-best NMT outputs using a SMT output (Ehara, 2017). Ehara (2017) shows under-translation can be reduced by the method. This time, we use the same technique. Figure 1 shows our system architecture.

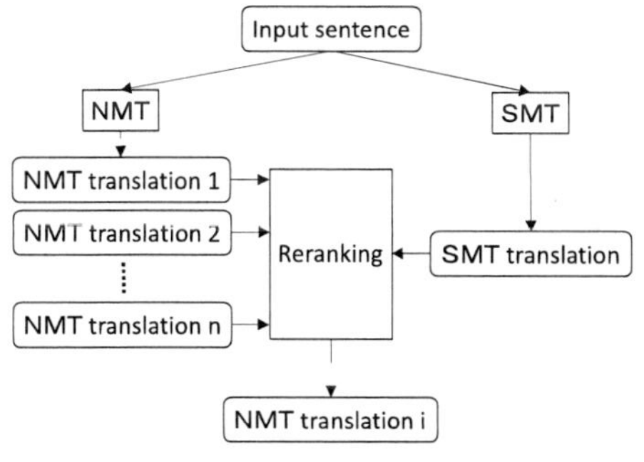

Figure 1: System architecture

An input sentence is fed to NMT part and to SMT part. N-best outputs of NMT are reranked by the SMT output as a reference. Reranking measure is BLEU, this time, instead of IMPACT in WAT2017. NMT translation i having highest BLEU score is output as a system output.

2 Experimental setting

In WAT2018 (Nakazawa et al., 2018), we participate four tasks: ASPEC en-ja, JPC zh-ja, JPC ko-ja and JPC en-ja tasks. We use OpenNMT (Minh-Thang Luong et al., 2015) in NMT part. Our SMT part is phrase-based SMT by Moses v.3 (Koehn et al., 2003) with default option settings. We adopt preordering in SMT for en-ja and zh-ja tasks. Option settings for NMT part is described in Ehara (2017). Segmentation policies for NMT are as follows. In JPC zh-ja task, zh part is segmented by a character and ja part is segmented by a word except for alpha-numeric and symbol character sequences. Alpha-numeric and symbol character sequences are segmented by a character. In JPC ko-ja task, ko part and ja part are both segmented by a character. In JPC en-ja task and ASPEC en-ja task, en parts and ja parts are both segmented by a sub word. For JPC en-ja task, vocabulary size of en part is 60,217 and vocabulary size of ja part is 94,542. For ASPEC en-ja task, vocabulary size of en part is 62,203 and vocabulary size of ja part is 107,145.

3 Experimental results

Experimental results are shown in Table 1 with training data size (number of sentences) and final epoch number of NMT training. Training data for JPC en-ja task include WAT2018's training data and NTCIR-10's training data (Goto et al., 2013). The differences of three data ID in four subtasks of

JPC en-ja task are epoch number of NMT training. They are 13, 18 and 20.

We can improve 1.5 to 3.0 BLEU score compared with the baseline scores.

JPO adequacy scores are similar to the last workshop's scores of EHR team (Adeq/2017).

Task	Data size	Sub task	Data ID	Epoch	BLEU	RIBES	Pairwise	JPO Adeq.	Adeq/2017
JPC zh-ja	1,000,000	N	2209	13	45.55	0.8567	--	--	--
		N1	2210	13	48.10	0.8583	--	4.22	4.31
		N2	2211	13	47.12	0.8617	--	4.22	--
		N3	2212	13	19.65	0.7673	--	--	--
		EP	2213	13	34.23	0.8051	--	--	--
JPC ko-ja	1,000,000	N	2214	13	71.70	0.9485	--	--	--
		N1	2215	13	71.45	0.9458	--	4.89	4.81
		N2	2216	13	73.29	0.9535	--	4.73	--
		N3	2217	13	53.83	0.9074	--	--	--
JPC en-ja	4,043,073	N	2283	13	44.71	0.8525	--	--	--
			2394	18	45.27	0.8549	--	--	--
			2475	20	45.39	0.8548	--	--	--
		N1	2284	13	47.57	0.8707	--	--	--
			2395	18	48.01	0.8734	--	--	--
			2476	20	48.03	0.8728	--	4.64	4.63
		N2	2285	13	41.54	0.8376	--	--	--
			2396	18	41.99	0.8405	--	--	--
			2477	20	42.12	0.8407	--	4.36	--
		N3	2286	13	50.04	0.8649	--	--	--
			2397	18	51.17	0.8642	--	--	--
			2478	20	51.42	0.8645	--	--	--
ASPEC en-ja	1,502,767	--	2245	13	37.97	0.8287	-0.500	--	--

Table 1: Experimental results

For ASPEC en-ja task, our result makes 37.97 BLEU score comparing that baseline result has 36.37 BLEU score. On the other hand, pairwise evaluation score of our system is minus 0.5. We calculate the difference of sentence level BLEU of our translation and baseline translation (diff BLEU)[1]. Figure 2 shows scattering graph of diff BLEU and pairwise evaluation score (sum of five evaluator's scores).

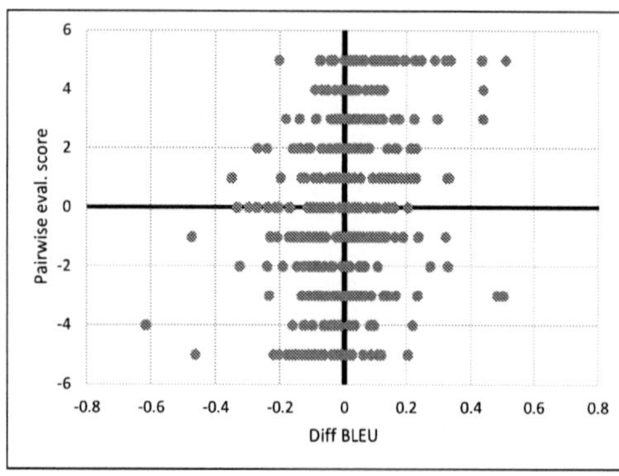

Figure 2: Scattering graph of diff BLEU and pairwise evaluation score (ASPEC en-ja task)

Data points in first quadrant and third quadrant have no contradiction in two scores. Data points in second quadrant and fourth quadrant have contradiction in two scores. Number of data in each quadrant is listed in Table 2. Several examples of contradicted data are examined in the next section.

Diff BLEU＼Pairwise	< 0	≧ 0
< 0	94	84
≧ 0	85	137

Table 2: Contingency table of diff BLEU and pairwise evaluation score.

We examine under- and over-translations in ASPEC en-ja task's 1,812 test data. The result is shown in Table 3. In Table 3, "reranked" means outputs with reranking, "unreranked" means outputs without reranking, "normal" means translation which includes neither under nor over translation, "under" means under-translation, "over" means over-translation and "under & over" means translation which includes both under and over translation.

		reranked				
		normal	under	over	under & over	total
unreranked	normal	1496	10	9	1	1516
	under	206	71	3	2	282
	over	4	0	6	0	10
	under & over	2	0	1	1	4
	total	1708	81	19	4	1812

Table 3: Number of under- and over-translation in unreranked translation and reranked translation for ASPEC en-ja task test data

From Table 3, we can see that in 1812 test sentences, 286 unreranked outputs include under-translation and only 85 reranked outputs include under-translation. On the other hand, in 1812 test sentences, 14 unreranked outputs include over-translation and 23 reranked outputs include over-translation. We can say our reranking technique decreases the number of under-translation, but cannot decrease the number of over-translation. Several examples of these data are described in the next section.

---

[1] Diff BLEU in Figure 2 is scaled from -1 to 1. On the other hand, BLEU in Table 1 is scaled from 0 to 100. NIST tool mteval-v13a.pl (ftp://jaguar.ncsl.nist.gov/mt/resources/mteval-v13a.pl)is used to calculate sentence level BLEU.

4 Analysis of translation results

4.1 Comparison of translation results with reranking and without reranking

We compare translation results with reranking and without reranking in this subsection for ASPEC en-ja task. We compute sentence level BLEU of both translation results. Table 4 shows the cases that the BLEU score of a translation with reranking is higher than the BLEU score of a translation without reranking. Table 5 shows the opposite cases.

In these tables, "snt. #" means sentence number of the test set, "src" means source sentence, "ref" means reference sentence, "smt" means translation result by the SMT part, "unreranked" means translation result without reranking, "reranked" means translation result with reranking by our method, "BLEU_f" means BLEU score of the "unreranked" and BLEU_r means BLEU score of the "reranked".

From Table 4, we can see several under-translations in the unreranked are corrected in reranked (see snt. # 1269 and 44).

item	value
snt. #	815
src	Method of the DCT is explained .
ref	DCT の 方法 に ついて 解説 した 。
smt	DCT の 方法 に ついて 解説 した 。
unreranked	DCT の 方法 を 説明 した 。
reranked	DCT の 方法 に ついて 解説 した 。
BLEU_f	0.2665
BLEU_r	1
remarks	BLEU_f is very low, however unreranked has similar meaning to ref.

snt. #	183
src	The dynamic equilibrium surface form is dependent on annealing condition and miss - cut direction of the substrate .
ref	動的 平衡 表面 形態 は アニーリング 条件 と 基板 の ミス カット 方向 に 依存 した 。
smt	動的 平衡 表面 形態 が アニーリング 条件 と 基板 の miss - cut 方向 に 依存 した 。
unreranked	動的 平衡 表面 形状 は 基板 の アニーリング 条件 と ミス カット 方向 に 依存 する 。
reranked	動的 平衡 表面 形態 は アニーリング 条件 と 基板 の ミス カット 方向 に 依存 した 。
BLEU_f	0.3921
BLEU_r	1
remarks	Dependee of "of the substrate" is " annealing condition and miss-cut direction" in unreranked that is incorrectly interpreted but is "miss-cut direction" in smt and reranked that is correctly interpreted.

snt. #	1236
src	This paper describes the application of the package software .
ref	業務 パッケージ ソフト の 適用 に ついて 述べた
smt	本稿 では , パッケージ ソフト の 適用 に ついて 述べた 。
unreranked	パッケージ ソフトウェア の 応用 に ついて 述べた 。
reranked	パッケージ ソフト の 適用 に ついて 述べた 。
BLEU_f	0.2336
BLEU_r	0.8409
remarks	"Application" is translated to "適用" in ref, smt and reranked and it is translated to "応用" in unreranked.

snt. #	1269
src	Survey items are as follows : 1) Trends of engineers (study in 1992 fiscal year and literature search) . 2) Survey on actual conditions and consciousness of engineers (questionnairing for each individual engineer) .
ref	調査 項目 は , 1) 技術 者 の 動向 (平成 4 年度 調査 と 文献 調査) , 2) 技術 者 の 実態 と 意識 に 関する 調査 (技術 者 個人 に 対する アンケート 調査) である 。
smt	調査 項目 は 以下 の 通り である 。 1 : 技術 者 (平成 4 年度 の 調査 と 文献 検索) 。 2) の 動向 , 技術 者 (個々 の 技術 者 に 対する アンケート 調査) の 実態 と 意識 に 関する 調査 。
unreranked	調査 項目 は 以下 の ようである 。
reranked	調査 項目 は , 1) 技術 者 の 動向 (平成 11 年度 の 研究 , 文献 調査) , 2) 技術 者 の 実態 と 意識 (個々 の 技術 者 ご との アンケート 調査) 。
BLEU_f	0.0019
BLEU_r	0.5796
remarks	Under-translation of unreranked is corrected in reranked.

snt. #	44
src	By measuring Josephson vortex flow resistance of slightly over doped (Tc = 86.0K) and intermediately doped (Tc = 82.5K) Bi2Sr2CaCu2O8 + δ (Bi - 2212) single crystals , the magnetic phase diagram was studied .
ref	僅かに 過剰 添加 (Tc = 86．0 K) 及び 中 程度 に 過剰 添加 (Tc = 82．5 K) した Bi 2 Sr 2 CaCu 2 O 8 + δ (Bi - 2 212) 単 結晶 の Josephson 渦 糸 フロー 抵抗 を 測定 して 磁 気 状態 図 を 調べた 。
smt	わずかに ドーピング した (Tc = 86．0 K 以上) と 中間 ドープ (Tc = 82．5 K) Bi 2 Sr 2 CaCu 2 O の Joseph son 渦 糸 流 抵抗 + δ (Bi - 2212) 単 結晶 を 測定 し , 磁 気 相 図 を 研究 した 。
unreranked	磁気 状態 図 を 調べた 。
reranked	わずかに ドープ した (Tc = 86．0 K) と 中間 ドープ (Tc = 8 2．5 K) Bi 2 Sr 2 CaCu 2 O 8 + δ (Bi - 2212) 単 結晶 の Josephson 渦 流 抵抗 を 測定 し , 磁気 相 図 を 研究 した 。
BLEU_f	0.0003
BLEU_r	0.5689
remarks	Under-translation of unreranked is corrected in reranked.

snt. #	1357
src	The electric power generation was the 380 micro watt .
ref	発電 量 は 380 マイクロ ワット であった 。
smt	発電 は 380 マイクロ ワット であった 。
unreranked	発電 は 380 μ W であった 。
reranked	発電 は 380 マイクロ ワット であった 。
BLEU_f	0.1703
BLEU_r	0.729
remarks	"Micro watt" is translated to "マイクロ ワット" in ref, smt and reranked and it is translated to "μ W" in unreranked.

snt. #	253
src	To begin with , this paper explains atomic energy level and transition between levels .
ref	先ず 原子 の エネルギー 準位 と 準位 間 の 遷移 から 説明 した 。
smt	本稿 では ， まず ， 原子 エネルギー 準位 と 準位 間 の 遷移 について 解説 した 。
unreranked	まず ， 原子 カ レベル と レベル 間 の 推移 について 解説 した 。
reranked	まず ， 原子 の エネルギー 準位 と 準位 間 の 遷移 について 解説 した 。
BLEU_f	0.077
BLEU_r	0.6119
remarks	"Atomic energy level" is incorrectly translated in reranked (原子 カ レベル), but in smt and reranked it is correctly translated (原子 の エネルギー 準位).

snt. #	303
src	The author also considered that on condition that the jointing part of two rows bonded with van der Waals force between main chains is a segement , Tg of linear polymer is the temperature when thermal expansion of the C-C bond from 0 ℃ becomes 1 % .
ref	また ， 線型 ポリマ の Tg は 主鎖 間 の van der Waals 力 で 結合 された 2 列 の 結合 部分 を セグメント と 考えて ， その C - C 結合 の 0 ℃ からの 熱 的な 伸び 率 が 1 % の 温度 とした 。
smt	また ， 主鎖 間 の ファンデルワールス 力 による 結合 した 2 列 の 接合 部 は segement である ことを 条件 に ， 線状 重合体 の Tg は 熱 expansition C - C 結合 の 0 ℃ から 1 % になると 温度 であると 考えた 。
unreranked	また ， 主鎖 間 の vanderWaals 力 に 結合 した 2 列 の 接合 部 が 偏析 する 条件 として ， 線形 高分子 の Tg は ， C - C 結合 の 熱 膨張 が 1 % になると 温度 になると 考えた 。
reranked	また ， 主鎖 間 の vanderWaals 力 に 結合 した 2 列 の 接合 部 が 偏析 する 条件 として ， 線状 高分子 の Tg は ， C - C 結合 の 熱 膨張 が 1 % になると 温度 は 温度 であると 考えた 。
BLEU_f	0.2003
BLEU_r	0.2052
remarks	Reranked includes over-translation "温度 は 温度 である ".

Table 4: Comparison of translation results with reranking and without reranking (case that the BLEU score of translation with reranking is higher than the BLEU score of translation without reranking)

item	value
snt. #	1527
src	This paper shows the optical system .
ref	光学 系 を 示した 。
smt	本稿 では ， 光学 系 を 示した 。
unreranked	光学 系 を 示した 。
reranked	本稿 では ， 光学 系 を 示した 。
BLEU_f	1
BLEU_r	0.4463
remarks	"This paper" is not translated in ref and unreranked.

snt. #	817
src	Therapy is mentioned afterwards .
ref	その後 の 治療法 について 言及 した 。
smt	その後 療法 が 挙げられる 。
unreranked	その後 の 治療法 に 言及 した 。
reranked	その後 療法 が 挙げられる 。
BLEU_f	0.6102
BLEU_r	0.0585
remarks	Worse translation of smt makes bad affects to reranked.

snt. #	509
src	Telomerase activity is high in reproductive cells and cancer cells .
ref	テロメラーゼ 活性 は 生殖 細胞 と 癌 細胞 で 高い 。
smt	テロメラーゼ 活性 は ， 生殖 細胞 と 癌 細胞 に 高い 。
unreranked	テロメラーゼ 活性 は 生殖 細胞 と 癌 細胞 で 高い 。
reranked	テロメラーゼ 活性 は ， 生殖 細胞 と 癌 細胞 に 高い 。
BLEU_f	1
BLEU_r	0.466
remarks	Mistranslation of case marker "に" in smt affects reranked.

snt. #	624
src	In the case of banking sites , the growth of large gully by water erosion was observed .
ref	一方 ， 盛り土 では 水食 による 大きな ガリ の 成長 が 観察 された 。
smt	盛土 サイト の 場合 には ， 水 による 侵食 により ， 大きな ガリー の 成長 を 観測 した 。
unreranked	盛土 サイト では ， 水 侵食 による 大きな ガリ の 成長 が 観察 された 。
reranked	盛土 サイト の 場合 ， 水 侵食 による 大きな ガリー の 成長 を 観測 した 。
BLEU_f	0.6342
BLEU_r	0.1135
remarks	Src, ref and unreranked are passive voice. Smt and reranked are active voice.

snt. #	1320
src	This paper described views on MEMS (micro electro mechanical system) studies in Singapore .
ref	シンガポール における MEMS (微小 電気 機械 システム) 研究 の 展望 を 述べた 。
smt	本稿 は ， MEMS (マイクロ エレクトロ メカニカル システム) についての 見解 ， シンガポール の 研究 について 述べた 。
unreranked	シンガポール における MEMS (マイクロ エレクトロ メカニカル システム) 研究 の 展望 を 述べた 。
reranked	シンガポール の MEMS (マイクロ エレクトロ メカニカル システム) 研究 についての 見解 を 述べた 。
BLEU_f	0.6739
BLEU_r	0.1762
remarks	"Views" is translated to "展望" in ref and unreranked and it is translated to "見解" in smt and reranked.

snt. #	1146
src	This was a case of a male , 66 years old .
ref	症例 は 66 歳 男性 。
smt	症例 は 66 歳 女性 であった 。
unreranked	症例 は 66 歳 男性 。
reranked	症例 は 66 歳 女性 。
BLEU_f	1
BLEU_r	0.5373
remarks	Mistranslation of "male" in smt "女性" affects reranked.

snt. #	544
src	The collection survey was performed on the reef coasts of the northern region of Ibaraki Prefecture .
ref	茨城 県 北部 地域 の 岩礁 海岸 で 採集 調査 を 行った 。
smt	採集 調査 礁 北部 地域 の 茨城 県 の 海岸 で 行った 。
unreranked	茨城 県 北部 の 礁 海岸 で 採集 調査 を 行った 。
reranked	採集 調査 は 茨城 県 北部 の 礁 海岸 で 行った 。
BLEU_f	0.5974
BLEU_r	0.1971
remarks	Smt has no meaning however reranked has similar meaning to ref and unreranked.

snt. #	1179
src	This paper surveys the safety of robot , and introduces the issues on safety of robot taken up through the EXPO .
ref	ロボット の 安全 性 を 概観 し，万博 を 通じて 取り 上げ られた ロボット の 安全 性 に 関する 課題 を 紹介 した 。
smt	本 論文 では，ロボット の 安全 性 について 調査 し，ロボット の 安全 性 に 関する 問題 を 取り 上げ 愛 を 紹介 した 。
unreranked	ロボット の 安全 性 を 概観 し，ロボット の 安全 性 に 関する 課題 を 紹介 した 。
reranked	ロボット の 安全 性 について 概観 し，ロボット の 安全 性 に 関する 問題 点 を 紹介 した 。
BLEU_f	0.6615
BLEU_r	0.424
remarks	Both unreranked and reranked include under-translation of " taken up through the EXPO (万博 を 通じて 取り 上げ られた)".

snt. #	866
src	By the mometasone furancarboxylate ointment , the pit was improved a little , and the pit derived from the normal skin was continued .
ref	フラン カルボン酸 モメタゾン 軟膏 に より，やや 陥 凹 は 軽快 したが，正常 皮膚 よりの 陥 凹 は 継続 した 。
smt	furancarboxylate モメタゾン 軟膏 外 用 により，ピット は やや 改善 し，正常 皮膚 由来 の ピット を 継続 した 。
unreranked	シス etasone フランカルボキシ 軟膏 軟膏 により，陥 凹 は やや 改善 し，正常 皮膚 からの 陥 凹 が 続いた 。
reranked	モメタゾンフランカルボン 酸 エステル 軟膏 により，ピット は やや 改善 し，正常 皮膚 からの 陥 凹 が 続いた 。
BLEU_f	0.2211
BLEU_r	0.1897
remarks	Unreranked includes over-translation "軟膏 軟膏".

snt. #	1313
src	Based on such design guidelines , engine and television of the DLP TMsystem are produced experimentally .
ref	このような 設計 指針 に 基づき，DLPTM 方式 の エンジン と テレビ を 試作 した 。
smt	このような 設計 指針 に 基づき，エンジン，DLP　TMsystem の テレビ を 試作 した 。
unreranked	この 設計 指針 に 基づき，DLPTM システム の エンジン と テレビ を 試作 した 。
reranked	このような 設計 指針 に 基づき，DLP システム の エンジン と テレビ を 試作 した 。
BLEU_f	0.7448
BLEU_r	0.7448
remarks	Reranked includes under-translation of "TM".

Table 5: Comparison of translation results with reranking and without reranking (case that the BLEU score of translation with reranking is lower than the BLEU score of translation without reranking)

4.2 Comparison of evaluation results by BLEU and pairwise evaluation

In this subsection, we examine the contradiction between BLEU score and pairwise evaluation score in ASPEC en-ja task. Several examples that diff BLEU≧0 and pairwise score＜0 are listed in Table 6. Several examples that diff BLEU＜0 and pairwise score≧0 are listed in Table 7.

In these tables, "baseline" means baseline translation result, "BLEU_b" means BLEU score of baseline and "pairwise" means pairwise evaluation score (sum of five evaluator's score).

Other abbreviations are explained in the previous subsection.

item	value
snt. #	365
src	Toxic substances in heavy oil is a cause of failure.
ref	重油 中 に 含ま れる 有害 物質 が 障害 の 原因 と なる 。
baseline	重油 中 の 有害 物質 は 故障 の 原因 である 。
reranked	重 質 油 中 の 有害 物質 が 障害 の 原因 と なって いる 。
BLEU_b	0.1027
BLEU_r	0.4261
pairwise	-1
remarks	Important information "heavy oil" is incorrectly translated to "重 質 油"in reranked. Long phase "有害 物質 が 障害 の" is same in ref and reranked, and "有害 物質 は 故障 の" in baseline has similar meaning.

snt. #	157
src	During the follow-up period 176 people died by malignant tumor.
ref	追跡 期間 中 に 176 名 が 悪性 腫瘍 により 死亡 した 。
baseline	追跡 期間 中 176 人 が 悪性 腫ようで 死亡 した 。
reranked	フォロー アップ 期間 中，悪性 腫ように より 死亡 した 。
BLEU_b	0.21
BLEU_r	0.3191
pairwise	-5
remarks	Important information "176 people" is not translated in reranked. Long phrase "悪性 腫瘍 により 死亡 した 。" is same in ref and reranked, and "悪性 腫ようで 死亡 した 。" in baseline has similar meaning.

snt. #	277
src	In addition, the neutronic characteristics of the demonstration reactor are introduced.
ref	この ほか 実証 炉 の 核 特性 について 紹介 した
baseline	さらに，実証 炉 の 中性子 特性 を 紹介 した 。
reranked	さらに，実証 炉 の 核 特性 を 紹介 した 。
BLEU_b	0.1836
BLEU_r	0.4035
pairwise	-4
remarks	"Neutronic characteristics" is literally translated to "中性子 特性" in baseline and non literally translated to "核 特性" in ref and reranked.

snt. #	118
src	A fractal analysis result of potentials related to events was applied to the survey of fluctuating conditions of intelligent activities.
ref	事象 関連 電位 の フラクタル 分析 を 行い，その 結果 を 知的な 活動 の 変動 的な 状態 の 調査 に 使った 。
baseline	事象 に 関連 した ポテンシャル の フラクタル 解析 結果 を，知的 活動 の 変動 条件 の 調査 に 適用 した 。
reranked	事象 関連 電位 の フラクタル 解析 結果 を，知的 活動 の 変動 条件 の 調査 に 適用 した 。
BLEU_b	0.1413
BLEU_r	0.2825
pairwise	-3
remarks	"Potentials related to events" is literally translated to "事象 に 関連 した ポテンシャル" in basline and non literally translated to "事象 関連 電位" in ref and reranked.

Table 6: Comparison of baseline translation and reranked translation (case that diff BLEU≧0 and pairwise score＜0)

From Table 6, we can see two reasons why diff BLEU≧0 and pairwise score＜0. First is that important information is differ in ref and reranked and not so important information that is expressed in long phrase is differ in ref and baseline and is same in ref and reranked. Because of it, diff BLEU $\geqq 0$ and pairwise score < 0. Second reason is that literal translation in baseline and non-literal translation in ref and reranked.

item	value
snt. #	128
src	No side effect was noted during treatment.
ref	治療 中 ， 副 作用 は 認め なかった 。
baseline	副 作用 は 認め なかった 。
reranked	治療 中 副 作用 は 認め られ なかった 。
BLEU_b	0.6065
BLEU_r	0.4033
pairwise	5
remarks	Important information "during treatment" is not translated in baseline. Long phrase "副 作用 は 認め なかった 。" is same in ref and baseline, and "副 作用 は 認め られ なかった 。" in reranked has similar meaning.

snt. #	76
src	Cutting, patterning polishing, and metalizing work of diamond films with laser beams are reviewed.
ref	レーザ に よる ダイヤモンド 膜 の 切断 ， パターニング ， 研摩 ， 金属 化 加工 に ついて 総 説 した 。
baseline	レーザ ビーム を 用いた ダイヤモンド 膜 の 切断 ， パターニング ， および メタライゼーション 作業 に ついて レビュー した 。
reranked	レーザ ビーム を 用いた ダイヤモンド 膜 の 切削 ， パターニング 研磨 ， 金属 化 に ついて レビュー した 。
BLEU_b	0.3412
BLEU_r	0.1592
pairwise	3
remarks	Important information "metalizing work" is literally translated to "メタライゼーション 作業" in baseline and non literally translated to "金属 化" in ref and reranked. Long phrase "ダイヤモンド 膜 の 切断 ， パターニング" is same in ref and baseline and "ダイヤモンド 膜 の 切削 ， パターニング" in reranked has similar meaning.

snt. #	36
src	Through the detailed analysis of the intensity dependence of excited light, this is judged to be due to photoionization.
ref	励起 光 強度 依存 性 の 詳細 解析 に より ， 光 イオン 化 に よる もの と 判断 した
baseline	励起 光 の 強度 依存 性 の 詳細な 解析 に より ， 光 イオン 化 に よる と 判断 した 。
reranked	励起 光 の 強度 依存 性 を 詳細に 解析 して ， これ は 光 イオン 化 に よる もの と 判断 した 。
BLEU_b	0.592
BLEU_r	0.4533
pairwise	3
remarks	Ref, baseline and reranked almost have similar meaning, Ref and baseline are literally near but less fluent than reranked.

Table 7: Comparison of baseline translation and reranked translation (case that diff BLEU < 0 and pairwise score $\geqq 0$)

The reason why diff BLEU < 0 and pairwise score $\geqq 0$ of example 1 and 2 (snt. # 128 and 76) is similar to the opposite case. The case of snt. # 36 is a little delicate. Three translations: ref, baseline and reranked have almost similar meaning but reranked has rather clear meaning and fluent expression.

5 Conclusion

We participate four tasks of WAT2018 with the technique of SMT reranked NMT. This technique can reduce under-translation that is frequently found in NMT. For over-translation, the technique, however, cannot reduce it.

References

Terumasa Ehara. 2017. SMT reranked NMT. *Proceedings of the 4th Workshop on Asian Translation (WAT2017)*, pages 119–126.

Isao Goto, Ka Po Chow, Bin Lu, Eiichiro Sumita and Benjamin K. Tsou. 2013. Overview of the Patent Machine Translation Task at the NTCIR-10 Workshop. *Proceedings of the 10th NTCIR Conference,* pages 260-286.

Toshiaki Nakazawa, Shohei Higashiyama, Chenchen, Ding, Raj Dabre, Anoop Kunchukuttan, Win Pa Pa, Isao Goto, Hideya Mino, Katsuhito Sudoh and Sadao Kurohashi. 2018. Overview of the 5th Workshop on Asian Translation, *Proceedings of the 5th Workshop on Asian Translation (WAT2018).*

Philipp Koehn, Franz J. Och and Daniel Marcu. 2003. Statistical Phrase-Based Translation. *Proceedings of HLTNAACL 2003*, pages 48-54.

Minh-Thang Luong, Hieu Pham and Christopher D. Manning. 2015. Effective Approaches to Attention-based Neural Machine Translation, *Proceedings of the 2015 Conference on Empirical Methods in Natural Language Processing*, pages 1412–1421.

English-Myanmar NMT and SMT with Pre-ordering: NICT's Machine Translation Systems at WAT-2018

Rui Wang   **Chenchen Ding**   **Masao Utiyama**   **Eiichiro Sumita**
National Institute of Information and Communications Technology (NICT)
3-5 Hikaridai, Seika-cho, Souraku-gun, Kyoto, 619-0289, Japan
{wangrui, chenchen.ding, mutiyama, eiichiro.sumita}@nict.go.jp

Abstract

This paper presents the NICT's participation (team ID: NICT) in the 5th Workshop on Asian Translation (WAT-2018) shared translation task, specifically Myanmar (Burmese) - English task in both translation directions. We built state-of-the-art neural machine translation (NMT) as well as phrase-based statistical machine translation (PBSMT) systems for these tasks. Our NMT systems were trained with the Transformer architecture on the provided parallel data. Pre-ordering technology is adopted to both NMT and PBSMT. Our NMT systems rank the first in English-to-Myanmar and the second in Myanmar-to-English according to the official human evaluation.

1   Introduction

This paper describes the machine translation systems[1] built for National Institute of Information and Communications Technology (NICT)'s participation in the the 5th Workshop on Asian Translation (WAT-2018) translation task (Nakazawa et al., 2018), specifically Myanmar (My) - English (En) for both translation directions. All of our systems are constrained, i.e., we used only the parallel adata provided by the organizers to train and tune our systems.

The remainder of this paper is organized as follows. In Section 2, we present the data preprocessing. In Section 3, we introduce the details

---

[1]This system is based on our WMT-2018 system (Marie et al., 2018).

of our NMT and SMT systems with pre-ordering technology. Empirical results obtained with our systems are analyzed in Section 4 and we conclude this paper in Section 5.

2   Data Preprocessing

As parallel data to train our systems, we used all the provided parallel data for all our targeted translation directions, including the training corpus "ALT" and "UCSY" and the"ALT" dev/test data. The statistics of our preprocessed parallel data are illustrated in Table 1.

Table 1: Statistics of our preprocessed parallel data.

Corpus	#lines	#tokens (My/En)
train(ALT)	17.9K	1.0M / 410.2K
train(UCSY)	208.6K	5.8M / 2.6M
dev(ALT)	0.9K	57.4K / 22.1K
test(ALT)	1.0K	58.3K / 22.7K

We used `Moses` tokenizer and truecaser for English. The truecaser was trained on the English data, after tokenization. For Myanmar, we used the original tokens. For cleaning, we only applied the `Moses` script `clean-n-corpus.perl` to remove lines in the parallel data containing more than 80 tokens and replaced characters forbidden by `Moses`.

Table 2: Results (BLEU-cased and official human evaluation) of our MT systems on the test set. We only submitted the top 2 systems on BLEU for human evaluation.

System	My→En (BLEU)	En→My (BLEU)	My→En (Human)	En→My (Human)
Moses	9.44	25.55	N/A	N/A
Moses Pre-order	N/A	25.75	N/A	N/A
Marian	16.32	26.02	7.250	42.50
Marian Pre-order	N/A	23.79	N/A	N/A
Marian ensemble	20.79	29.89	20.50	61.00

3 MT Systems

3.1 NMT

To build competitive NMT systems, we chose to rely on the Transformer architecture (Vaswani et al., 2017) since it has been shown to outperform, in quality and efficiency, the two other mainstream architectures for NMT known as deep recurrent neural network (deep-RNN) and convolutional neural network (CNN). We chose `Marian`[2] (Junczys-Dowmunt et al., 2018) to train our NMT systems since it supports many state-of-the-art features and is one of the fastest NMT frameworks publicly available.[3]

All our NMT systems were consistently trained on 4 GPUs,[4] with the following parameters for `Marian`:

```
--type transformer --max-length
80 --dec-depth 6 --normalize 1
--save-freq 5000 --workspace
8000 --disp-freq 500
--beam-size 12 --overwrite
--cost-type ce-mean-words
--keep-best --enc-depth 6
--transformer-dropout 0.1
--valid-mini-batch 16 --valid-freq
5000 --learn-rate 0.0003
--lr-decay-inv-sqrt 16000
--lr-warmup 16000 --lr-report
--sync-sgd --devices 0 1 2
3 --dim-vocabs 50000 50000
--exponential-smoothing
```

```
--optimizer-params 0.9 0.98 1e-09
--clip-norm 5 --tied-embeddings
--mini-batch-fit --early-stopping
5 --label-smoothing 0.1
--valid-metrics ce-mean-words
perplexity translation
```

We performed NMT decoding with an ensemble of a total of 4 models according to the best BLEU (Papineni et al., 2002) and the perplexity scores, produced by 4 independent training runs.

3.2 SMT

We also trained phrase-based SMT systems using `Moses`. Word alignments and phrase tables were trained on the tokenized parallel data using `mgiza`. Source-to-target and target-to-source word alignments were symmetrized with the `grow-diag -final-and` heuristic. We simply trained regular phrase-based models and used the default distortion limit of 6. We trained two 5-gram language models on the entire target side of the parallel data, with SRILM (Stolcke, 2002). To tune the SMT model weights, we used MERT (Och, 2003) and selected the weights giving the best BLEU score on the development data.

3.3 Pre-ordering

We also tried a classic pre-ordering method for English-to-Myanmar translation task. Specifically, the dependency-based head finalization in Ding et al. (2014) is exactly reproduced in our experiment. The source English part is pre-ordered before being input into NMT and SMT systems.

---

[2] `https://marian-nmt.github.io/`, version 1.4.0

[3] It is fully implemented in pure C++ and supports multi-GPU training.

[4] NVIDIA® Tesla® P100 16Gb.

4 Results

Our systems are evaluated on the ALT test set and the results[5] are shown in Table 2. Our observations from are as follows:

1) Our NMT (`Marian`) system performed much better than SMT (`Moses`) system in My-to-En. That is, nearly 7 BLEU scores. However, there is no significant difference in En-to-My.

2) Pre-ordering did not show significant improvement in the NMT systems, while it improved translation quality by 0.2 BLEU points in the SMT system.

3) Ensemble decoding significantly outperformed decoding with a single NMT model.

5 Conclusion

We presented in this paper the NICT's participation in the WAT-2018 shared translation task. Our primary NMT submissions to the task performed the best submitted system according to the official human evaluation. Our results also confirmed the slight positive impact of using pre-ordering in PBSMT.

References

Chenchen Ding, Ye Kyaw Thu, Masao Utiyama, Andrew Finch, and Eiichiro Sumita. 2014. Empirical dependency-based head finalization for statistical chinese-, english-, and french-to-myanmar (burmese) machine translation. In *Proceedings of IWSLT*, pages 184–191.

Marcin Junczys-Dowmunt, Roman Grundkiewicz, Tomasz Dwojak, Hieu Hoang, Kenneth Heafield, Tom Neckermann, Frank Seide, Ulrich Germann, Alham Fikri Aji, Nikolay Bogoychev, André F. T. Martins, and Alexandra Birch. 2018. Marian: Fast neural machine translation in C++. In *Proceedings of ACL 2018, System Demonstrations*, Melbourne, Australia.

Benjamin Marie, Rui Wang, Atsushi Fujita, Masao Utiyama, and Eiichiro Sumita. 2018. NICT's neural and statistical machine translation systems for the WMT18 news translation task. In *Proceedings of the Third Conference on Machine Translation, Volume 2: Shared Task Papers*, Brussels, Belgium, October. Association for Computational Linguistics.

Toshiaki Nakazawa, Shohei Higashiyama, Chenchen Ding, Raj Dabre, Anoop Kunchukuttan, Win Pa Pa, Isao Goto, Hideya Mino, Katsuhito Sudoh, and Sadao Kurohashi. 2018. Overview of the 5th workshop on asian translation. In *Proceedings of the 5th Workshop on Asian Translation (WAT2018)*, Hong Kong, China, December.

Franz Josef Och. 2003. Minimum error rate training in statistical machine translation. In *Proceedings of the 41st Annual Meeting of the Association for Computational Linguistics*, pages 160–167, Sapporo, Japan.

Kishore Papineni, Salim Roukos, Todd Ward, and Wei-Jing Zhu. 2002. Bleu: a method for automatic evaluation of machine translation. In *Proceedings of 40th Annual Meeting of the Association for Computational Linguistics*, pages 311–318, Philadelphia, Pennsylvania, USA, July. Association for Computational Linguistics.

Andreas Stolcke. 2002. Srilm-an extensible language modeling toolkit. In *Proceedings International Conference on Spoken Language Processing*, pages 257–286, Seattle.

Ashish Vaswani, Noam Shazeer, Niki Parmar, Jakob Uszkoreit, Llion Jones, Aidan N Gomez, Ł ukasz Kaiser, and Illia Polosukhin. 2017. Attention is all you need. In I. Guyon, U. V. Luxburg, S. Bengio, H. Wallach, R. Fergus, S. Vishwanathan, and R. Garnett, editors, *Advances in Neural Information Processing Systems 30*.

---

[5]The results of BLEU are based on our own evaluation. For the official results, please refer to `http://lotus.kuee.kyoto-u.ac.jp/WAT/evaluation/index.html`.

Combination of Statistical and Neural Machine Translation
for Myanmar–English

Benjamin Marie   **Atsushi Fujita**   **Eiichiro Sumita**
National Institute of Information and Communications Technology
3-5 Hikaridai, Seika-cho, Soraku-gun, Kyoto, 619-0289, Japan
{bmarie, atsushi.fujita,eiichiro.sumita}@nict.go.jp

Abstract

This paper presents the NICT's machine translation system combining neural and statistical machine translation for the WAT2018 Myanmar–English translation task. For both translation directions, we built state-of-the-art statistical (SMT) and neural (NMT) machine translation systems and combined them to improve translation quality. Our NMT systems were trained with the Transformer architecture using the provided parallel data. Our systems combining SMT and NMT are ranked first for this task according to BLEU. This paper also describes the impact of using a small quantity of back-translated monolingual data.

1 Introduction

This paper describes neural (NMT) and statistical machine translation systems (SMT) built for the participation of the National Institute of Information and Communications Technology (NICT) to the WAT2018 Myanmar–English translation task (Nakazawa et al., 2018).[1] We present systems built using only the parallel data provided by the organizers. For contrastive experiments, we also present systems that use monolingual data not provided by the organizers. For both translation directions, we trained NMT and SMT systems, and combined them through n-best list reranking using several informative features (Marie and Fujita, 2018). This simple combination method achieved the best results among the submitted MT systems for this task according to BLEU (Papineni et al., 2002). We also

show that the use of monolingual data can dramatically improve translation quality.

The remainder of this paper is organized as follows. In Section 2, we introduce the data preprocessing. In Section 3, we describe the details of our NMT and SMT systems. The back-translation of monolingual data used by some of our systems is described in Section 4. Then, the combination of NMT and SMT is described in Section 5. Empirical results achieved by our systems are showed and analyzed in Section 6, and Section 7 concludes this paper.

2 Data preprocessing

To train our systems, we used all the bilingual data provided by the organizers. The provided bilingual data comprise two different corpora: the training data provided by the ALT project[2] and additional training data, UCSY corpus, constructed by the University of Computer Studies, Yangon (UCSY). Since no monolingual corpus was provided, we submitted for human evaluation the outputs of systems trained only on the parallel data. For contrastive experiments, we also built systems using monolingual data. For English, we used the monolingual corpora provided by the WMT18 shared News Translation Task. As for Myanmar, we experimented with two monolingual corpora: Myanmar Wikipedia and Myanmar CommonCrawl. The Wikipedia corpus was created from the entire Myanmar Wikipedia dumped on 2017/06/01. The CommonCrawl cor-

---

[1] The team ID of our participation is "NICT-4".

[2] `http://www2.nict.go.jp/astrec-att/`
`member/mutiyama/ALT/index.html`

pus consists of sentences in the Myanmar language[3] from the first quarter of the CommonCrawl data crawled during April 2018. These Myanmar monolingual corpora, especially the CommonCrawl corpus crawled from various websites, contain a large portion of useless data. For instance, many lines in the corpus are made of long sequences of numbers or punctuation marks. For cleaning, we decided to remove lines in both corpora that fulfill at least one of the following conditions:

- more than 25% of its tokens are numbers or punctuation marks.

- contains less than 4 tokens

- contains more than 80 tokens

For contrastive experiments, we also prepared CommonCrawl and Wikipedia corpora for English and cleaned them in the same manner. For the CommonCrawl corpus, we sampled 2M lines from the entire CommonCrawl corpus provided by WMT18, while for the Wikipedia corpus we sampled 1M lines from the entire dump of the English Wikipedia of 2017/06/01.

We tokenized and truecased English data respectively with the tokenizer and truecaser of Moses (Koehn et al., 2007). The truecaser was trained on the English side of the parallel data. Truecasing was performed on all the tokenized data. For Myanmar, the provided bilingual data were already tokenized into writing units and Romanized.[4] However, we were not able to take advantage of this preprocessing and chose to reverse it and tokenize the bilingual and monolingual data by ourselves with an in-house tokenizer. We did not apply truecasing on the Myanmar data. Note that for the en→my task, the outputs generated in the Myanmar language must be processed as done by the organizers before submission.

For cleaning bilingual data, we only applied the Moses script `clean-n-corpus.perl` to remove lines in the parallel data containing more than 80

Data set	#sent. pairs	#tokens (my)	#tokens (en)
Train	226.6k	4.4M	3.4M
Development	993	37.8k	25.4k
Test	1,007	38.8k	25.9k

Table 1: Statistics of our preprocessed parallel data.

Corpus	#lines	#tokens
WMT (English)	338.7M	7.5B
Wikipedia (English)	1M	11.8M
CommonCrawl (English)	2M	44.5M
Wikipedia (Myanmar)	1.2M	13.0M
CommonCrawl (Myanmar)	1.5M	56.6M

Table 2: Statistics of our preprocessed monolingual data.

tokens and escaped characters forbidden by Moses. Note that we did not perform any punctuation normalization.

To tune/validate and evaluate our systems, we used the official development and test sets chosen for the task: the ALT test data consisting of translations of English texts sampled from English Wikinews.

Tables 1 and 2 present the statistics of the parallel and monolingual data, respectively, after preprocessing.

3 MT Systems

3.1 NMT

To build competitive NMT systems, we chose to rely on the Transformer architecture (Vaswani et al., 2017) since it has been shown to outperform, in quality and efficiency, the two other mainstream architectures for NMT known as deep recurrent neural network (deep RNN) and convolutional neural network (CNN). We chose Marian[5] (Junczys-Dowmunt et al., 2018) to train and evaluate our NMT systems since it supports state-of-the-art features and is one of the fastest NMT framework publicly available. In order to limit the size of the vocabulary of the NMT models, we further segmented tokens in the parallel data into sub-word units via byte pair encoding (BPE) (Sennrich et al., 2016b) using 8k operations for both languages.[6] All

---

[3]We used `fasttext` and its pretrained models for language identification: `https://fasttext.cc/blog/2017/10/02/blog-post.html`

[4]The preprocessing was performed, and can be reversed with this script: `http://www2.nict.go.jp/astrec-att/member/mutiyama/ALT/myan2roma.py`

[5]`https://marian-nmt.github.io/`, version 1.6

[6]The number of operations was chosen among 8k,16k,32k according to the best BLEU score obtained on the development set. We observed around 2 BLEU points of difference between

our NMT systems were consistently trained on 4 GPUs,[7] with the following parameters for Marian:

```
--type transformer --max-length 80
--mini-batch-fit --valid-freq 5000
--save-freq 5000 --workspace 10000
--disp-freq 500 --beam-size 12
--normalize 1 --valid-mini-batch
16 --overwrite --early-stopping
5 --cost-type ce-mean-words
--valid-metrics ce-mean-words
perplexity translation --keep-best
--enc-depth 4 --dec-depth 4
--transformer-dropout 0.1
--learn-rate 0.001 --dropout-src
0.1 --dropout-trg 0.1 --lr-warmup
16000 --lr-decay-inv-sqrt 16000
--lr-report --label-smoothing 0.1
--devices 0 1 2 3 --dim-vocabs
8000 8000 --optimizer-params
0.9 0.98 1e-09 --clip-norm 5
--sync-sgd --exponential-smoothing.
```

3.2 SMT

We also trained SMT systems using Moses. Word alignments and phrase tables were trained on the tokenized parallel data using `mgiza`. Source-to-target and target-to-source word alignments were symmetrized with the `grow-diag-final-and` heuristic. We trained phrase-based SMT models and `MSLR` (monotone, swap, discontinuous-left, discontinuous-right) lexicalized reordering models. We also used the default distortion limit of 6. We trained two 4-gram language models, one on the WMT monolingual data for English, and on the Wikipedia data for Myanmar, concatenated to the target side of the parallel data, and another one on the target side of the parallel data only, using `LMPLZ` (Heafield et al., 2013). To tune the SMT model weights, we used `kb-mira` (Cherry and Foster, 2012) and selected the weights giving the best BLEU score for the development data during 15 iterations.

8k and 32k.

[7]NVIDIA® Tesla® P100 16Gb.

Back-translation	# backtr.	my→en	en→my
None (baseline)	0	19.0	27.6
Wikipedia	300k	20.1	29.0*
	1M	23.3	27.9
CommonCrawl	300k	23.2	22.5
	1M	25.1*	17.6

Table 3: BLEU scores for our NMT systems on the official test set of the tasks. The "Corpus" column denotes the origin of the back-translated data and the "#backtr." column denotes the number of back-translated sentences mixed with the bilingual data for training. "*" indicates the best configuration for each task used for experiments with back-translated data presented in Section 6.

4 Back-Translation of Monolingual Data for NMT

Parallel data for training NMT can be augmented with synthetic parallel data, generated through a so-called back-translation, to significantly improve translation quality (Sennrich et al., 2016a). To perform back-translation, we used an NMT system, trained on the parallel data provided by the organizers, to translate target monolingual sentences into the source language. Then, the back-translated sentences were simply mixed with the original parallel data to train from scratch a new source-to-target NMT system. However, since our monolingual data were not provided by the organizers, we did not use back-translation to generate our primary submissions for human evaluation.

We compared systems using back-translations of either Wikipedia or CommonCrawl. We also experimented using 300k or 1M back-translated sentences for training. The results are reported in Table 3. For my→en, the use of back-translations significantly improved the translation quality, especially in the configurations where we used 1M back-translated sentences. Since the improvements are significantly larger with CommonCrawl data, we chose this corpus for additional experiments presented in Section 6. For en→my, using only 300k back-translated sentences from Wikipedia led to the best results but with only 1.6 BLEU points of improvements over the baseline system, which did not use back-translated data. Using CommonCrawl corpus systematically decreased the translation quality with up to 10 BLEU points from the baseline system. We

Feature	Description
L2R (4)	Scores given by each of the 4 left-to-right Marian models
R2L (1)	Score given by each the right-to-left Marian model
LEX (4)	Sentence-level translation probabilities, for both translation directions
LM (1 or 2)	Scores given by the language models used by the Moses baseline systems
LEN (2)	Difference between the length of the source sentence and the length of the translation hypothesis, and its absolute value

Table 4: Set of features used by our reranking systems. The "Feature" column refers to the same feature name used in Marie and Fujita (2018). The numbers between parentheses indicate the number of scores in each feature set.

speculate that our Myanmar CommonCrawl corpus is too noisy to be useful to train an NMT model.

5 Combination of NMT and SMT

Our primary submissions for the task were the results of a simple combination of NMT and SMT. As demonstrated by Marie and Fujita (2018), and despite the simplicity of the method used, combining NMT and SMT makes MT more robust and can significantly improve translation quality, even though SMT greatly underperforms NMT. Following Marie and Fujita (2018), our combination of NMT and SMT works as follows.

5.1 Generation of n-best Lists

We first independently generated the 100-best translation hypotheses with 4 NMT models, independently trained, and also with the ensemble of these 4 NMT models. We also generated 100-best translation hypotheses with our SMT system. We then merged all these 6 lists generated by different systems, without removing duplicated hypotheses, which resulted in a list of 600 diverse translation hypotheses for each source sentence. Finally, we rescored all the hypotheses in the list with a reranking framework using features to better model the fluency and the adequacy of each hypothesis. This method can find a better hypothesis in these merged n-best lists than the one-best hypothesis originated by the individual systems.

5.2 Reranking Framework and Features

We chose `kb-mira` as a rescoring framework and used a subset of the features proposed in Marie and Fujita (2018). All the following features we used are described in details by Marie and Fujita (2018). As listed in Table 4, it includes the scores given by

4 left-to-right NMT models independently trained. We also used as features the scores given by one right-to-left NMT model. We computed sentence-level translation probabilities using the lexical translation probabilities learned by `mgiza` during the training of our SMT systems. The two language models trained for SMT for each translation direction were also used to score the n-best translation hypotheses. We used only one language model trained on the target side of the parallel data for our primary submission. To account for hypotheses length, we added the difference, and its absolute value, between the number of tokens in the translation hypothesis and the source sentence.

The reranking framework was trained on n-best lists generated by decoding of the development data that we used to validate the training of NMT systems and to tune the weights of SMT models.

6 Results

Our results are presented in Table 5. As expected, SMT performed significantly worse than NMT for both translation directions (#1 vs #3), especially for my→en with 9.5 BLEU points difference. Introducing a larger language models trained on monolingual data improved translation quality (#1 vs #2), especially for my→en, owing to the very large monolingual data. Even though our monolingual data for en→my were significantly smaller and noisier, we could still obtain an improvement of 0.5 BLEU points.

For NMT without back-translation, ensembling 4 models for decoding was very effective with 3.0 and 2.0 BLEU points of improvements (#3 vs #4), respectively for my→en and en→my. As discussed in Section 4, introducing back-translation significantly improved the translation quality.

ID	System	my→en	en→my
1.	Moses	9.5	23.1
2.	Moses w/ big LM	11.4	23.6
3.	Marian single	19.0	27.6
4.	Marian ensemble of 4	22.0	29.6
5.	Marian single w/ backtr.	25.1	29.0
6.	Marian ensemble of 4 w/ backtr.	27.8	31.8
7.	Moses (#1) + Marian ensemble of 4 (#4)	22.5	30.5
8.	Moses w/ big LM (#2) + Marian ensemble of 4 w/ backtr. (#6)	29.1	32.3

Table 5: BLEU scores for our MT systems on the official test set of the tasks. "big LM" denotes the use of a language model trained on large monolingual data. "backtr" denotes the use or not of back-translated monolingual data. "Moses + Marian" denotes our n-best list combination described in Section 5: #7 combines systems trained only on the parallel data provided by the organizers, while #8 does so the best SMT and the best NMT systems realized using additional monolingual data. We submitted systems #4 and #7 for human evaluation.

Combining SMT and NMT, without using large monolingual data, slightly improved the translation quality (#4 vs #7) by 0.5 and 0.9 BLEU points for my→en and en→my, respectively. Combining "Moses big LM" and "Marian ensemble of 4 w/ backtr." further improved translation quality (#6 vs #8) by 1.3 and 0.5 BLEU points, respectively.

While our combination of SMT and NMT (#7) achieved the best BLEU scores among the submitted systems, it consistently underperformed our best NMT system (#4) according to human evaluation. We speculate that this is the consequence of the adoption of some SMT outputs that may be more adequate to the given source sentence but less fluent than the NMT outputs. In future work, we will perform further analysis to better understand the results, given the translation task, the specificities of the Myanmar–English language pair, and the methodology of the human evaluation used for WAT.

7   Conclusion

In this paper, we showed that combining SMT and NMT can further improve the translation quality over a very strong NMT system, even though SMT largely underperforms NMT. Moreover, we showed that the use of monolingual data significantly improved the translation quality for Myanmar–English. In order to allow participants to build state-of-the-art MT systems, we strongly encourage WAT organizers to provide monolingual data for future editions of the workshop. The gap in translation quality between NMT systems that use and do not use monolingual data has been constantly enlarging every year and it is expected to be even more significant in the near future (Edunov et al., 2018).

Acknowledgments

The method used in this participation was developed under the program "Promotion of Global Communications Plan: Research, Development, and Social Demonstration of Multilingual Speech Translation Technology" of the Ministry of Internal Affairs and Communications (MIC), Japan.

References

Colin Cherry and George Foster. 2012. Batch tuning strategies for statistical machine translation. In *Proceedings of the 2012 Conference of the North American Chapter of the Association for Computational Linguistics: Human Language Technologies*, pages 427–436, Montréal, Canada, June. Association for Computational Linguistics.

Sergey Edunov, Myle Ott, Michael Auli, and David Grangier. 2018. Understanding back-translation at scale. In *Proceedings of the 2018 Conference on Empirical Methods in Natural Language Processing*, pages 489–500, Brussels, Belgium. Association for Computational Linguistics.

Kenneth Heafield, Ivan Pouzyrevsky, Jonathan H. Clark, and Philipp Koehn. 2013. Scalable modified Kneser-Ney language model estimation. In *Proceedings of the 51st Annual Meeting of the Association for Computational Linguistics (Volume 2: Short Papers)*, pages 690–696, Sofia, Bulgaria, August. Association for Computational Linguistics.

Marcin Junczys-Dowmunt, Roman Grundkiewicz, Tomasz Dwojak, Hieu Hoang, Kenneth Heafield, Tom Neckermann, Frank Seide, Ulrich Germann, Alham Fikri Aji, Nikolay Bogoychev, André F. T. Martins, and Alexandra Birch. 2018. Marian: Fast neural machine translation in C++. In *Proceedings of ACL 2018, System Demonstrations*, pages 116–121, Melbourne, Australia, July. Association for Computational Linguistics.

Philipp Koehn, Hieu Hoang, Alexandra Birch, Chris Callison-Burch, Marcello Federico, Nicola Bertoldi, Brooke Cowan, Wade Shen, Christine Moran, Richard Zens, Chris Dyer, Ondrej Bojar, Alexandra Constantin, and Evan Herbst. 2007. Moses: Open source toolkit for statistical machine translation. In *Proceedings of the 45th Annual Meeting of the Association for Computational Linguistics Companion Volume Proceedings of the Demo and Poster Sessions*, pages 177–180, Prague, Czech Republic. Association for Computational Linguistics.

Benjamin Marie and Atsushi Fujita. 2018. A smorgasbord of features to combine phrase-based and neural machine translation. In *Proceedings of the 13th Conference of the Association for Machine Translation in the Americas (Volume 1: Research Papers)*, pages 111–124, Boston, USA. Association for Machine Translation in the Americas.

Toshiaki Nakazawa, Shohei Higashiyama, Chenchen Ding, Raj Dabre, Anoop Kunchukuttan, Win Pa Pa, Isao Goto, Hideya Mino, Katsuhito Sudoh, and Sadao Kurohashi. 2018. Overview of the 5th workshop on asian translation. In *Proceedings of the 5th Workshop on Asian Translation (WAT2018)*, Hong Kong, China, December.

Kishore Papineni, Salim Roukos, Todd Ward, and Wei-Jing Zhu. 2002. Bleu: a method for automatic evaluation of machine translation. In *Proceedings of 40th Annual Meeting of the Association for Computational Linguistics*, pages 311–318, Philadelphia, Pennsylvania, USA, July. Association for Computational Linguistics.

Rico Sennrich, Barry Haddow, and Alexandra Birch. 2016a. Improving neural machine translation models with monolingual data. In *Proceedings of the 54th Annual Meeting of the Association for Computational Linguistics (Volume 1: Long Papers)*, pages 86–96, Berlin, Germany. Association for Computational Linguistics.

Rico Sennrich, Barry Haddow, and Alexandra Birch. 2016b. Neural machine translation of rare words with subword units. In *Proceedings of the 54th Annual Meeting of the Association for Computational Linguistics (Volume 1: Long Papers)*, pages 1715–1725, Berlin, Germany, August. Association for Computational Linguistics.

Ashish Vaswani, Noam Shazeer, Niki Parmar, Jakob Uszkoreit, Llion Jones, Aidan N. Gomez, Łukasz Kaiser, and Illia Polosukhin. 2017. Attention is all you need. In *Proceedings of the 30th Neural Information Processing Systems Conference (NIPS)*, pages 5998–6008.

TMU Japanese-Chinese Unsupervised NMT System
for WAT 2018 Translation Task

Longtu Zhang and **Yuting Zhao** and **Mamoru Komachi**
Tokyo Metropolitan University
Graduate School of System Design
6-6 Asahigaoka, Hino, Tokyo 191-0065, Japan
{zhang-longtu, zhao-yuting}@ed.tmu.ac.jp   komachi@tmu.ac.jp

Abstract

This paper describes the unsupervised
neural machine translation system of
Tokyo Metropolitan University for the
WAT 2018 translation task, focusing on
Chinese–Japanese translation.   Neural
machine translation (NMT) has recently
achieved impressive performance on some
language pairs, although the lack of large
parallel corpora poses a major practical
problem for its training.   In this work,
only monolingual data are used to train
the NMT system through an unsupervised
approach. This system creates synthetic
parallel data through back-translation and
leverages language models trained on both
source and target domains.   To enhance
the shared information in the bilingual
word embeddings further, a decomposed
ideograph and stroke dataset for ASPEC
Chinese–Japanese Language pairs was also
created. BLEU scores of 32.99 for ZH-
JA and 26.39 for JA-ZH translation were
recorded, respectively (both using stroke
data). [1]

1 Introduction

Neural machine translation (NMT) (Bahdanau
et al., 2014; Cho et al., 2014; Sutskever et al.,
2014) systems have achieved great success in recent years and outperform traditional statistical machine translation (SMT) (Sennrich et al.,

2016a; Wu et al., 2016; Zhou et al., 2016) systems. Nevertheless, one of its major challenges
has been that it is necessary for NMT models
to be trained using large parallel data, meaning
that they can fail when the training data is not
big enough (Koehn and Knowles, 2017; Isabelle
et al., 2017). Unfortunately, the lack of large
parallel corpora is a practical problem for the
vast majority of language pairs, and these are often non-existent for low-resource languages. On
the other hand, monolingual data is much easier to find; many languages with limited parallel
data still possess significant amounts of monolingual data.

Lample et al. (2018) have proposed an
unsupervised   NMT   model   that   is   effective on similar language pairs, such as
English–French and English–German.   In
this work, Chinese–Japanese language pair is
used because they also share a lot of characters which can be used to replace the need
for bilingual dictionaries. New sub-character
datasets were also created to enhance the
shared information.   The byte-pair encodings
(BPE) (Sennrich et al., 2016c) vocabularies
were shared between the two related languages
by jointly trained both monolingual corpora.
FastText (Bojanowski et al., 2017) was then
used to generate cross-lingual embeddings.
Following this, two encoder–decoder language
models were trained on noisy data on either
monolingual corpora, respectively.   For the
translation models, back-translation (Sennrich
et al., 2016b) was used to handle both direc-

---

[1] Our team ID for the submission to this shared
task (Nakazawa et al., 2018) is TMU.

tions in tandem, from source to target and from target to source (the former generates data to train the later and vice versa). The goal of this back-translation model is to generate a source sentence for each target sentence in the monolingual corpus. The loss is computed based on monolingual data in four-ways: the source and target language models, and the source and target back-translation models. Finally, the model was tested on the translation models only.

The main findings of this paper are summarized as follows:

- The effectiveness of unsupervised NMT is quite promising in Chinese–Japanese language pairs, even if the shared tokens are not as high as 95% (Lample et al., 2018).

- Enhancing the shared information between language pairs will further promote the performance of unsupervised NMT.

2 Data Preparation

Chinese and Japanese are two logographic languages that utilize structuralized strokes to form ideographs and structuralized ideographs to form characters (Japanese also has Kanas that function as phonetic letters). According to UNICODE 10.0 standard, there are 36 strokes ("—", "丨", "丿", "乀", etc.) composing hundreds of ideographs [2], and further composing 90,000+ of different characters. Table 1 shows examples of Chinese characters and how strokes and ideographs compose different characters.

ASPEC–JC (Japanese Chinese language pairs) parallel corpora (Nakazawa et al., 2016) were used in the experiments. There are 672,315 sentences in training set, and 2,090 and 2,107 sentences in the development and test sets, respectively. Note that although this corpus is bilingual, it was used monolingually in the models for this task. Ideally, a larger monolingual dataset (such as Wikipedia) should be used to obtain better performance.

Character	Semantic ideograph	Phonetic ideograph	Pinyin
驰 run	马 horse	也	chí
池 pool	水(氵) water	也	chí
施 impose	方 direction	也	shī
弛 loosen	弓 bow	也	chí
地 land	土 soil	也	dì
驱 drive	马 horse	区	qū

Table 1: Examples of Chinese characters (Pinyin is the official Romanization of Chinese characters according to its pronunciation.). Note that sometimes a ideograph can also be a character itself (like "马"); some ideographs denote the semantic meaning of the character (semantic ideographs); some denote the pronunciation (phonetic ideographs). Both semantic ideographs and phonetic ideographs can be shared across different characters for similar functions, such that "驰" and "驱" both with "马" have related meanings, while characters with "也" usually pronounce similarly.

Because neither Chinese nor Japanese have natural word boundaries, MeCab (Kudo et al., 2004) was used to pre-tokenize Japanese with the IPADic dictionary, and Jieba to pre-tokenize Chinese with its default dictionary. Then, a BPE sub-word model was trained on concatenated Chinese and Japanese monolingual data with a vocabulary size of 30,000 using fastBPE [3], in order to reduce the vocabulary size and eliminate the presence of unknown words (OOV).

Further, unsupervised NMT models rely heavily on shared information between the source and target data. Therefore, to enhance this information, new ideographs and stroke datasets were created. As opposed to Zhang and Komachi (2018), who utilized three corpora for different language pairs, namely, ASPEC–JC (Japanese Chinese), ASPEC–JE (Japanese English) and Casia2015 [4] (Chinese English) to create decomposed datasets, only ASPEC–JC was chosen in this work in order to focus on the shared information between Chinese and Japanese characters. Another difference is that CHISE was used instead of CNS11643 charset

---

[2]The number depends on how to define ideographs (usually around 500+); sometimes there are standalone ideographs that can be regard as characters as well.

[3]https://github.com/glample/fastBPE

[4]http://nlp.nju.edu.cn/cwmt-wmt/

Language	Word
JA-character	風 景
JA-ideograph	□几重 □日京
JA-stroke	□□丿乙日丿□□□丨フ一□日丨一、 日□□□丨フ日一一日日、一日□丨フ 一□丨□丿、
ZH-character	风 景
ZH-ideograph	□几乂 □日京
ZH-stroke	□□丿乙□丿、 日□□□丨フ日一一日日、一日□丨フ 一□丨□丿、
EN	landscape

Table 2: Examples of decomposition of a Japanese word "風景" and Chinese word "风景", both meaning "landscape" in English.

for the decomposition information. The CHISE Project [5] provides decomposition mappings for Unicode CJK characters using 12 Ideographic Description Characters, 394 ideographs, and 19 special symbols for "unclear" ideographs. This mapping can help create new datasets. For ideograph datasets, the CHISE mappings were used directly; for stroke dataset, the ideographs and special symbols were manually transcribed to stroke sequences in the CHISE format, and then recursively decomposed characters into strokes. The examples are in Table 2. Similarly, BPE sub-word models were trained by and applied to these stroke and ideograph datasets with a vocabulary size of 30,000.

3 Architecture Description

Three key principles underpin the approach to unsupervised neural machine translation used in this model. The design is largely based on Lample et al. (2018)'s implementation of unsupervised NMT systems.

3.1 Shared BPE Embeddings

Instead of initializing and mapping the bilingual word embeddings based on a bilingual seed dictionary and two monolingual embeddings for unsupervised NMT models (Artetxe et al., 2018),

---

[5] http://www.chise.org/

a bilingual embedding is directly trained in two steps: first, the data is segmented using relevant BPE models trained on concatenated monolingual data of character-, ideograph- and stroke-level corpora; second, relying on the shared information between these corpora, word embeddings are trained directly using fastText (Bojanowski et al., 2017). This method is used not only because finding a readily available sub-word level bilingual embedding is almost impossible, but also because it is found to be efficient enough to encode the shared information directly into one space.

3.2 Encoder–Decoder Language Models

Artetxe et al. (2018) designed a shared encoder for both source and target languages, while Lample et al. (2018) used two different encoders for different languages, where the weights were only shared in last layers. Here, the latter design is followed. Two encoder-decoder models are used as the language models of the source and target languages. The encoders will encode monolingual sentences into latent representations for respective decoders, and the decoders learn to decode the same sentences based on these latent representations. Random blank-outs are added to the input sentences as noise to improve the quality of the language model training.

3.3 Back-Translation

The original idea of back-translation (Sennrich et al., 2016b) was to enhance the training of a single NMT model (source–target) using the output of another readily available NMT model (target–source). The difference between the back-translation in the present system and the original one is that two back-translation models are trained together with the two encoder–decoder language models. There is no readily available model, but all models in the architecture learn to encode and generate from scratch.

Specifically, for one translation direction, the forward NMT model translates the source sentences into the target sentences and the backward NMT model translates the target into the

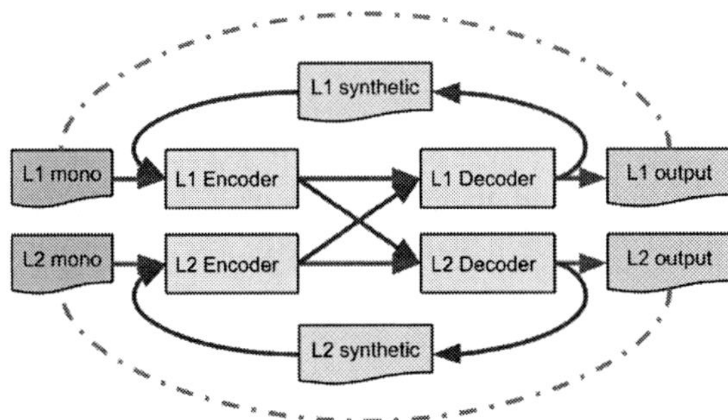

Figure 1: The architecture of unsupervised NMT model. The green arrows indicate the direction of data flow in encoder–decoder language models; the red arrows indicate the direction of data flow in back-translation models. The dotted lines are losses computed from output of the decoders and the original inputs.

source. These models generate sentences separately and then use the resulting translations to train each other. From another perspective, by combining the translation with its original sentence, a pseudo-parallel corpus is created, which is utilized to train the model to reconstruct the original sentence from its translation. More specifically, from the perspective of the two encoders, the models learn to encode both ground truth and synthetic monolingual sentences into latent representations; from the perspective of the two decoders, the models generate good sentences from latent representations, from encoders in both languages.

Figure 1 shows the illustration of the architecture of unsupervised NMT models.

4 Experiments

4.1 Setup

The baseline system in this work was an unsupervised NMT model trained on Chinese–Japanese charcater level data. This was to confirm the effectiveness of the model. Then, two experiments were completed, one for the ideograph model and the other for the stroke model. As discussed in the "Dataset Preparation" section, this is to enhance the shared information between the two languages. Understanding the importance of this in unsu-

pervised NMT models is one of the main goals of this work.

4.2 Training

The system developed in this work was implemented based on Lample et al. (2018) [6]. Transformer (Vaswani et al., 2017) cells were used as the basic units in the encoders and decoders through the PyTorch 0.4.0 toolkit, and the numbers of both the encoder and decoder layers were set to 4. The dimension of the token embeddings and the hidden layers was set to 512. The Adam optimizer (Kingma and Ba, 2015) was used, with a learning rate of 0.0001 and a batch size of 32. A maximum length of 175 tokens per sentence for each type of dataset and a dropout rate of 0.1 was set. It is worth mentioning that the random blank-out rate was set to 0.1 in the last experiment. BLEU scores (Papineni et al., 2002) of the translation in both directions were evaluated at every epoch, and training was stopped when the scores from the last ten epochs did not improve.

5 Results

BLEU scores of 7.01 for translation from ZH-JA and 7.73 for JA-ZH were recorded, respectively, at the time of result submission. However, after bug-fixing and fine-tuning, the best scores increased to 31.99 and 25.87 respectively (both using stroke data).

The results of the baseline systems and the two experiments on sub-character level data are recorded in Table 3. The two sub-character level models outperform the character level baseline model. Moreover, the stroke model performs better than the ideograph model. The translation examples can be found in Table 4.

6 Discussion

6.1 Effectiveness of Unsupervised NMT Model

According to Lample et al. (2018), the source data and target data should share 95% of the tokens in order to make the model effective.

---

[6]`https://github.com/facebookresearch/`
`UnsupervisedMT`

Level	Direction	BLEU
Character	JA–ZH	24.18
	ZH–JA	29.79
Ideograph	JA–ZH	25.76
	ZH–JA	32.61
Stroke	JA–ZH	**26.39**
	ZH–JA	**32.99**

Table 3: BLEU scores of 3 unsupervised NMT models on 6 translation directions. The stroke data has the best BLEU scores in both the JA–ZH and ZH–JA translation directions

However, according to the baseline and experiments in this paper, it seems that only 66.89% of shared tokens on character level data are required to generate good translations. Although the BLEU scores of both translation directions is not as good as the most basic supervised NMT model using RNNSearch (Zhang and Komachi, 2018), it is still promising, since the training data used in this work is much smaller than the original setting (Lample et al., 2018).

On the other hand, the testing output produced by the model was closely investigated. In both translation directions, translations were produced which do not use the exact terms in the reference, but instead use synonymous expressions. Several native speakers were asked to judge the grammaticality, fluency, and naturalness of the output translations, and many of the translations were thought to be better than the references. For example in Table 4, the character-level model Chinese translation "中显示" was very close to the reference "所示" semantically, and this translation was consistent in ideograph- and stroke-level models. This might be because of the encoder–decoder language models in the architecture, which successfully grasp the features of the language and express it in the translation. Therefore, if semantic-based metrics (instead of n-gram based metrics, like BLEU) could be introduced to NMT evaluation, the performance of unsupervised NMT could be better reflected in their BLEU scores.

6.2 Shared Information

Zhang and Komachi (2018) proposed that in logographic languages, sub-character decompositions could help supervised NMT models. It is found that sub-character decompositions (ideographs and strokes) are also helpful in unsupervised NMT models. This is largely due to the increase in shared information. Furthermore, since strokes are smaller units than ideographs, and they contain more shared information, the model performance is improved. For example in Table 4, despite the fact that translations produced by ideograph and stroke models were better than that of character model, stroke model was even slightly better than ideograph model. The stroke model translated Japanese "表現" into Chinese "表达", which was considered more precise than ideograph model's "名词". This might be due to the similarity of characters between Chinese and Japanese; and stroke model, as a model of finer granularity of sub-character level, successfully took advantage of this shared information.

Current unsupervised models still perform poorly on distant language pairs, so if the shared information between distant languages can be improved, unsupervised NMTs may be created for more general purpose.

7 Conclusion

The effectiveness of unsupervised NMT models is investigated for another language pair: Chinese–Japanese. The unsupervised NMT system is quite promising for similar languages, even if the monolingual dataset is not large. However, to evaluate its performance more successfully, better semantic-based metrics are required.

Acknowledgments

This work was partially supported by JSPS Grant-in-Aid for Young Scientists (B) Grant Number JP16K16117.

Type	Sentence
Reference–JA	図 3 に 「 会 」 が 固有 表現 である か 否 か を 判定 する 2 つ の 例文 を 示した .
Reference–ZH	图 3 所示 的 是 2 个 关于 判断 " 会 " 是否是 固有 表达 的 例句 。
Charcater–JA	図 3 に 示す よう な 2 つ の 判断 について 「 会 」 が 固有 表現 である か どう か を 判断 する 例文 を 示す .
Character–ZH	图 3 中 显示 了 判定 " 会 " 是 固有 名词 还是 有 2 个 例句 。
Ideograph–JA	図 3 に 示す よう に 2 つ の 判断 「 会 」 が 固有 表現 である か どうか について の 例文 を 示す .
Ideograph–ZH	图 3 中 显示 了 判定 " 会 " 是否是 固有 名词 的 2 个 例句 。
Stroke–JA	図 3 に 示す の は , 2 つ の 判断 について 「 会 」 が 固有 表現 の 例文 で ある か どうか で ある
Stroke–ZH	图 3 中 显示 了 判定 " 会 " 是否是 固有 表达 的 2 个 例句 。
English	Figure 3 showed 2 example sentences of judging whether "会" is an inherent expression.

Table 4: Translation examples from 3 unsupervised NMT models in 6 translation directions. Note that even if the produced translations are not the exact words from the reference sentences, they are synonymous. Furthermore, the stroke model can generate more accurate translations semantically than the ideograph model.

References

Mikel Artetxe, Gorka Labaka, Eneko Agirre, and Kyunghyun Cho. 2018. Unsupervised neural machine translation. In *International Conference on Learning Representations*.

Dzmitry Bahdanau, Kyunghyun Cho, and Yoshua Bengio. 2014. Neural machine translation by jointly learning to align and translate. In *ICLR 2015*.

Piotr Bojanowski, Edouard Grave, Armand Joulin, and Tomas Mikolov. 2017. Enriching word vectors with subword information. In *Transactions of the Association for Computational Linguistics (TACL)*, pages 135–146.

Kyunghyun Cho, Bart van Merrienboer, Caglar Gulcehre, Dzmitry Bahdanau, Fethi Bougares, Holger Schwenk, and Yoshua Bengio. 2014. Learning phrase representations using RNN encoder–decoder for statistical machine translation. In *The 2014 Conference on Empirical Methods In Natural Language Processing*, pages 1724–1734.

Pierre Isabelle, Colin Cherry, and George Foster. 2017. A challenge set approach to evaluating machine translation. In *Proceedings of the 2017 Conference on Empirical Methods in Natural Language Processing*, pages 2476–2486.

Diederick P Kingma and Jimmy Ba. 2015. Adam: A method for stochastic optimization. In *International Conference on Learning Representations (ICLR)*.

Philipp Koehn and Rebecca Knowles. 2017. Six challenges for neural machine translation. In *Proceedings of the First Workshop on Neural Machine Translation*, pages 28–39.

Guillaume Lample, Myle Ott, Alexis Conneau, Ludovic Denoyer, and Marc'Aurelio Ranzato. 2018. Phrase-based & neural unsupervised machine translation. In *Proceedings of the 2018 Conference on Empirical Methods in Natural Language Processing (EMNLP)*, pages 5039–5049.

Toshiaki Nakazawa, Manabu Yaguchi, Kiyotaka Uchimoto, Masao Utiyama, Eiichiro Sumita, Sadao Kurohashi, and Hitoshi Isahara. 2016. Aspec: Asian scientific paper excerpt corpus. In Nicoletta Calzolari (Conference Chair), Khalid Choukri, Thierry Declerck, Sara Goggi, Marko Grobelnik, Bente Maegaard, Joseph Mariani, Helene Mazo, Asuncion Moreno, Jan Odijk, and Stelios Piperidis, editors, *Proceedings of the Tenth International Conference on Language Resources and Evaluation (LREC 2016)*, may.

Toshiaki Nakazawa, Shohei Higashiyama, Chenchen Ding, Raj Dabre, Anoop Kunchukuttan, Win Pa Pa, Isao Goto, Hideya Mino, Katsuhito Sudoh, and Sadao Kurohashi. 2018. Overview of the 5th workshop on asian translation. In *Proceedings of the 5th Workshop on Asian Translation (WAT2018)*, Hong Kong, China, December.

Kishore Papineni, Salim Roukos, Todd Ward, and Wei-Jing Zhu. 2002. Bleu: a method for automatic evaluation of machine translation. In

Proceedings of the 40th Annual Meeting on As-sociation for Computational Linguistics, pages 311–318.

Rico Sennrich, Barry Haddow, and Alexandra Birch. 2016a. Edinburgh neural machine translation systems for WMT 16. In *Proceedings of the First Workshop on Neural Machine Translation*, pages 371–376.

Rico Sennrich, Barry Haddow, and Alexandra Birch. 2016b. Improving neural machine translation models with monolingual data. In *Proceedings of the 54th Annual Meeting of the Association for Computational Linguistics (Volume 1: Long Papers)*, pages 86–96.

Rico Sennrich, Barry Haddow, and Alexandra Birch. 2016c. Neural machine translation of rare words with subword units. In *Proceedings of the 54th Annual Meeting of the Association for Computational Linguistics (Volume 1: Long Papers)*, volume 1, pages 1715–1725.

Ilya Sutskever, Oriol Vinyals, and Quoc V. Le. 2014. Sequence to sequence learning with neural networks. In *Advances in Neural Information Processing Systems*, pages 3104–3112.

Ashish Vaswani, Noam Shazeer, Niki Parmar, Jakob Uszkoreit, Llion Jones, Aidan N. Gomez, Lukasz Kaiser, and Illia Polosukhin. 2017. Attention is all you need. In *Advances in Neural Information Processing Systems*, pages 6000–6010.

Yonghui Wu, Mike Schuster, Zhifeng Chen, Quoc V. Le, Mohammad Norouzi, Wolfgang Macherey, Maxim Krikun, Yuan Cao, Qin Gao, Klaus Macherey, Jeff Klingner, Apurva Shah, Melvin Johnson, Xiaobing Liu, Łukasz Kaiser, Stephan Gouws, Yoshikiyo Kato, Taku Kudo, Hideto Kazawa, Keith Stevens, George Kurian, Nishant Patil, Wei Wang, Cliff Young, Jason Smith, Jason Riesa, Alex Rudnick, Oriol Vinyals, Greg Corrado, Macduff Hughes, and Jeffrey Dean. 2016. Google's neural machine translation system: Bridging the gap between human and machine translation. *CoRR*, abs/1609.08144.

Lontu Zhang and Mamoru Komachi. 2018. Neural machine translation of logographic language using sub-character level information. In *Proceedings of the Third Conference on Machine Translation*, pages 17–25.

Jie Zhou, Ying Cao, Xuguang Wang, Peng Li, and Wei Xu. 2016. Deep recurrent models with fast-forward connections for neural machine translation. In *Transactions of the Association for Computational Linguistics (TACL)*, pages 371–383.

Statistical Machine Translation Using 5-grams Word Segmentation in Decoding

Aye Thida **Nway Nway Han** **Sheinn Thawtar Oo**

AI Research Lab, University of Computer Studies, Mandalay, Myanmar

{ayethida, nwaynwayhan, sheinthawtaroo}@ucsm.edu.mm

Abstract

This paper presents UCSMNLP's submission to the WAT 2018 Translation Tasks focusing on the Myanmar-English translation for mixed domain tasks. In statistical machine translation (SMT), word segmentation is a necessary step to generate more fluent translation results. Myanmar is one of the low resource languages and many researches are supposed to develop word segmentation for Myanmar language. However, there are no public tools for Myanmar word segmentation. This paper addresses the problem of word segmentation for Myanmar language in SMT by developing syllable, 5-grams and longest matching word segmentation with monolingual lexicon. This paper describes the phrase-based statistical machine translation (PBSMT) with batch version of MIRA tuning using 5-grams word segmentation for English-Myanmar language pairs in both directions. The experimental results showed that the baseline SMT with 5-grams could outperform the baseline system in terms of BLEU, RIBES and AMFM scores.

1 Introduction

In Natural Language Processing (NLP), machine translation system is one of the important tasks to communicate one language to another. In Myanmar script, sentences are clearly delimited by a sentence boundary maker but words are not always delimited by spaces. Words are composed of one or more syllables and that are not usually separated by white space. Sometimes spaces are used to separating the phrases for easier reading, but it is not essential, and these spaces are rarely used in short sentences.

Syllable and word segmentation are the necessary steps for statistical machine translation. This paper describes the phrase-based statistical machine translation (PBSMT) using 5-grams word segmentation for English-Myanmar language pairs in both directions.

In this work, we focus on comparing baseline PBSMT and PBSMT with 5-grams. Section 2 describes our system description. Section 3 describes the experimental setup. Section 4 describes the results and observations of our experiments. Finally, section 5 concludes the report.

2 System Description

In this section, we describe the methodology used in the machine translation experiments for this paper. This system mainly relies on the phrase-based statistical machine translation system and focus on comparing baseline PBSMT and PBSMT with 5-grams. It is implemented using the Moses toolkit (Philipp and Haddow, 2009).

2.1 Syllable 5-grams

Many other western languages use alphabetic writing system like English. However, Myanmar language uses a syllabic writing system and every syllable has a meaning is interestingly. This system firstly introduced how to do the 5-grams word segmentation. One 5-grams word consists of 5 syllables and one longest word includes maximum number of syllables in Myanmar Lexicon of Words (MLW). This system used Myanmar word segmentation by using MLW with a set of heuristics to identify word boundaries in text. In Myanmar lexicon, there are 39854 different words from myPOS corpus (draft released 1.0)[1] and myG2P[2] dictionary (Thu et al., 2016).

2.2 Phrase-based Statistical Machine Translation (PBSMT)

A PBSMT translation model is based on phrasal units. Here, a phrase is simply a contiguous sequence of words and generally, not a linguistically motivated phrase. A phrase-based translation model typically gives better translation performance than word-based models. We describe a simple phrase-based translation model consisting of phrase-pair probabilities extracted from corpus and a basic reordering model, and an algorithm to extract the phrases to build a phrase-table.

2.3 Phrase-based Statistical Machine Translation with 5-grams (PBSMT_5grams)

PBSMT with 5-grams Myanmar word segmentation uses Myanmar lexicon, which includes 39854 different words from myPOS corpus and myG2P dictionary. Table 1 shows the precision, recall and F1 scores for different segmentations. In segmentation experiments, we used the test corpus sentences from WAT-18 Myanmar-English dataset as reference corpus and segmented with 5-grams on these sentences. To evaluate the performance of the segmentation, we against the result of our segmenter with reference data. According to our experiment, the accuracy of longest segmentation is better than 5-grams segmentation. This system firstly applies the phrase-based statistical machine translation (PBSMT) using 5-grams word segmentation for English-Myanmar language pairs in both directions.

Segmentation	Precision	Recall	F1
5-grams	35.8	34.5	35.1
longest	38.9	35.4	37.0

Table 1: Precision, Recall and F1 scores for different segmentations

3 Experiments

To evaluate the translation quality of baseline PBSMT and PBSMT with 5-grams, our analysis looked through the translation tasks of two corpora, the ALT corpus and UCSY corpus.

3.1 Corpus Statistics

This system used parallel data for Myanmar-English translation tasks at WAT2018 which consists of two corpora, the ALT corpus and UCSY corpus. The ALT corpus is one part from the Asian Language Treebank (ALT) Project, consists of nearly twenty thousand Myanmar-English parallel sentences from news articles. The UCSY corpus is constructed by the NLP Lab, University of Computer Studies, Yangon (UCSY), and Myanmar. This corpus consists of over 200 thousand Myanmar-English parallel sentences collected from different domains, including news articles and textbooks.

In this experiment, the training data was combined with ALT and UCSY corpus. And then, removing mismatch sentences from training corpus. After cleaning sentences from training corpus, 226601 parallel sentences were remained. Table-2 shows data statistics used for the experiments.

Set	#Sentences
TRAIN	226,601
DEV	993
TEST	1,007

Table 2: Statistics of data sets

For the baseline, Moses tokenizer is used for both English and Myanmar language of the parallel data. Table-3 shows data statistics used for baseline PBSMT.

Set	#Sentences	#Tokens	
		En	Myan
TRAIN	226,601	743,028	170,216
DEV	993	25,360	54,268
TEST	1,007	25,903	55,022

Table 3: Statistics of data sets for BaseLine

For 5-grams PBSMT, Moses tokenizer is used for English language and 5-grams word segmenter

---

[1] https://github.com/ye-kyaw-thu/myPOS

[2] https://github.com/ye-kyaw-thu/myG2P

Source-	BLEU Scores		RIBES Scores		AMFM Scores	
Target	PBSMT	PBSMT (5-grams)	PBSMT	PBSMT (5-grams)	PBSMT	PBSMT (5-grams)
en-my	6.79	**19.17**	53.07	**55.40**	45.88	**61.52**
my-en	3.51	**6.01**	52.61	**53.63**	47.05	**51.90**

Table 5: BLEU, RIBES and AMFM scores for PBSMT, PBSMT with 5-grams (with Batch-Mira tuning)

is used for Myanmar language. Table-4 shows data statistics used for 5-grams PBSMT.

Set	#Sentences	#Tokens	
		Eng	Myan
TRAIN	226,601	743,028	170,216
DEV	993	25,360	65,028
TEST	1,007	25,903	66,040

Table 4: Statistics of data sets for 5-grams

3.2 Moses SMT system

We used the PBSMT system provided by the Moses toolkit (Philipp and Haddow, 2009) for training PBSMT statistical machine translation systems. According to our knowledge, there is no publicly available word segmenter for Myanmar language. Thus, we used 5-grams word segmenter only for Myanmar language which is developed by the NLP Lab, University of Computer Studies, Mandalay (UCSM), Myanmar, aiming to promote machine translation research on Myanmar language. The segmented word of source language was aligned with the segmented word of target language using MGIZA++ (Gao and Vogel, 2008). This system used grow-diag-final-and heuristic (Koehn et al., 2003) for the symmetrized alignment and msd-bidirectional-fe (Tillmann, 2004) option for the lexicalized reordering model was trained with. Although the sentences in test data are long, this system used (default 6) distortion limit in MOSES. The language model was trained by KENLM (Heafield, 2011) with interpolated modified Kneser-Ney discounting (Heafield et al., 2013). To do the tuning for decoder parameters, this system used Batch (J=60) with MIRA tuning (Cherry and Foster, 2012) and Moses decoder (version 2.1.1) for decoding.

3.3 Evaluation

This system reports the translation quality of those methods in terms of Bilingual Evaluation Understudy (BLEU) (Papineni et al., 2002), Rank-based Intuitive Bilingual Evaluation Measure (RIBES) (Isozaki et al., 2010) and Adequacy-Fluency Metrics (AMFM) (Banchs, et al., 2015).

In PBSMT without tuning method, this system gets -96.5 pairwise human evaluation score in English to Myanmar translation and -99.5 in Myanmar to English translation.

To get the more influent translation results, this system used the Batch-Mira tuning method. Table 5 shows the BLEU, RIBES and AMFM scores for PBSMT and PBSMT with 5-grams by using batch size 60 with mira tuning. Due to time constraint, the results of PBSMT with 5-grams by using batch-mira tuning method could not be submitted for manual evaluation.

4 Results and Discussion

The BLEU, AMFM and RIBES score results for machine translation experiments with PBSMT and PBSMT with 5-grams segmentation are shown in Table 5. The highest scores of the different approaches are indicated as bold numbers. Comparing to existing baselines of PBSMT, PBSMT with 5-grams approach achieved higher scores in our experiments.

According the results from Table 5, the PBSMT with 5-grams outperforms the baseline PBSMT in terms of BLEU, RIBES and AMFM score from English to Myanmar translation. On the other hand, from Myanmar to English translation, the PBSMT with 5-grams better than the baseline PBSMT in terms of BLEU, RIBES and AMFM score.

Further experimentation is required to see the PBSMT with n-grams segmentation and analyze which one performs better on English-Myanmar in both directions. One way to test this is by increasing the n-grams (longest) segmentation even further.

Our experimental results indicate that in terms of adequacy (as measured by BLEU score), the PBSMT with 5-grams approach produced the higher quality translations than baseline. However in some sentences, PBSMT with 5-grams approach cannot translate in name entities. Likewise, the PBSMT with 5-grams is better word order (as measured by the RIBES score) than the baseline but this system requires to get correct word order in long sentences for both directions. In terms of both semantic and syntactic components of the translation process, the AMFM scores of PBSMT with 5-grams give higher scores than baseline that provide a more balanced view on Myanmar-English bidirectional translation quality.

For Myanmar Language, PBSMT with 5-grams segmentations approach is not suitable to get the adequate and fluent translation results. As an example, the Myanmar word "တပ်မတော်ဒုတိယ ကာကွယ်ရေးဦးစီးချုပ်" is translated to "Deputy Chief of Defense" in English. Therefore, we need to test n-grams (longest) segmentation to get better translation results. Moreover, according to our experiments, automatic evaluation metrics can sometimes be misleading. In Myanmar-English bilingual language translation, the word order difference of two languages is one of the difficulties in machine translation to get influent results. Therefore, human evaluation with bilingual judges (Vilar et al., 2007) would be required to get better qualities of the machine translation approaches for Myanmar-English language pair.

5 Conclusion

This paper compared two approaches of PBSMT: baseline PBSMT and PBSMT with 5-grams segmentation approach for Myanmar-English language pairs in both directions. Although the evaluation results of PBSMT with 5-grams with batch-mira tuning are better than baseline PBSMT, this approach is not suitable to get the adequate and fluent translation results. In future, we would like to investigate the better model by modifying the PBSMT with 5-grams approach to improve the translation quality of statistical machine translation for Myanmar-English in both directions.

References

Banchs, R.E., D'Haro, L.F. and Li, H., 2015. Adequacy-fluency metrics: Evaluating MT in the continuous space model framework. *IEEE/ACM Transactions on Audio, Speech and Language Processing (TASLP)*, *23*(3), pp.472-482.

Chen, S.F. and Goodman, J., 1999. An empirical study of smoothing techniques for language modeling. *Computer Speech & Language*, *13*(4), pp.359-394.

Cherry, C. and Foster, G., 2012, June. Batch tuning strategies for statistical machine translation. In *Proceedings of the 2012 Conference of the North American Chapter of the Association for Computational Linguistics: Human Language Technologies* (pp. 427-436). Association for Computational Linguistics.

Gao, Q. and Vogel, S., 2008, June. Parallel implementations of word alignment tool. In *Software engineering, testing, and quality assurance for natural language processing* (pp. 49-57). Association for Computational Linguistics.

Heafield, K., 2011, July. KenLM: Faster and smaller language model queries. In *Proceedings of the Sixth Workshop on Statistical Machine Translation* (pp. 187-197). Association for Computational Linguistics.

Heafield, K., Pouzyrevsky, I., Clark, J.H. and Koehn, P., 2013. Scalable modified Kneser-Ney language model estimation. In *Proceedings of the 51st Annual Meeting of the Association for Computational Linguistics (Volume 2: Short Papers)* (Vol. 2, pp. 690-696).

Isozaki, H., Hirao, T., Duh, K., Sudoh, K. and Tsukada, H., 2010, October. Automatic evaluation of translation quality for distant language pairs. In *Proceedings of the 2010 Conference on Empirical Methods in Natural Language Processing* (pp. 944-952). Association for Computational Linguistics.

Koehn, P. and Haddow, B., 2009, March. Edinburgh's submission to all tracks of the WMT2009 shared task with reordering and speed improvements to Moses. In *Proceedings of the Fourth Workshop on Statistical Machine Translation* (pp. 160-164). Association for Computational Linguistics.

Koehn, P., Och, F.J. and Marcu, D., 2003, May. Statistical phrase-based translation. In *Proceedings of the 2003 Conference of the North American Chapter of the Association for Computational Linguistics on Human Language Technology-Volume 1* (pp. 48-54). Association for Computational Linguistics.

Nakazawa, T., Higashiyama, S., Ding, C., Dabre, R., Kunchukuttan, A., Pa, W.P., Goto, I., Mino, H., Sudoh, K. and Kurohashi, S., 2018, December. Overview of the 5th Workshop on Asian Translation.

In *Proceedings of the 5th Workshop on Asian Translation (WAT2018)*.

Och, F.J. and Ney, H., 2000, October. Improved statistical alignment models. In *Proceedings of the 38th Annual Meeting on Association for Computational Linguistics* (pp. 440-447). Association for Computational Linguistics.

Papineni, K., Roukos, S., Ward, T. and Zhu, W.J., 2002, July. BLEU: a method for automatic evaluation of machine translation. In *Proceedings of the 40th annual meeting on association for computational linguistics* (pp. 311-318). Association for Computational Linguistics.

Thu, Y.K., Pa, W.P., Sagisaka, Y. and Iwahashi, N., 2016. Comparison of grapheme-to-phoneme conversion methods on a myanmar pronunciation dictionary. In *Proceedings of the 6th Workshop on South and Southeast Asian Natural Language Processing (WSSANLP2016)* (pp. 11-22).

Tillmann, C., 2004, May. A unigram orientation model for statistical machine translation. In *Proceedings of HLT-NAACL 2004: Short Papers* (pp. 101-104). Association for Computational Linguistics.

Vilar, D., Leusch, G., Ney, H. and Banchs, R.E., 2007, June. Human evaluation of machine translation through binary system comparisons. In *Proceedings of the Second Workshop on Statistical Machine Translation* (pp. 96-103). Association for Computational Linguistics.

CVIT-MT Systems for WAT-2018

Jerin Philip[†], Vinay P. Namboodiri[‡] and C.V. Jawahar[†]
[†] CVIT, IIIT Hyderabad, [‡] IIT-Kanpur
`jerin.philip@research.iiit.ac.in`
`vinay.pn@cse.iitk.ac.in, jawahar@iiit.ac.in`

Abstract

This document describes the machine translation system used in the submissions of IIIT-Hyderabad (CVIT-MT) for the WAT-2018 English-Hindi translation task. Performance is evaluated on the associated corpus provided by the organizers. We experimented with convolutional sequence to sequence architectures. We also train with additional data obtained through backtranslation.

1 Introduction

Innovations in Neural Machine Translation (NMT) have led to success in many machine translation tasks, often outperforming Statistical Machine Translation (SMT) techniques. Similar to many other language pairs, NMT based approaches have been attempted for the English-Hindi language pair as well (e.g. the WAT-2017 submission (Wang et al., 2017)). Hindi continue to remain as a low resource language demanding further attention from Natural Language Processing (NLP, Machine Learning ML and other related communities. The Hindi-English pair has limited availability of sentence level aligned bitext as parallel corpora.

Lack of sufficient data for Indian languages motivated us to explore techniques that can help in low-resource situations. Recent works (such as (Edunov et al., 2018; Lample et al., 2018)) point to the use of iterative backtranslation to improve translation in low resource languages or under the unavailability of parallel corpora.

This paper describes an overview of the submission from IIIT Hyderabad (CVIT-MT) in WAT-2018(Nakazawa et al., 2018) for for the Hindi-English and English-Hindi translation tasks of the mixed domain tasks. In Section 2, we describe the components constituting our pipeline, following which in Section 3 we provide the details of the data used and procedure used for the training. Section 4 summarizes our results for WAT-2018. Finally in Section 5 we include additional results using newer architectures. We conclude our observations in Section 6.

2 System Description

In this section, we describe the details associated with the tokenization, architecture and data augmentation. These are the three components that helped in obtaining superior results on the corpus provided by the organizers of WAT-2018.

2.1 Tokenization

A popular method of addressing rare-words without compromising coverage of the entire corpus was Byte Pair Encoding (BPE) (Sennrich et al., 2016b), which used a deterministic greedy compression based algorithm to bring the vocabulary down to a finite feasible value.

SentencePiece (Kudo, 2018) builds on top of byte pair encoding. Unlike BPE, which is agnostic to language, SentencePiece gives the most likely derivation of a sentence composed of subword units. This setting reduces to character level in case a completely unknown sentence/word is provided, and the translation model also learns to transliterate. We use SentencePiece for its merits mentioned above.

2.2 Convolutional Sequence to Sequence Learning

In our submission, we employ the Convolutional Sequence to Sequence architecture (CONVS2S) (Gehring et al., 2017). CONVS2S follows an encoder decoder architecture. This has the advantage of being faster than the popular Recurrent Neural Network (RNN) based encoder decoder architectures with attention. This is because the context is built through multiple inputs stacking k convolution blocks ($O(\frac{n}{k})$) with the ability to build in parallel representations for multiple parts of the sentence, unlike through time in the RNN ($O(n)$).

A 1-D convolutional filter of width w with two channels at the output sliding over the embeddings of the text inputs constitute a basic convolutional block. Output of one channel builds up context representation and the other is used to enable gating through Gated Linear Units (GLUs) (Dauphin et al., 2017). The encoder is constructed by stacking k of the above setup, creating a receptive field controlled by w and k. The decoder is similar to the encoder in architecture, with a fully connected layer projecting output to vocabulary size.

2.3 Backtranslation

Backtranslation is a widely tried and tested data augmentation method, proposed for aiding NMT in languages low on parallel resources using available monolingual data by Sennrich *et. al* (2016a). The method works by first training a model in the low to high resource direction followed by using this model on monolingual data. The process provides more authentic sentences in the resource-scarce language and close approximation of its translation in the high resource language. It has been empirically shown that synthetic data alone generated through backtranslation can attain upto 83% of the performance using proper bitext (Edunov et al., 2018).

In the next section, we describe how the components explained above are implemented and used in training - including generating dataset, preprocessing and filtering the training samples, hyperparameters of the architectures in place and evaluations.

3 Experimental Setup

3.1 Dataset

In our experiments, we use the training data provided by organizers. In addition, we also use data obtained from translated Hindi content available on Internet. Top level statistics of the data used are provided in Table 1.

Dataset	Pairs	Tokens	
		hi	en
IITB train	1,492,827	22.2M	20.6M
IITB train†	923,377	20.3M	18.9M
National News	2,495,129	41.2M	39.0M
Backtranslated	5,653,644	77.5M	91.9M
IITB dev	505	10,656	10,174
IITB test	2,507	49,394	57,037

Table 1: Descriptions of the corpora used, IITB train† is a filtered version of the IITB train corpus.

The training corpus provided by the organizers, hereafter denoted by IITB-corpus consists of data from mixed domains. There are roughly 1.5M samples in training data from diverse sources, while the development and test sets are from newspaper crawls. In addition to this, monolingual data collected by the organizers from several sources are used in our backtranslation enabled attempts at training an NMT system. There are 45M samples in the monolingual corpus provided.

We enhanced the training data with additional pairs, but automatically translated. Note that no manual translation was used to create additional data. We obtain 2.5M Hindi sentences automatically translated to English from newspapers and similar resources, obtained from Internet. This data is some what domain specific. They are primarily, from news articles related to national news. This is mentioned as National News in Table 1.

We also create a parallel corpus through backtranslation using the organizers monolingual Hindi data hereafter denoted by Backtranslated, the details of which are also included in Table 1 and the methods of creation elaborated in Section 3.3.

3.2 Data Processing

We train separate SentencePiece models using official implementation available online [1] with vocabulary restricted to 8000 units to function as a learned tokenizer for both English and Hindi. We use the unigram model, which gives language aware tokenization.

To filter any noisy content from IITB corpus, *langdetect*[2] and removed every pair which had probability of being in the respective language less than 0.95. This gave us roughly 0.92M pairs for training, from IITB corpus and is indicated as IITB train[†] in Table 1. English data is kept true-cased, which we found to have better results consistently with our NMT model.

3.3 Training

In our experiments we use the fairseq [3] toolkit. For the tasks in this submission we use the CONVS2S model.

The encoder and decoder embeddings have a dimension of 512. The hidden units in the encoder and decoder are also 512 dimensional, following Gehring *et. al* (2017). We use convolutional filters of width 3 and 20 layers stacked for both the encoder and decoder. A dropout with probability 0.1 is put in-place right after the embeddings layer for better generalization. The training is run in batches of maximum 4000 tokens at a time, which is on an average 140 sample sentences per batch. The model is trained to minimize the categorical cross-entropy loss at the token level using Nestorov accelerated gradient descent. Decoding is performed through beam search with a beam width of 10.

We run training using four NVIDIA 1080Ti-s until validation loss hasn't improved for 3 epochs straight. The training time was roughly 2 days and stopping around 30-40 epochs.

We keep our model hyperparameters constant as specified across experiments and work with different combinations of corpora created from augmenting the National News dataset and official parallel corpora. For creating the Backtranslated corpus, we use a model trained to translate from Hindi to English

using both National News and IITB corpus. We filter the obtained pairs using confidence of translation obtained from the beam-score and further to pairs with a length between 10 and 30 tokens.

3.4 Evaluations

We report Bilingual Evaluation Understudy (BLEU) (Papineni et al., 2002), Rank-based Intuitive Bilingual Evaluation Score (RIBES) (Isozaki et al., 2010), Adequacy-fluency metrics (AM-FM) (Banchs et al., 2015) for all our attempts and scores from WAT-2018 human evaluations(Human in Table 2) when available.

BLEU is computed as the geometric mean of unigram, bigram, trigram and 4-gram precision multiplied by a brevity penalty (BP). BLEU ranges from 0 to 1, but the values reported in Tables 2 and 3 are in percentages. RIBES, also giving a value in $[0, 1]$ was proposed to tackle shortcomings of BLEU in distant language pairs, where changes in word ordering deteriorates BLEU.

4 Discussions

The results using our systems for WAT-2018 are presented in Table 2 (see some additional results in Table 3). The first part of the table consists of results on combinations of datasets and augmentations. All values are for models trained from scratch. In the second part, the current leader board is indicated for comparison. Note that entries in this part don't correspond to a single submission, but the values corresponding to the best in the respective metric.

Our submission based on the combination National News and IITB corpus tops human evaluation in Hindi to English, and ranks second in English to Hindi. We demonstrate the possibility of distilling knowledge of online available sources into a usable translation model. We successfully use the CONVS2S architecture along with SentencePiece to obtain results comparable to the top submissions. Our experiments also indicates data augmentation using backtranslation positively works for the Hindi-English pair.

5 Additional Transformer Experiments

In this section, we present a set of experiments and results post WAT-2018 involving the Transformer

---

[1] https://github.com/google/sentencepiece
[2] https://github.com/Mimino666/langdetect
[3] http://github.com/pytorch/fairseq (formerly fairseq-py)

Dataset	en-hi				hi-en			
	BLEU	RIBES	AM-FM	Human	BLEU	RIBES	AM-FM	Human
IITB train[†]	13.25	0.695113	0.647220	-	11.83	0.675462	0.572900	-
National News	18.77	0.748008	0.697630	-	19.53	0.745764	0.614260	-
+IITB train[†]	19.69	0.758365	0.699810	69.50	20.63	0.751883	0.623240	72.25
Backtranslated	16.77	0.714197	0.664330	50.50	-	-	-	-
2017 Best	21.39	0.749660	0.688770	64.50	22.44	0.750921	0.629530	68.25
2018 Best	20.28	0.761582	0.704220	77.00	17.80	0.731727	0.611090	67.25

Table 2: Quantitative results of translating English to Hindi and vice versa.

Architecture (Vaswani et al., 2017). Two variants of the architecture - Transformer Base and Transformer Big outperformed then state of the art CONVS2S models in the WMT German-English and French-English translation tasks.

We used the Transformer-Base architecture in further experiments with the National News + IITB corpus where CONVS2S performed the best, with the rest of the pipeline being kept same as described before. We went with the default hyperparameters provided by *fairseq* framework - which did not give us impressive results.

Following Popel and Bojar (2018), we modified the hyperparameters for initial warm-up steps of 16000 without any learning rate decay, starting from a learning rate of 0.25, followed by an exponential decay of learning rate. We also had to enable delayed gradient updates (Ott et al., 2018) to simulate a larger batch on smaller GPU before the model demonstrated any learning. During inference time, we averaged checkpoints of the model at different epochs once the loss on the development set had plateaued to obtain better results than a single checkpoint.

Architecture	BLEU	RIBES	AM-FM
CONVS2S	19.69	0.758365	0.699810
Transformer	21.10	0.771549	0.712200
+Averaging	**21.57**	**0.773923**	**0.712110**

Table 3: Transformer-Base vs CONVS2S on National News + IITB corpus, for English to Hindi direction.

In Table 3, we compare the performance of the transformer with that CONVS2S. Consistent with observations in languages like German-English and French-English, the transformer network produces better results than CONVS2S on all metrics. The averaged model performs the best in all metrics in English to Hindi translation task, at the time of writing this paper.

6   Observations

We believe that NMT is a promising approach for Indian language machine translation for obtaining reasonably accurate solutions. Our initial results reported here confirms this. In addition, we believe, the popular data augmentation methods are effective and feasible for many low-resource machine translation settings. We see the direct utility of the advances in NMT for many western language pairs on English-Hindi in terms of ideas and architectures. At the same time, we also believe, there is much more to do for making them effective on Indian languages.

Acknowledgments

We thank the organizers for systematically setting up this task, and for the very useful resources. We also thank the larger language processing group at IIIT Hyderabad for the encouragement, support and insights.

References

Rafael E Banchs, Luis F D'Haro, and Haizhou Li. 2015. Adequacy-fluency metrics: Evaluating MT in the continuous space model framework. *IEEE/ACM Transactions on Audio, Speech and Language Processing (TASLP)*, 23(3):472–482.

Yann N Dauphin, Angela Fan, Michael Auli, and David Grangier. 2017. Language Modeling with Gated Convolutional Networks. In *International Conference on Machine Learning*, pages 933–941.

Sergey Edunov, Myle Ott, Michael Auli, and David Grangier. 2018. Understanding Back-Translation at Scale. In *Proceedings of the 2018 Conference on Empirical Methods in Natural Language Processing*, pages 489–500.

Jonas Gehring, Michael Auli, David Grangier, Denis Yarats, and Yann N Dauphin. 2017. Convolutional Sequence to Sequence Learning. In *International Conference on Machine Learning*, pages 1243–1252.

Hideki Isozaki, Tsutomu Hirao, Kevin Duh, Katsuhito Sudoh, and Hajime Tsukada. 2010. Automatic evaluation of translation quality for distant language pairs. In *Proceedings of the 2010 Conference on Empirical Methods in Natural Language Processing*, pages 944–952. Association for Computational Linguistics.

Taku Kudo. 2018. Subword regularization: Improving neural network translation models with multiple subword candidates. In *Proceedings of the 56th Annual Meeting of the Association for Computational Linguistics (Volume 1: Long Papers)*, pages 66–75. Association for Computational Linguistics.

Guillaume Lample, Alexis Conneau, Ludovic Denoyer, and Marc'Aurelio Ranzato. 2018. Unsupervised machine translation using monolingual corpora only. In *International Conference on Learning Representations (ICLR)*.

Toshiaki Nakazawa, Shohei Higashiyama, Chenchen Ding, Raj Dabre, Anoop Kunchukuttan, Win Pa Pa, Isao Goto, Hideya Mino, Katsuhito Sudoh, and Sadao Kurohashi. 2018. Overview of the 5th workshop on asian translation. In *Proceedings of the 5th Workshop on Asian Translation (WAT2018)*, Hong Kong, China, December.

Myle Ott, Sergey Edunov, David Grangier, and Michael Auli. 2018. Scaling neural machine translation. In *Proceedings of the Third Conference on Machine Translation: Research Papers*, pages 1–9. Association for Computational Linguistics.

Kishore Papineni, Salim Roukos, Todd Ward, and Wei-Jing Zhu. 2002. BLEU: a method for automatic evaluation of machine translation. In *Proceedings of the 40th annual meeting on association for computational linguistics*, pages 311–318. Association for Computational Linguistics.

Martin Popel and Ondřej Bojar. 2018. Training Tips for the Transformer Model. *The Prague Bulletin of Mathematical Linguistics*, pages 43–70.

Rico Sennrich, Barry Haddow, and Alexandra Birch. 2016a. Improving Neural Machine Translation Models with Monolingual Data. In *Proceedings of the 54th Annual Meeting of the Association for Computational Linguistics (Volume 1: Long Papers)*, volume 1, pages 86–96.

Rico Sennrich, Barry Haddow, and Alexandra Birch. 2016b. Neural Machine Translation of Rare Words with Subword Units. In *Proceedings of the 54th Annual Meeting of the Association for Computational Linguistics (Volume 1: Long Papers)*, volume 1, pages 1715–1725.

Ashish Vaswani, Noam Shazeer, Niki Parmar, Jakob Uszkoreit, Llion Jones, Aidan N Gomez, Łukasz Kaiser, and Illia Polosukhin. 2017. Attention is all you need. In *Advances in Neural Information Processing Systems*, pages 5998–6008.

Boli Wang, Zhixing Tan, Jinming Hu, Yidong Chen, et al. 2017. XMU neural machine translation systems for WAT 2017. In *Proceedings of the 4th Workshop on Asian Translation (WAT2017)*, pages 95–98.

The RGNLP Machine Translation Systems for WAT 2018

Atul Kr. Ojha
SSIS, Jawaharlal Nehru University,
New Delhi, India
shashwatup9k@gmail.com

Koel Dutta Chowdhury
ADAPT Centre, Dublin City University
Dublin, Ireland
koel.chowdhury@adaptcentre.ie

Chao-Hong Liu
ADAPT Centre, Dublin City University
Dublin, Ireland
chaohong.liu@adaptcentre.ie

Karan Saxena
LTI, Carnegie Mellon University
Pittsburgh, PA, USA
karansax@cs.cmu.edu

Abstract

This paper presents the system description of Machine Translation (MT) system(s) for Indic Languages Multilingual Task for the 2018 edition of the WAT Shared Task. In our experiments, we (the RGNLP team) explore both statistical and neural methods across all language pairs. (We further present an extensive comparison of language-related problems for both the approaches in the context of low-resourced settings.) Our PBSMT models were highest score on all automaticevaluation metrics in the English into Telugu, Hindi, Bengali, Tamil portion of the shared task.

1 Introduction

The Statistical Machine Translation (SMT) (Brown et al., 1993) has been a growing area in the Machine Translation (MT) for the last two decades in comparison to the Rule-based Machine Translation (RBMT), especially after the availability of Moses open source toolkit (Koehn et al., 2007). However, recent years have witnessed a surge in application of neural model for solving machine translation tasks. There are many NMT open source toolkits available such as OpenNMT (Klein et al., 2017), Neural Monkey (Helcl et al., 2017), Nematus (Sennrich et al., 2017) etc. With the goal of preventing low resource Indic languages from being left behind in the advancement of NMT, we take the first step towards applying neural methods for English⇆Indic Language pairs in the 2018 WAT Indic Languages Multilingual Task[1].

---

[1] http://lotus.kuee.kyoto-u.ac.jp/WAT/indic-multilingual/index.html

Our submission results show that despite being trained on the same training data, there are inconsistencies in translation quality between the SMT and NMT system. While NMT approaches continue to be a challenging problem in low-resource scenarios (Koehn et al., 2017), it clearly outperforms phrase based SMT model in terms of evaluation metrics for rich-resourced language pairs such as English-German, French-English, German-French, Russian-English, English-Czech, English-Chinese etc.

2 System Overview

We built 42 bidirectional MT systems (including 28 PBSMT and 14 NMT) for English⇄Indic language pairs. These were trained using both phrase-based statistical and neural network approaches. The system details are given below:

(a) **Phrase-based SMT Systems with KenLM and SRILM language model:** We built our phrase-based statistical MT systems using the Moses toolkit (Koehn et al., 2007). We use the GIZA++ (Och et al., 2003) toolkit with the grow-diag-final-and heuristic for extracting phrases from the corresponding parallel corpora. In addition, we use both KenLM and SRILM toolkits (Stolcke, 2002) to build 4-gram and 5-gram language models respectively. The KeNLM follows probing and TRIEs which renders the system to train faster (Heafield, 2011) while the SRILM follows TRIE (Stolcke, 2002). We use the scripts from Moses tokenizer to tokenize and lowercasing the English representations of our experiments.

(b) **Neural Machine Translation Systems on Long-Short Term Memory (LSTM) network:** To build our Neural Machine

Translation systems we use OpenNMT-py (the pytorch port of Open-NMT toolkit (Klein et al., 2017)). Our settings follow the Open-NMT training guidelines that indicate that the default training setup is reasonable for training any language pairs. Specifically, we use a 2-layer LSTM (Hochreiter et al, 1997) The model is trained for 13 epochs, using Adam (Kingma and Ba, 2015) with learning rate 0.002 and mini-batches of 40 with 500 hidden units, a vocabulary size of 50002 and 50004 respectively for the source and target-side of the data. We maintain a static NMT-setup using same hyper-parameters setting across all language pairs.

(c) Direct Assessment and Ablation Study: We evaluate our systems using three standard MT evaluation metrics- BLEU, RIBES, and AMFM scores. In addition to these, evaluation is also performed against direct Human evaluation metrics based on the JPOadequacy (Nakazawa, et al., 2016) for English and Hindi. 5 evaluators took part in the task over a period of approx.10 days to evaluate the translated outputs at sentence level. The final decisions were prepared by the means of voting. The scores were calculated and shared by WAT 2018 which have been shown and discussed in section 4 in detail.

3   Experiments

In this section, we briefly describe the experimental settings used to develop the PBSMT and NMT systems for seven Indic languages:

Data Sets

The data was provided by the WAT 2018 organizers under the **Indic Languages Multilingual Task**(Nakazawa et al., 2018). The parallel corpora were distributed as the '**Indic Languages Multilingual Parallel Corpus'**. These parallel corpora have been extracted from the Opus (OpenSubtitles) website which comes under the domain of spoken language. The detailed statistics of the parallel and monolingual corpora are demonstrated in Table-1 and 2 which used to train the MT systems. The parallel data was further divided into training, tuning and testing sets. The detailed information of the split is presented in Table-1.In terms of

data volume, English⇆Singhalese language pair was the largest while English⇆Telugu language pair consists of minimum number of sentences. The similar trend is observed for the monolingual part of the corpora, with English having highestnumber of sentences and Telugu having the lowest.

Language Pair	Training	Tuning	Testing	Total Parallel sentences (including training, tuning and testing)
English⇄Hindi	84557	500	1000	86057
English⇄Bengali	337428	500	1000	338928
English⇄Malayalam	359423	500	1000	360923
English⇄Tamil	26217	500	1000	27717
English⇄Telugu	22165	500	1000	23665
English⇄Singhalese	521726	500	1000	523226
English⇄Urdu	26619	500	1000	28119

Table 1: Statistics of Parallel Sentences of the Indic Multilingual Languages

Language	Monolingual Sentences
English	2891079
Hindi	104967
Bengali	453859
Malayalam	402761
Tamil	30268
Telugu	24750
Singhalese	705793
Urdu	29086

Table 2: Statistics of Monolingual Corpus of the Indic Multilingual Languages

3.1   Pre-Processing

For scope of this work, we perform the following Pre-processing steps. I Both types of corpora were tokenized, cleaned (removing sentences of length over 40 words). We also true-cased the English representations of the corpora. These processes were performed using Moses scripts. The tokenization of Indic languages was done by the RGNLP team tokenizer. The pre-processing of the Indic languages were done using tokenizer[2] provided by the RGNLP team to ensure the canonical Unicode representation.

3.2   Development of RGNLP Systems

In the next step, we developed three MT models perlanguage pair: two different phrase-based statistical machine translation system using

---

[2]https://github.com/shashwatup9k/

different language models and one neural MT system using the encoder-decoder framework.

3.2.1 Training and Developments of PBMST

Systems: As above mentioned, we used the Moses open source tool the PBSMT system. The systems were trained independently and combined in a log-linear scheme in which each model was assigned a different weight using the Minimum Error Rate Training (Och et al., 2003) tuning algorithm. To investigate the role that language model has to play in terms of translation output, we used two different language model toolkits, namely KenLM and SRILM for building the 5-grams and 4-grams language models respectively. We used 500 parallel sentences for all language pairs to tune the systems.

3.2.2 Training and Developments of NMT

Systems: We use the OpenNMT toolkit for developing the NMT systems. We trained on a two layers of LSTM network with 500 hidden units at the both encoder and decoder models for 13 epochs. We have limited the variability of the parameters by using the default hyper-parameters configuration. Any unknown words in the translation were replaced with the word in the source language having the highest attention weight.

Finally, we translated the given test data using all 42 MT systems and performed some post-processing such as de-tokenization, de-truecasing to further improve the accuracy of the translated outputs.

4 Results and Analysis

In this section, we describe the following three things: (a) automatic evaluation results, (b) Human evaluation, and (c) Comparative Analysis of the PBSMT and NMT systems.

(a) Automatic Evaluation Results:

Evaluation is measured with the reference set provided the shared task organizers using the standard MT evaluation metrics. We present only the highest scoring system results across all language pair evaluated, in this paper. In order to gain a quantitative insight into specific differences, at least in terms of evaluation

metrics, we highlight some results in Figure 1 and 2 as follows:

We see from the results that for PBSMT systems, the English-Hindi language pair produced best results in terms of all three metrics (44.08 in BLEU, 0.751in RIBES, and 0.699in AMFM) while the Malayalam-English language pair scored the lowest for all three metrics (8.74 BLEU).

For the NMT systems, the English⇆Hindi, English-Urdu scored the highest (21, 0.60, 0.47 in BLEU, RIBES and AMFM, respectively) while English-Singhalese scored 0.97 BLEU with respect to the SMT counter-part. Our PBSMT system highestand secondhighestscoreswith respect to BLEU and other evaluation metrics respectively across all language pair evaluated (shown in the Figure3 and 4).

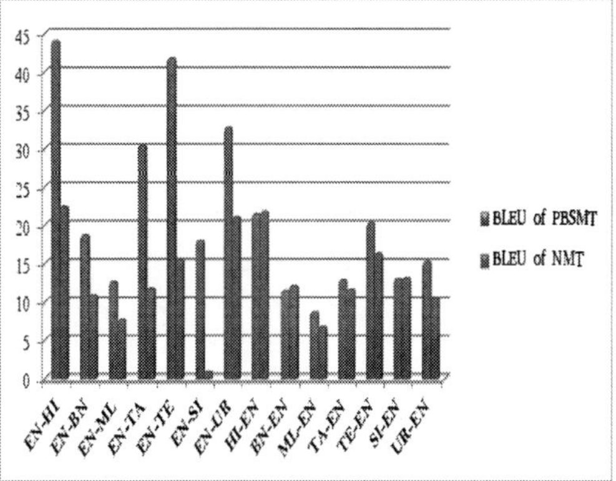

Figure 1: Accuracy of the English⇌Indic Languages of PBSMT and NMT Systems at the BLEU

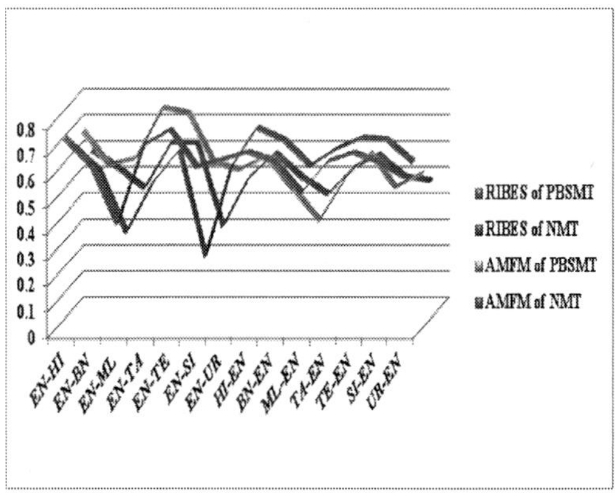

Figure 2: Accuracy of the English⇌Indic Languages of PBSMT& NMT Systems at the RIBES and AMFM

(b) Human Evaluation Results: In this section, we report the human evaluation accuracy of only English⇄HindiMT systems on adequacy. Figures 3 and 4 demonstrate the Pairwise and Adequacy results of English-Hindi and Hindi-English systems compared with other top MT systems. The Pairwise scores of our English-Hindi and Hindi-English systems were 15.50 and 22.25, respectively while the Adequacy of these pairs were 1.45 and 1.46. Both the Figures 3 and 4 clearly show that our systems hold the third rank in the human evaluation.

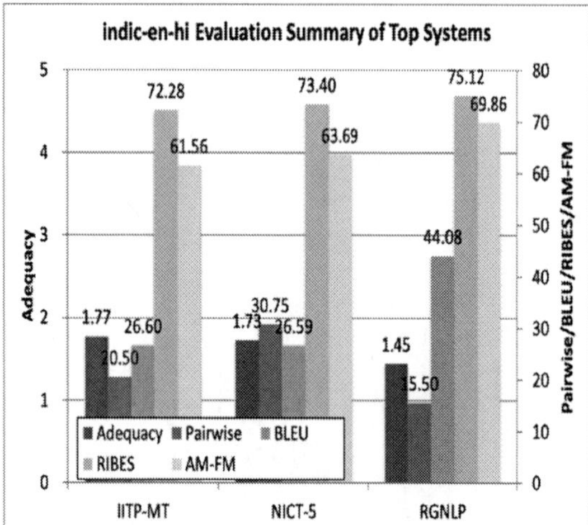

Figure 3: Comparative Evaluation of English-HindiMT Systems

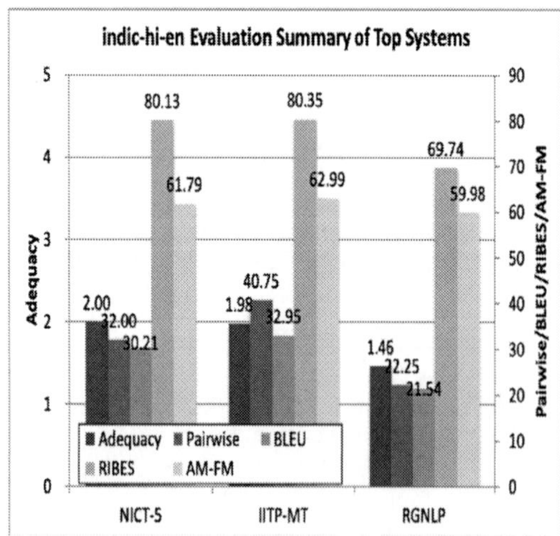

Figure 4: Comparative Evaluation of Hindi-English MT Systems

(c) Comparative Analysis of the PBSMT and NMT Systems: During comparison of the PBMST and NMT systems, the Indic-English language pairs of the NMT systems accuracies were the highest in BLEU, RIBES and AMFM metrics compared to other MT systems (Indic-English PBSMT, and English⇄Indic PBSMT and NMT), as shown in Figure 1 and 2. When we compare English-Hindi and Hindi-English both PBSMT and NMT systems at the adequacy level, the NMT's performance was worse (the accuracy was in negative). It happened because the NMT's result was affected majorly by over-generation, OOV (Out-of-Vocabulary), NER issues, and word-order and unable to produce output of some source sentences. The PBSMT's results were also affected by OOV, word-order, NER issues; nevertheless, it was able to produce output of each source sentence.

5 Conclusions

In this paper, two major points have been discussed. The first is development of the MT systems for English⇄Indic language pairs at the WAT2018 shared task and the second is the comparison of phrase-based statistical and neural based MT systems. The phrase-based and neural based MT systems were evaluated by automatic metrics on BLEU, RIBES and AMFM. To evaluate the adequacy of the PBSMT and NMT systems, the English-Hindi and Hindi-English MT systems were shared by five evaluators who evaluated these systems at the sentence level. The results of adequacy of systems were prepared via voting. Finally, we have compared and analyzed PBSMT and NMT systems and discussed their major problems.

Acknowledgements

We are grateful to the organizers of WAT2018 for providing us the Indic Language Multilingual Parallel and Monolingual Corpus and evaluation scores. We would also like to acknowledge the ADAPT Centre for Digital Content Technology which is funded under the SFI Research Centre Programme (Grant No. 13/RC/2106) and is co-funded under the European Regional Development Fund. This project has partially received funding from the European Union's Horizon 2020 Research and Innovation programme under the Marie Skłodowska-Curie Actions (Grant No. 734211).

References

Heafield, K. (2011, July). KenLM: Faster and smaller language model queries. In Proceedings of the Sixth Workshop on Statistical Machine Translation (pp. 187-197). Association for Computational Linguistics.

Helcl, J., &Libovický, J. (2017). Neural Monkey: An open-source tool for sequence learning. The Prague Bulletin of Mathematical Linguistics, 107(1), 5-17.

Hochreiter, S., &Schmidhuber, J. (1997). Long short-term memory. Neural computation, 9(8), 1735-1780.

Kingma, D. P., & Ba, J. (2014). Adam: A method for stochastic optimization. arXiv preprint arXiv:1412.6980.

Klein, G., Kim, Y., Deng, Y., Senellart, J., & Rush, A. M. (2017). Opennmt: Open-source toolkit for neural machine translation. arXiv preprint arXiv:1701.02810.

Koehn, P., & Knowles, R. (2017). Six challenges for neural machine translation. arXiv preprint arXiv:1706.03872.

Koehn, P., Hoang, H., Birch, A., Callison-Burch, C., Federico, M., Bertoldi, N., ... & Dyer, C. (2007, June). Moses: Open source toolkit for statistical machine translation. In Proceedings of the 45th annual meeting of the ACL on interactive poster and demonstration sessions (pp. 177-180). Association for Computational Linguistics.

Koehn, P., Och, F. J., &Marcu, D. (2003, May). Statistical phrase-based translation. In Proceedings of the 2003 Conference of the North American Chapter of the Association for Computational Linguistics on Human Language Technology-Volume 1 (pp. 48-54). Association for Computational Linguistics.

Och, F. J., & Ney, H. (2003). A systematic comparison of various statistical alignment models. Computational linguistics, 29(1), 19-51.

Sennrich, R., Firat, O., Cho, K., Birch, A., Haddow, B., Hitschler, J., ... &Nădejde, M. (2017). Nematus: a toolkit for neural machine translation. arXiv preprint arXiv:1703.04357.

Stolcke, A. (2002). SRILM-an extensible language modeling toolkit. In Seventh international conference on spoken language processing.

Nakazawa, T., Higashiyama, S., Ding, C., Dabre, R., Kunchukuttan, A., Pa, W. P., Goto, I., Mino, H., Sudoh, K., &Kurohashi, S. (2018, December). Overview of the 5th Workshop on Asian Translation. In Proceedings of the 5th Workshop on Asian Translation (WAT2018) at Hong Kong, China.

Nakazawa, T., Mino, H., Goto, I., Neubig, G., Kurohashi, S., Sumita, E. (2016). Overview of the2nd Workshop on Asian Translation. Retrieved from: http://lotus.kuee.kyoto-u.ac.jp/WAT/WAT2015/papers/submissions/W15s/W15-5001.Presentation.pdf

IITP-MT at WAT2018: Transformer-based Multilingual Indic-English Neural Machine Translation System

Sukanta Sen, Kamal Kumar Gupta, Asif Ekbal, Pushpak Bhattacharyya

Department of Computer Science and Engineering

Indian Institute of Technology Patna

{sukanta.pcs15,kamal.pcs17,asif,pb}@iitp.ac.in

Abstract

This paper describes the systems submitted by the IITP-MT team to WAT 2018 multilingual Indic languages shared task. We submit two multilingual neural machine translation (NMT) systems (Indic-to-English and English-to-Indic) based on Transformer architecture and our approaches are similar to many-to-one and one-to-many approaches of Johnson et al. (2017). We also train separate bilingual models as baselines for all translation directions involving English. We evaluate the models using BLEU score and find that a single multilingual NMT model performs better (up to 14.81 BLEU) than separate bilingual models when the target is English. However, when English is the source language, multilingual NMT model improves only for low-resource language pairs (up to 11.60 BLEU) and degrades for relatively high-resource language pairs over separate bilingual models.

1 Introduction

In this paper, we describe our submission to multilingual Indic languages shared task at 5th Workshop on Asian Translation (WAT 2018) (Nakazawa et al., 2018). This task covers 7 Indic languages (Bengali, Hindi, Malayalam, Tamil, Telugu, Sinhalese and Urdu) and English. The objective of this shared task is to build translation models for XX-EN language pairs. By XX, we denote the set of 7 Indic languages. In this task, we submit two (single models for Indic-to-English and English-to-Indic) multilingual neural machine translation systems to translate between Indic languages and English. Unlike the European languages, most of the Indian languages do not have enough-sized parallel English translations. The parallel corpora used in this shared task have 22k to 521k parallel sentences (see Table 1), which is insufficient for NMT training. NMT is a data hungry approach and it is not possible to have sufficient amount of parallel training data for all language pairs. So building multilingual translation model by means of sharing parameters with high-resource languages is a common practice to improve the performance of low-resource language pairs. Sharing of parameters between low-resource and high-resource language pairs helps low-resource pairs to learn better model compared to model trained separately. However, it has been seen that training multiple languages together sometimes degrades the performance of some language pairs compared to a separate single bilingual model as languages may have different linguistic properties.

Recent success of end-to-end bilingual NMT systems (Kalchbrenner and Blunsom, 2013; Cho et al., 2014; Sutskever et al., 2014; Bahdanau et al., 2015) quickly gave the rise of multilingual NMT in various ways (Dong et al., 2015; Firat et al., 2016; Johnson et al., 2017). Most of the existing multilingual NMT involve non-Indic languages and are based on attentional encoder-decoder approach. We use the Transformer architecture (Vaswani et al., 2017) with subword (Sennrich et al., 2016) as basic translation unit. We develop two multilingual translation models: one is for XX→EN (7 Indic languages to English) and another is for EN→XX (English to 7 Indic languages). We also train separate bilingual model as a baseline for each translation direction involving English. We evaluate the multilingual models against the bilingual models using BLEU (Papineni et al., 2002) metric. We found that multilingual NMT is better than bilingual models for all XX→EN directions, however for EN→XX directions, multilingual NMT performs better than bilingual NMT for low-resource language pairs only.

In the next section, we briefly mention some notable multilingual NMT works. We describe our submitted systems in section 3 which includes description on datasets, preprocessing, experimental setup. Results are described in section 4. Finally, the work is concluded in section 5.

2   Related Works

Dong et al. (2015) implemented a system with one-to-many mapping of languages. They translated a source language to multiple target languages where each target language decoder deals with its own attention network. Firat et al. (2016) used a single attentional network that was shared among all source-target language pairs. They used separate encoder decoder for each source and target language. Thus, the number of parameters increases as the number of language increases. Johnson et al. (2017) came up with a simple but effective approach for multilingual translation. They mixed all parallel data and trained a standard attentional encoder-decoder NMT model without any change. They used an additional token before each source sentence to specify its target language. We apply this simple approach of combining training data and then we train transformer based NMT models for building multilingual translation systems (many-to-one and one-to-many) for Indic languages.

3   System Description

In this section, we describe datasets, preprocessing of data and experimental setup of our systems.

3.1   Datasets

We use the Indic Languages Multilingual Parallel Corpus[1] consisting of the following languages: Bengali, Hindi, Malayalam, Tamil, Telugu, Sinhalese,

Urdu and English. It contains 7 parallel corpora for 7 Indic languages (translated into English), and 8 monolingual corpora. These corpora have been collected from OPUS[2] and belongs to the spoken language (OpenSubtitles) domain. For experiments, we use parallel corpora only. Training data size is presented in Table 1. For each language pair, development set and test set have 500 and 1,000 parallel sentences, respectively. Before feeding the data for training, we tokenize, truecase, subword the original corpora as preprocessing. We tokeninze English data using Moses tokenizer[3] and the Indic_NLP library[4] tool is used for tokenizing Indic language data. Tokenized English sentences are truecased using Moses truecaser script. There is no need to truecase Indic languages as they are case-insensitive.

Language Pair	#Sentences
Bengali (BN) - English	337,428
Hindi (HI) - English	84,557
Malayalam (ML) - English	359,423
Tamil (TA) - English	26,217
Telugu (TE) - English	22,165
Urdu (UR) - English	26,619
Sinhalese (SI) - English	521,726

Table 1: Training data size for each language pair.

3.2   Subword Unit

NMT works with fixed vocabulary size. To deal with large vocabulary of Indic languages, we subword each bilingual corpora independently. Sennrich et al. (2016) introduced Byte-pair-encoding (BPE) based subword unit for dealing with rare words problem in NMT. It helps to decrease the vocabulary size and to deal with unseen tokens at training and test time. With variable size of training data (see Table 1) and morphological variations among languages, vocabulary size for each language is also different. Original vocabulary size, number of BPE merge, and vocabulary size after applying BPE are shown in Table 2.

---

[1] http://lotus.kuee.kyoto-u.ac.jp/WAT/indic-multilingual/indic_languages_corpus.tar.gz

[2] http://opus.nlpl.eu

[3] https://github.com/moses-smt/mosesdecoder/blob/RELEASE-3.0/scripts/tokenizer/tokenizer.perl

[4] https://bitbucket.org/anoopk/indic_nlp_library

Data Pair	Source			Target		
	Original Vocab	**Merge**	**Final Vocab**	**Original Vocab**	**Merge**	**Final Vocab**
BN-EN	90,482	8,000	8,394	56,498	5,000	5,248
HI-EN	24,470	4,000	4,286	24,380	4,000	4,150
ML-EN	253,360	10,000	10,351	58,320	5,000	5,273
SI-EN	169,603	9,000	9,392	72,093	7,000	7,417
TA-EN	18,723	3,500	3,675	18,723	2,000	2,114
TE-EN	12,728	2,000	2,230	9,929	1,500	1,633
UR-EN	13,581	3,000	3,268	12,854	2,000	2,126

Table 2: Original vocabulary size, number of BPE merge and final vocabulary size after applying BPE for each training data pair. We decided the BPE merge values without any rigorous exploration.

3.3 Experimental Setup

We train 2 multilingual models namely XX→EN (Indic languages to English) and EN→XX (Englsih to Indic languages) and 14 bilingual models (7 for Indic languages to English, and 7 for English to Indic languages). All of these models are based on Transformer (Vaswani et al., 2017) network. For training the models, we use Sockeye (Hieber et al., 2017), a toolkit for NMT. Each token in training, development and test sets are split in subword units in preprocessing stage. Along with that an additional token[5] indicating which Indic language a sentence pair belong to is added at the beginning of every source[6] sentence. Then parallel data of all pairs are appended in one parallel corpus with Indic languages in one side and English on other side, for training a single multilingual model for each of EN→XX and XX→EN directions. These tokens are added with development and test sets too and likewise, development sets are also appended in a single development set. We set embedding dimension of 512, hidden dimension of 512, learning rate of 0.0002, dropout rate of 0.2. We use Adam (Kingma and Ba, 2015) optimizer. We keep minibatch size of 2000 words[7], and maximum sentence length is restricted to 50. Rest of the hyperparameters are set to the default values of Sockeye. Training is completed on meeting early-stopping criteria

(BLEU based, 10 patience) on development set. Finally, the best model is used for translating the test sets.

System			Bi	Multi	▲
BN			18.24	20.05	+1.81
HI			27.11	32.95	+5.84
ML			10.56	19.94	+9.38
SI	→	**EN**	18.22	21.35	+3.13
TA			11.58	22.42	+10.84
TE			16.15	30.96	+14.81
UR			20.02	26.56	+6.54
	BN		13.38	13.27	-0.11
	HI		24.25	26.60	+2.35
	ML		20.92	13.50	-7.42
EN	→	**SI**	12.75	10.64	-2.11
	TA		11.88	18.81	+6.93
	TE		14.21	25.81	+11.60
	UR		18.73	21.48	+2.75

Table 3: BLEU scores of our {BN, HI, ML, SI, TA, TE, UR}→EN and EN→{BN, HI, ML, SI, TA, TE, UR} systems; Bi: Bilingual Model; Multi: Multilingual Model; ▲ denotes improvement of multilingual model over bilingual model.

4 Results

BLEU scores of bilingual and Multilingual systems are shown in Table 3. For Indic languages to English (XX→EN), BLEU score increases in each pair of multilingual system compared to bilingual system of that pair. Here, at target side decoder has

---

[5]We use the followings tokens: BN##, HI##, ML##, SI##, TA##, TE##, UR##

[6]Source can be either English or any Indic language depending on translation direction.

[7]Sockeye supports word based batching too.

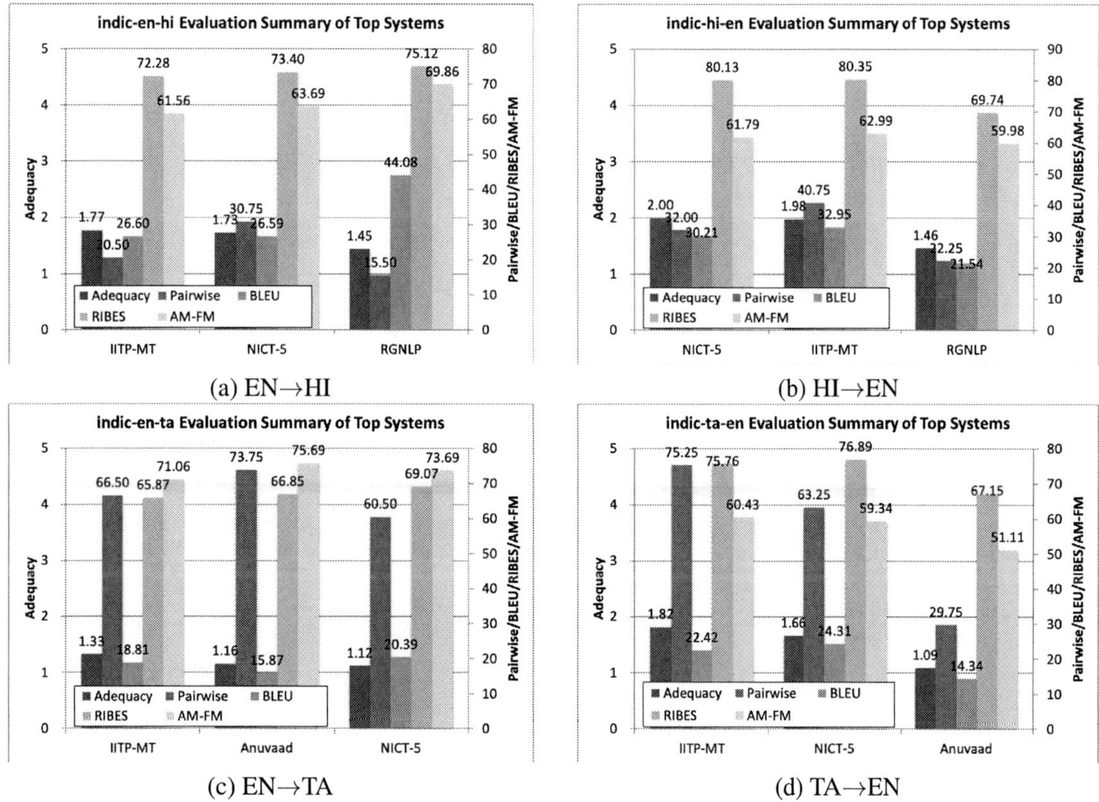

(a) EN→HI   (b) HI→EN

(c) EN→TA   (d) TA→EN

Figure 1: Official bar charts showing Adequacy, Pairwise Human Evaluation, BLEU, RIBES and AM-FM scores of top systems for multilingual Indic languages shared task at WAT 2018.

to deal with only one language i.e. English (EN). It shows sharing of parameters improves the performance of high-resource language pairs ({BN, ML, SI}→EN) as well as low-resource language pairs ({HI, TA, TE, UR}→EN). Unlike XX→EN, BLEU scores of EN→XX improve only for low-resource language pairs (EN→{HI, TA, TE, UR}) at the cost of BLEU scores of high-resource language pairs (EN→{BN, ML, SI}). For EN→XX multilingual system, a single decoder has to deal with multiple languages with different vocabulary and different linguistic features; that is why it is difficult for a single decoder to handle information of each target language.

For multilingual shared task, the official Pairwise Human evaluation and Adequacy scores (Nakazawa et al., 2018) were released for four translation directions only: EN→HI, HI→EN, EN→TA and TA→EN. Figure 1 shows the comparison of Pair-

wise Human evaluation and Adequacy scores along with BLEU, RIBES (Isozaki et al., 2010), AM-FM (Banchs et al., 2015) scores of top three systems for each of the four translation directions.

5 Conclusion

In this paper, we described our submission to WAT 2018 multilingual Indic languages shared task. We submitted two multilingual NMT models: many-to-one (7 Indic languages to English) and one-to-many (English to 7 Indic languages). Our multilingual NMT is based on Transformer architecture. We evaluated our models using BLEU score and found that multilingual NMT performs better than separately trained bilingual NMT models when the target side has only one language (English) and the improvement is higher for low-resource languages (up to 14.81 BLEU points). However, performance of multilingual NMT degrades compared to bilingual models for the relatively high-resource languages when the target has many languages.

References

Dzmitry Bahdanau, Kyunghyun Cho, and Yoshua Bengio. 2015. Neural machine translation by jointly learning to align and translate. *International Conference on Learning Representation(ICLR)*.

Rafael E Banchs, Luis F D'Haro, and Haizhou Li. 2015. Adequacy-fluency metrics: Evaluating mt in the continuous space model framework. *IEEE/ACM Transactions on Audio, Speech and Language Processing (TASLP)*, 23(3):472–482.

Kyunghyun Cho, Bart Van Merriënboer, Dzmitry Bahdanau, and Yoshua Bengio. 2014. On the properties of neural machine translation: Encoder-decoder approaches. In *Proceedings of SSST-8, Eighth Workshop on Syntax, Semantics and Structure in Statistical Translation*, pages 103–111.

Daxiang Dong, Hua Wu, Wei He, Dianhai Yu, and Haifeng Wang. 2015. Multi-task learning for multiple language translation. In *Proceedings of the 53rd Annual Meeting of the Association for Computational Linguistics and the 7th International Joint Conference on Natural Language Processing (Volume 1: Long Papers)*, pages 1723–1732. Association for Computational Linguistics.

Orhan Firat, Kyunghyun Cho, and Yoshua Bengio. 2016. Multi-way, multilingual neural machine translation with a shared attention mechanism. In *Proceedings of the 2016 Conference of the North American Chapter of the Association for Computational Linguistics: Human Language Technologies*, pages 866–875. Association for Computational Linguistics.

Felix Hieber, Tobias Domhan, Michael Denkowski, David Vilar, Artem Sokolov, Ann Clifton, and Matt Post. 2017. Sockeye: A toolkit for neural machine translation. *arXiv preprint arXiv:1712.05690*.

Hideki Isozaki, Tsutomu Hirao, Kevin Duh, Katsuhito Sudoh, and Hajime Tsukada. 2010. Automatic evaluation of translation quality for distant language pairs. In *Proceedings of the 2010 Conference on Empirical Methods in Natural Language Processing*, pages 944–952. Association for Computational Linguistics.

Melvin Johnson, Mike Schuster, Quoc V. Le, Maxim Krikun, Yonghui Wu, Zhifeng Chen, Nikhil Thorat, Fernanda Viégas, Martin Wattenberg, Greg Corrado, Macduff Hughes, and Jeffrey Dean. 2017. Google's multilingual neural machine translation system: Enabling zero-shot translation. *Transactions of the Association for Computational Linguistics*, 5:339–351.

Nal Kalchbrenner and Phil Blunsom. 2013. Recurrent continuous translation models. In *Proceedings of the 2013 Conference on Empirical Methods in Natural Language Processing*, pages 1700–1709.

Diederik P Kingma and Jimmy Ba. 2015. Adam: A method for stochastic optimization. *International Conference on Learning Representation(ICLR)*.

Toshiaki Nakazawa, Shohei Higashiyama, Chenchen Ding, Raj Dabre, Anoop Kunchukuttan, Win Pa Pa, Isao Goto, Hideya Mino, Katsuhito Sudoh, and Sadao Kurohashi. 2018. Overview of the 5th workshop on asian translation. In *Proceedings of the 5th Workshop on Asian Translation (WAT2018)*, Hong Kong, China, December.

Kishore Papineni, Salim Roukos, Todd Ward, and Wei-Jing Zhu. 2002. BLEU: a Method for Automatic Evaluation of Machine Translation. In *Proceedings of the 40th annual meeting on association for computational linguistics*, pages 311–318, Philadelphia, Pennsylvania.

Rico Sennrich, Barry Haddow, and Alexandra Birch. 2016. Neural machine translation of rare words with subword units. In *Proceedings of the 54th Annual Meeting of the Association for Computational Linguistics (Volume 1: Long Papers)*, pages 1715–1725. Association for Computational Linguistics.

Ilya Sutskever, Oriol Vinyals, and Quoc V Le. 2014. Sequence to sequence learning with neural networks. In *Advances in neural information processing systems*, pages 3104–3112.

Ashish Vaswani, Noam Shazeer, Niki Parmar, Jakob Uszkoreit, Llion Jones, Aidan N Gomez, Łukasz Kaiser, and Illia Polosukhin. 2017. Attention is all you need. In *Advances in Neural Information Processing Systems*, pages 5998–6008.

Multilingual Indian Language Translation System at WAT 2018: Many-to-one Phrase-based SMT

Tamali Banerjee[1], Anoop Kunchukuttan[2], Pushpak Bhattacharya[1]
[1] Department of Computer Science and Engineering,
Indian Institute of Technology Bombay.
{tamali,pb}@cse.iitb.ac.in
[2] Microsoft AI and Research, India.
ankunchu@microsoft.com

Abstract

This paper describes our trained models of phrase-based statistical machine translation (PBSMT) systems for Indic→English and English→Indic language-pairs, which has been submitted to the WAT 2018 shared task. In addition, we have introduced many-to-one statistical machine translation (SMT). This new approach produced comparable results in terms of translation accuracy with respect to the result of baseline SMT.

1 Introduction

India is one of the most linguistically diverse countries in the world. According to the Census of India of 2001, India has 122 major languages and 1599 other languages. These languages span four major language families. North-Indian languages such as Hindi, Bengali, Sindhi belong to the Indo-Aryan branch of the Indo-European language family, whereas South-Indian languages such as Tamil, Telugu and Malayalam belong to the Dravidian language family. These are the major language families, in addition to the Austro-Asiatic and Tibeto-Burman languages spoken by a small section of the population. In addition to the similarities between languages belonging to the same language families, there are many similarities between the four language families on account of contact over a long period of time. Hence, India is referred to as a *linguistic area* (Emeneau, 1956). This relatedness manifests itself in the form of lexical, structural and morphological similarities between these languages (Bhattacharyya et al., 2016).

In the WAT 2018 shared task (Nakazawa et al., 2018), we participated as team 'Anuvaad' and trained Indic→English and English→Indic baseline SMT systems along with our proposed many-to-one Indic→English system. In neural machine translation (NMT) (Cho et al., 2014; Sutskever et al., 2014; Bahdanau et al., 2015), multilingual transfer learning approaches (includes many-to-one, one-to-many, or many-to-many translation) have shown significant improvement in translation quality with minimal increase in network complexity, especially in the case of resource-poor languages (Johnson et al., 2017; Firat et al., 2016; Dong et al., 2015). However, SMT is still superior, when the training corpus is not big enough (Koehn and Knowles, 2017). Hence, we experimented with a multilingual many-to-one SMT system for Indic language to English translation using significantly less amount of data as compared to NMT.

2 Many-to-one SMT

Despite, the huge success of NMT, SMT can still be used to achieve comparable transnational outcome in case of data scarcity (Koehn and Knowles, 2017). In order to train a SMT system, the learning of language model and translation model requires lesser amount of data as compared to learning of NMT system (Koehn and Knowles, 2017).

Mathematically, SMT is represented as-

$$\hat{e} = \arg\max_e(P(e|f)) = \arg\max_e(P(e).P(f|e)) \tag{1}$$

where, e is a sentence of English language and f

is a sentence of foreign language.

An SMT system selects the best translated English sentence e given a foreign sentence f. The *argmax* computation is expressed as a product of language model $P(e)$ and translation model $P(f|e)$. It produces the English sentence which exhibits highest probability value for a given sentence f.

In many-to-one SMT model, the translation model needs to be trained on merged corpus of all Indic→English language-pair, wherein, all bilingual corpora are transliterated into a certain script-pair (Kunchukuttan et al., 2015). Further, the language model is trained on the merged form of the target language corpus.

3 Experimental Setup

We trained 14 bilingual SMT systems for 7 Indic-English language-pairs (such as Bengali, Hindi, Malayalam, Tamil, Telugu, Urdu and Sinhalese individually paired with English) in both directions. Additionally, we trained a many-to-one SMT system which was used to translate a sentence from any of these 7 Indic languages to English.

We trained our systems using training data *Indic Languages Multilingual Parallel Corpus* comprised of OpenSubtitles domain data provided by WAT 2018 organizers for shared task experiment. The data-set contains parallel corpora of 7 Indic languages as mentioned above along with their English translation. We did not use any monolingual corpus for this experiment. We extracted the data in individual files for training, tuning and testing. Table 1 shows the statistics of the data split.

.

3.1 Pre-processing

We process the corpus through appropriate filters for normalization, tokenization and truecasing using the scripts available in Moses (Koehn et al., 2007) and the Indic NLP Library[1]. Further, the training sentence length was limited to 50 words.

Following the above preprocessing steps, we generated corpora of all Indian languages transliterated in Devanagari script using the BrahmiNet transliteration system (Kunchukuttan et al., 2015), which is

---

[1]`https://github.com/anoopkunchukuttan/indic_nlp_library`

Language-pairs	Train	Dev	Test
bn-en	337,428	500	1000
hi-en	84,557	500	1000
ml-en	359,423	500	1000
ta-en	26,217	500	1000
te-en	22,165	500	1000
ur-en	26,619	500	1000
si-en	521,726	500	1000

Table 1: Indic-English corpora (bn- Bengali, hi- Hindi, ml- Malayalam, ta- Tamil, te- Telugu, ur- Urdu, si- Sinhalese individually paired with en-English) split statistics. The number indicates the number of sentences in the split (train, dev an test).

based on the transliteration module in Moses (Durrani et al., 2014). This data was used to train our many-to-one SMT system.

4 Models trained

For all our experiments, we trained the models using the Moses implementation (Koehn et al., 2007) with 3-gram language model and using the *grow-diag-final-and* heuristic for extracting phrases. We trained two types of SMT systems, baseline SMT system and many-to-one SMT system. 14 baseline SMT systems were trained using 7 parallel corpora as shown in Table 2.

In order to train the multilingual SMT system, first, we merged all these corpora into a single bilingual corpus, wherein, sentences of Indic languages were transliterated into Devanagari script. Transliteration is important here to leverage the lexical similarity among Indic languages (Kunchukuttan and Bhattacharyya, 2016). This was followed by the training of translation model with the mentioned 7 Indic-English bilingual corpora.

5 Postprocessing

Output translations of Indic→English language-pairs were detokenized using Moses (Koehn et al., 2007). However, for English→Indic language-pairs we did not perform any postprocessing step.

	Baseline				Many-to-one			
	BLEU	**RIBES**	**AMFM**	**Human**	**BLEU**	**RIBES**	**AMFM**	**Human**
bn→en	14.17	0.689672	0.454990	-	13.98	0.669154	0.447900	-
hi→en	25.57	0.720866	0.599880	0.750	22.45	0.709235	0.558850	5.750
ml→en	11.25	0.566812	0.376260	-	11.51	0.600102	0.365770	-
ta→en	14.34	0.671535	0.511130	29.750	14.09	0.673058	0.487250	29.250
te→en	24.05	0.729178	0.606850	-	22.13	0.714266	0.569170	-
ur→en	18.03	0.630810	0.541890	-	18.31	0.635688	0.519810	-
si→en	16.44	0.692275	0.492410	-	16.92	0.692236	0.484710	-
en→bn	11.34	0.601570	0.532680	-	-	-	-	-
en→hi	26.49	0.692385	0.657180	11.000	-	-	-	-
en→ml	14.23	0.422574	0.567090	-	-	-	-	-
en→ta	15.87	0.668548	0.756890	73.750	-	-	-	-
en→te	21.02	0.728584	0.744230	-	-	-	-	-
en→ur	21.62	0.628279	0.534550	-	-	-	-	-
en→si	11.71	0.580957	0.535950	-	-	-	-	-

Table 2: Translation accuracies of baseline and many-to-one SMT systems. bn- Bengali, hi- Hindi, ml- Malayalam, ta- Tamil, te- Telugu, ur- Urdu, si- Sinhalese individually paired with en-English.

6   Result and Discussion

Table 2 shows translation accuracies of baseline PB-SMT and many-to-one PBSMT in terms of Bilingual Evaluation Understudy (BLEU) (Papineni et al., 2002), Rank-based Intuitive Bilingual Evaluation Score (RIBES) (Group and others, 2013), Adequacy-Fluency Metrics (AMFM) (Banchs et al., 2015) and human evaluation score (HUMAN) (only for hi-en and ta-en translation models).

From the results of our experiment, we did not get any discernible improvement in translation quality by using many-to-one PBSMT compared to the baseline PBSMT systems. The many-to-one SMT approach shows minor improvement in BLEU scores for 3 Indic languages namely Malayalam, Urdu and Sindhi, and minor degradation in BLEU scores for 2 Indic languages Bengali and Tamil. A noticeable reduction was observed in BLEU scores for both Hindi and Telugu. However, only a single translation model was required for all language pairs. Thus only a single model needs to be maintained and hosted. Of course, the phrase table for the multilingual model is substantially larger than the individual models (see Table 3 for phrase table size statistics).

Language-pairs	No. of Phrases in Phrase-table
XX→en	15,829,552
bn→en	3,897,808
hi→en	931,612
ml→en	3,753,408
ta→en	228,846
te→en	167,668
ur→en	335,617
si→en	6,270,747

Table 3: Number of phrases in phrase-table of many-to-one (XX→en) and bilingual models.

7   Conclusion

In this paper, we have described our submissions to WAT 2018. Our multilingual PBSMT was comparable to each baseline PBSMT model, but we did not observe any major gains. However, this is only an initial study where various models have not been explored. Further investigation can help to understand if many-to-one SMT approach is useful. Many-to-one approach could also be useful for translation of code-mixed sentences.

Acknowledgments

We would like to thank Raj Dabre for his valuable inputs.

References

Dzmitry Bahdanau, KyungHyun Cho, and Yoshua Bengio. 2015. Neural machine translation by jointly learning to align and translate. In *In Proceedings of the International Conference on Learning Representations (ICLR)*.

Rafael E Banchs, Luis F D'Haro, and Haizhou Li. 2015. Adequacy-fluency metrics: Evaluating mt in the continuous space model framework. *IEEE/ACM Transactions on Audio, Speech and Language Processing (TASLP)*, 23(3):472–482.

Pushpak Bhattacharyya, Mitesh Khapra, and Anoop Kunchukuttan. 2016. Statistical Machine Translation Between Related Languages. In *Annual Conference of the North American Chapter of the Association for Computational Linguistics: Tutorials*.

Kyunghyun Cho, Bart van Merrienboer, Caglar Gulcehre, Dzmitry Bahdanau, Fethi Bougares, Holger Schwenk, and Yoshua Bengio. 2014. Learning phrase representations using rnn encoder–decoder for statistical machine translation. In *Proceedings of the 2014 Conference on Empirical Methods in Natural Language Processing (EMNLP)*, pages 1724–1734.

Daxiang Dong, Hua Wu, Wei He, Dianhai Yu, and Haifeng Wang. 2015. Multi-task learning for multiple language translation. In *Proceedings of the 53rd Annual Meeting of the Association for Computational Linguistics and the 7th International Joint Conference on Natural Language Processing (Volume 1: Long Papers)*, volume 1, pages 1723–1732.

Nadir Durrani, Hassan Sajjad, Hieu Hoang, and Philipp Koehn. 2014. Integrating an unsupervised transliteration model into statistical machine translation. In *Proceedings of the 14th Conference of the European Chapter of the Association for Computational Linguistics, volume 2: Short Papers*, pages 148–153.

Murray B Emeneau. 1956. India as a lingustic area. *Language*, 32(1):3–16.

Orhan Firat, Kyunghyun Cho, and Yoshua Bengio. 2016. Multi-way, multilingual neural machine translation with a shared attention mechanism. In *Proceedings of NAACL-HLT*, pages 866–875.

Linguistic Intelligence Research Group et al. 2013. Ntt communication science laboratories. ribes: Rank-based intuitive bilingual evaluation score.

Melvin Johnson, Mike Schuster, Quoc V Le, Maxim Krikun, Yonghui Wu, Zhifeng Chen, Nikhil Thorat, Fernanda Viégas, Martin Wattenberg, Greg Corrado, et al. 2017. Google's multilingual neural machine translation system: Enabling zero-shot translation. *Transactions of the Association of Computational Linguistics*, 5(1):339–351.

Philipp Koehn and Rebecca Knowles. 2017. Six challenges for neural machine translation. In *Proceedings of the First Workshop on Neural Machine Translation*, pages 28–39.

Philipp Koehn, Hieu Hoang, Alexandra Birch, Chris Callison-Burch, Marcello Federico, Nicola Bertoldi, Brooke Cowan, Wade Shen, Christine Moran, Richard Zens, et al. 2007. Moses: Open source toolkit for statistical machine translation. In *Proceedings of the 45th annual meeting of the ACL on interactive poster and demonstration sessions*, pages 177–180. Association for Computational Linguistics.

Anoop Kunchukuttan and Pushpak Bhattacharyya. 2016. Orthographic syllable as basic unit for smt between related languages. In *Proceedings of the 2016 Conference on Empirical Methods in Natural Language Processing*, pages 1912–1917.

Anoop Kunchukuttan, Ratish Puduppully, and Pushpak Bhattacharyya. 2015. Brahmi-net: A transliteration and script conversion system for languages of the indian subcontinent. In *Proceedings of the 2015 Conference of the North American Chapter of the Association for Computational Linguistics: Demonstrations*, pages 81–85.

Toshiaki Nakazawa, Shohei Higashiyama, Chenchen Ding, Raj Dabre, Anoop Kunchukuttan, Win Pa Pa, Isao Goto, Hideya Mino, Katsuhito Sudoh, and Sadao Kurohashi. 2018. Overview of the 5th workshop on asian translation. In *Proceedings of the 5th Workshop on Asian Translation (WAT2018)*, Hong Kong, China, December.

Kishore Papineni, Salim Roukos, Todd Ward, and Wei-Jing Zhu. 2002. Bleu: a method for automatic evaluation of machine translation. In *Proceedings of the 40th annual meeting on association for computational linguistics*, pages 311–318. Association for Computational Linguistics.

Ilya Sutskever, Oriol Vinyals, and Quoc V Le. 2014. Sequence to sequence learning with neural networks. In *Advances in neural information processing systems*, pages 3104–3112.

TMU Japanese–English Neural Machine Translation System using Generative Adversarial Network for WAT 2018

Yukio Matsumura   **Satoru Katsumata**   **Mamoru Komachi**

Tokyo Metropolitan University
Tokyo, Japan

{matsumura-yukio, katsumata-satoru}@ed.tmu.ac.jp, komachi@tmu.ac.jp

Abstract

This paper describes our neural machine translation (NMT) system. We implemented an attention-based recurrent neural network (RNN) encoder–decoder as a baseline. Additionally, we implemented a generative adversarial network (GAN) and reconstructor models in our NMT. We experimented with our NMT system on the shared tasks at the 5th Workshop on Asian Translation (WAT 2018). We participated in the scientific paper subtasks of the Japanese–English and English–Japanese translation tasks. The experimental results demonstrate that the ensemble of baseline systems achieved 25.85 and 36.14 points in Japanese–English and English–Japanese translations, respectively, in terms of BLEU scores. Furthermore, we found that GAN NMT can translate fluently.

1 Introduction

In recent years, neural machine translation (NMT) has been researched all over the world. Once the encoder–decoder NMT (Sutskever et al., 2014; Cho et al., 2014), which combines two recurrent neural networks (RNNs), was proposed, NMT gained huge popularity in the machine translation community.

However, the conventional encoder–decoder NMT works poorly on long sequences. Attention-based NMT (Bahdanau et al., 2015; Luong et al., 2015) can provide better prediction of output words by using the weights of each hidden state of the encoder as the context vector. It contributed to improvement of translation quality, especially in long sentences.

Transformer (Vaswani et al., 2017) is an extension of attention-based NMT; however, it is different from previous NMTs. They proposed a self-attention network and positional encoding. Thereby, NMT achieved high-quality translation without using RNN and convolutional neural network (CNN).

Nevertheless, NMT has several problems such as over-translation, wherein some words are translated repeatedly or unnecessary words are generated and under-translation, wherein some words remain mistakenly untranslated. Furthermore, an objective function of NMT is optimized by word unit; therefore, it cannot be guaranteed that the output of NMT is optimized as a sentence. This may become the cause of over- and under-translation.

In this paper, we describe the NMT system that was tested on the shared tasks at the 5th Workshop on Asian Translation (WAT 2018) (Nakazawa et al., 2018). We implemented an attention-based RNN encoder–decoder as a baseline. Furthermore, we implemented a generative adversarial network (GAN) and reconstructor models in our NMT.

GAN NMT comprises a generator and a discriminator. The discriminator should distinguish between true or generated sentences, whereas the generator aims to generate a sentence close to its correct translation, which the discriminator cannot distinguish. The goal of this adversarial training is to have the generator predict a target sentence close to its correct translation from given source sentence. Additionally, the objective function of this approach considers a term that is optimized by sentence unit. GAN is reported to improve translation quality (Yang et al., 2018).

Reconstructor NMT comprises an encoder–decoder and reconstructor. The reconstructor back-translates from hidden states of the decoder into the source sentence. On training, the NMT considers both: forward and back-translations. This approach can reduce over- and under-translation in forward translation because back-translation fails if there is a lack of information. The effect of this approach in English–Japanese translation is reported in (Matsumura et al., 2017).

We experimented with our NMT system for Japanese–English and English–Japanese scientific paper translation subtasks. The experimental results demonstrate that the ensemble of baseline systems achieved 25.85 and 36.14 points in Japanese–English and English–Japanese translations, respectively, in terms of BLEU (Papineni et al., 2002) scores. Furthermore, we found that GAN NMT can translate fluently in English-Japanese pairwise evaluation.

2 Attention-based NMT

In this section, we describe our baseline NMT system[1]. This system is based on the attention-based NMT (Luong et al., 2015). We adopted a bi-directional long short-term memory (LSTM) as the encoder and a unidirectional LSTM as the decoder.

2.1 Encoder

The source sentence is input as a sequence of one-hot word vectors: $(\boldsymbol{X} = [\boldsymbol{x}_1, \cdots, \boldsymbol{x}_{|\boldsymbol{X}|}])$, where $|\boldsymbol{X}|$ is the length of the source sentence.

At each time step i, the source word embedding vector: $\boldsymbol{e}_i^s$ is computed by the following equation.

$$\boldsymbol{e}_i^s = \tanh(\boldsymbol{W}_x \boldsymbol{x}_i) \tag{1}$$

where $\boldsymbol{W}_x \in \mathbb{R}^{q \times v_s}$ is a weight matrix, q is the dimension of the word embeddings, and v_s is the size of the source vocabulary.

The hidden state $\bar{\boldsymbol{h}}_i$ of the encoder is computed by the following equation:

$$\bar{\boldsymbol{h}}_i = \overrightarrow{\boldsymbol{h}_i}^{(L)} + \overleftarrow{\boldsymbol{h}_i}^{(L)} \tag{2}$$

where L is the number of layers. Here, the forward state $\overrightarrow{\boldsymbol{h}_i}^{(l)}$ and the backward state $\overleftarrow{\boldsymbol{h}_i}^{(l)}$ are computed

by

$$\overrightarrow{\boldsymbol{h}_i}^{(l)} = \text{LSTM}(\overrightarrow{\boldsymbol{h}_i}^{(l-1)}, \overrightarrow{\boldsymbol{h}_{i-1}}^{(l)}) \tag{3}$$

and

$$\overleftarrow{\boldsymbol{h}_i}^{(l)} = \text{LSTM}(\overleftarrow{\boldsymbol{h}_i}^{(l-1)}, \overleftarrow{\boldsymbol{h}_{i+1}}^{(l)}) \tag{4}$$

where l is the layer number. Note that $\overrightarrow{\boldsymbol{h}_i}^{(0)}$ and $\overleftarrow{\boldsymbol{h}_i}^{(0)}$ are regarded as $\boldsymbol{e}_i^s$.

2.2 Decoder

Similar to the source sentence, the target sentence is input as a sequence of one-hot word vectors: $(\boldsymbol{Y} = [\boldsymbol{y}_1, \cdots, \boldsymbol{y}_{|\boldsymbol{Y}|}])$, where $|\boldsymbol{Y}|$ is the length of the target sentence.

At each time step j, the hidden state $\boldsymbol{h}_j^{(l)}$ of each layer of the decoder is represented by the following equation.

$$\boldsymbol{h}_j^{(l)} = \text{LSTM}(\boldsymbol{h}_j^{(l-1)}, \boldsymbol{h}_{j-1}^{(l)}) \tag{5}$$

Note that $\boldsymbol{h}_j^{(0)}$ is regarded as the concatenation of the target word embedding vector $\boldsymbol{e}_{j-1}^t$ and the attentional hidden state $\tilde{\boldsymbol{h}}_{j-1}$ at the previous time step: $[\boldsymbol{e}_{j-1}^t : \tilde{\boldsymbol{h}}_{j-1}]$. In this system, the first hidden state $\boldsymbol{h}_1^{(l)}$ of each layer is initialized by the hidden state of the encoder as follows:

$$\boldsymbol{h}_1^{(l)} = \overrightarrow{\boldsymbol{h}_{|\boldsymbol{X}|}}^{(l)} + \overleftarrow{\boldsymbol{h}_1}^{(l)}. \tag{6}$$

The target word embedding vector $\boldsymbol{e}_j^t$ is computed as:

$$\boldsymbol{e}_j^t = \tanh(\boldsymbol{W}_y \boldsymbol{y}_j) \tag{7}$$

where $\boldsymbol{W}_y \in \mathbb{R}^{q \times v_t}$ is a weight matrix and v_t is the target vocabulary size. The attentional hidden state $\tilde{\boldsymbol{h}}_j$ is represented as:

$$\tilde{\boldsymbol{h}}_j = \tanh(\boldsymbol{W}_a[\boldsymbol{h}_j^{(L)} : \boldsymbol{c}_j] + \boldsymbol{b}_a) \tag{8}$$

where $\boldsymbol{W}_a \in \mathbb{R}^{r \times 2r}$ is a weight matrix, $\boldsymbol{b}_a \in \mathbb{R}^r$ is a bias vector, and r is the number of hidden units.

The context vector $\boldsymbol{c}_j$ is a weighted sum of each hidden state $\bar{\boldsymbol{h}}_i$ of the encoder. It is represented as:

$$\boldsymbol{c}_j = \sum_{i=1}^{|\boldsymbol{X}|} \alpha_{ij} \bar{\boldsymbol{h}}_i. \tag{9}$$

Its weight α_{ij} is a normalized probability distribution, which is computed using a dot product of hidden states as follows:

$$\alpha_{ij} = \frac{\exp(\bar{\boldsymbol{h}}_i^{\mathrm{T}} \boldsymbol{h}_j^{(L)})}{\sum_{k=1}^{|\boldsymbol{X}|} \exp(\bar{\boldsymbol{h}}_k^{\mathrm{T}} \boldsymbol{h}_j^{(L)})}. \tag{10}$$

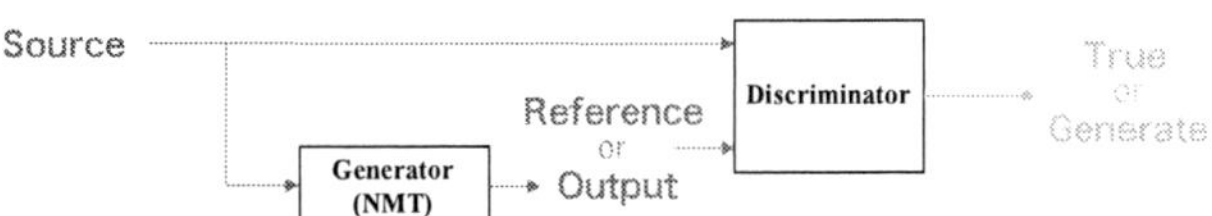

Figure 1: Overview of GAN NMT.

The conditional probability of the output word $\hat{y}_j$ is computed as:

$$p(\hat{y}_j|Y_{<j}, X) = \text{softmax}(W_p \tilde{h}_j + b_p) \quad (11)$$

where $W_p \in \mathbb{R}^{v_t \times r}$ is a weight matrix and $b_p \in \mathbb{R}^{v_t}$ is a bias vector.

2.3 Training

The objective function of this system is

$$\mathcal{L}(\theta) = \frac{1}{D} \sum_{d=1}^{D} \sum_{j=1}^{|Y|} \log p(y_j^{(d)}|Y_{<j}^{(d)}, X^{(d)}, \theta) \quad (12)$$

where D denotes the number of data and θ denotes the model parameters. The model parameters in word embedding are pretrained using GloVe (Pennington et al., 2014). All other model parameters are randomly initialized.

2.4 Testing

To achieve better predictions, we adopted beam search and ensemble decoding. In beam search, the system retains hypotheses of beam size n at each time step. During the subsequent time step, for each hypothesis, it computes n hypotheses; further, it retains n hypotheses out of the total n^2 hypotheses. In ensemble decoding, the conditional probability of the output word $\hat{y}_j$ is the average of each model's score $p^{(m)}$. It is computed by

$$p(\hat{y}_j|Y_{<j}, X) = \frac{1}{M} \sum_{m=1}^{M} p^{(m)}(\hat{y}_j|Y_{<j}, X) \quad (13)$$

where M denotes the number of models. They reduce the risk of predicting wrong words.

3 GAN NMT

Herein, we describe GAN NMT[2] based on Yang et al. (2018). It comprises two networks: a generator

[2]https://github.com/yukio326/GAN-NMT

which generates a target sentence, and a discriminator which distinguishes a generated sentence from its true translation as shown in Figure 1.

3.1 Generator

The generator attempts to generate a target sentence close to its correct translation from a given source sentence. We use the attention-based NMT described in Section 2 as the generator network.

3.2 Discriminator

The discriminator predicts whether the target sentence is true or generated by the given source and target sentences. At each time step i, the hidden state f_i^s corresponding to the source embedding vector e_i^s in Equation 1 is represented as:

$$f_i^s = \overrightarrow{f_i^s}(L) + \overleftarrow{f_i^s}(L). \quad (14)$$

Here, the forward state $\overrightarrow{f_i^s}(l)$ and the backward state $\overleftarrow{f_i^s}(l)$ are computed by

$$\overrightarrow{f_i^s}(l) = \text{LSTM}(\overrightarrow{f_i^s}(l-1), \overrightarrow{f_{i-1}^s}(l)) \quad (15)$$

and

$$\overleftarrow{f_i^s}(l) = \text{LSTM}(\overleftarrow{f_i^s}(l-1), \overleftarrow{f_{i+1}^s}(l)). \quad (16)$$

Note that $\overrightarrow{f_i^s}(0)$ and $\overleftarrow{f_i^s}(0)$ are regarded as e_i^s. The sentence vector of source sentence $\bar{f}^s$ is computed by

$$\bar{f}^s = \text{average}\left(\left[f_1^s, f_2^s, \cdots, f_{|X|}^s\right]\right). \quad (17)$$

Similarly, at each time step j, the hidden state f_j^s corresponding to the target embedding vector e_j^t in Equation 7 is represented as

$$f_j^t = \overrightarrow{f_j^t}(L) + \overleftarrow{f_j^t}(L). \quad (18)$$

Here, the forward state $\overrightarrow{f_j^t}(l)$ and the backward state $\overleftarrow{f_j^t}(l)$ are computed by

$$\overrightarrow{f_j^t}(l) = \text{LSTM}(\overrightarrow{f_j^t}(l-1), \overrightarrow{f_{j-1}^t}(l)) \quad (19)$$

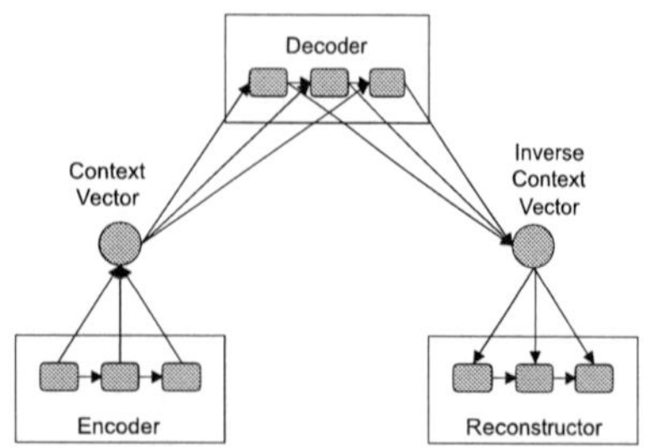

Figure 2: Overview of reconstructor NMT.

and

$$\overleftarrow{\boldsymbol{f}}_j^{t(l)} = \text{LSTM}(\overleftarrow{\boldsymbol{f}}_j^{t(l-1)}, \overleftarrow{\boldsymbol{f}}_{j+1}^{t}{}^{(l)}). \quad (20)$$

Note that $\overrightarrow{\boldsymbol{f}}_j^{t(0)}$ and $\overleftarrow{\boldsymbol{f}}_j^{t(0)}$ are regarded as $\boldsymbol{e}_j^t$. The sentence vector of target sentence $\bar{\boldsymbol{f}}^t$ is computed by

$$\bar{\boldsymbol{f}}^t = \text{average}\left(\left[\boldsymbol{f}_1^t, \boldsymbol{f}_2^t, \cdots, \boldsymbol{f}_{|\boldsymbol{Y}|}^t\right]\right). \quad (21)$$

Finally, the probability that the target sentence is true is predicted by the dot product of the source and target sentence vectors as follows:

$$p(\boldsymbol{X}, \boldsymbol{Y}) = \text{sigmoid}(\bar{\boldsymbol{f}}^s \cdot \bar{\boldsymbol{f}}^t). \quad (22)$$

3.3 Training

GAN must be trained adversarially. The discriminator should distinguish between true or generated sentences, whereas the generator aims to generate a sentence close to its correct translation, which the discriminator cannot distinguish. Alternatively, the objective function of the generator differs from that of the discriminator.

The objective functions of the generator and discriminator networks are defined by the following:

Generator

$$\mathcal{L}_G(\boldsymbol{\theta}, \boldsymbol{\gamma}) = \frac{1}{D} \sum_{d=1}^{D} \left\{ \sum_{j=1}^{|\boldsymbol{Y}|} \log p(\boldsymbol{y}_j^{(d)} | \boldsymbol{Y}_{<j}^{(d)}, \boldsymbol{X}^{(d)}, \boldsymbol{\theta}) \right.$$
$$\left. + \log p(\boldsymbol{X}^{(d)}, \hat{\boldsymbol{Y}}^{(d)} | \boldsymbol{\gamma}) \right\}. \quad (23)$$

train	974,198
dev	1,790
test	1,812

Table 1: Number of Japanese–English parallel sentences.

Discriminator

$$\mathcal{L}_D(\boldsymbol{\gamma}) = \frac{1}{D} \sum_{d=1}^{D} \left\{ \log p(\boldsymbol{X}^{(d)}, \boldsymbol{Y}^{(d)} | \boldsymbol{\gamma}) \right.$$
$$\left. + \log \left\{ 1 - p(\boldsymbol{X}^{(d)}, \hat{\boldsymbol{Y}}^{(d)} | \boldsymbol{\gamma}) \right\} \right\}. \quad (24)$$

where $\boldsymbol{\gamma}$ is the model parameters in the discriminator. In the objective function of generator, the second term considers the sentence unit information. We applied pre-training to both generator and discriminator using the baseline.

4 Reconstructor NMT

Next, we describe reconstructor NMT[3] based on Tu et al. (2017) as shown in Figure 2. It comprises two components: encoder–decoder and reconstructor, which back-translates from hidden states of the decoder into the source sentence. On training, the NMT considers both forward and back-translations. This approach can reduce over- and under-translation in forward translation because back-translation fails if there is a lack of information.

4.1 Encoder–Decoder

We use the attention-based NMT described in Section 2 as the encoder–decoder network. Difference from Matsumura et al. (2017) is an encoder–decoder network. Their encoder–decoder network is based on Bahdanau et al. (2015).

4.2 Reconstructor

The reconstructor back-translates hidden states of the decoder into the source sequence. At each time step i, the hidden state $\boldsymbol{h}_i^{\prime(l)}$ of each layer of the reconstructor is represented as:

$$\boldsymbol{h}_i^{\prime(l)} = \text{LSTM}(\boldsymbol{h}_i^{\prime(l-1)}, \boldsymbol{h}_{i-1}^{\prime(l)}) \quad (25)$$

---

[3] https://github.com/yukio326/Reconstructor-NMT

Model	BLEU	RIBES	AMFM	HUMAN
Baseline	24.94	0.757955	0.596590	-
GAN NMT	25.17	0.757413	0.595850	-
Reconstructor NMT	24.98	0.759238	0.599110	-
Ensemble of six baselines	**25.85**	**0.761450**	**0.600730**	-20.000
Ensemble of two models each	25.45	0.759790	0.598770	-

Table 2: Japanese–English translation results.

Model	BLEU	RIBES	AMFM	HUMAN
Baseline	35.17	0.827386	0.749190	-
GAN NMT	35.09	0.827650	0.750350	-
Reconstructor NMT	34.89	0.826013	0.752100	-
Ensemble of six baselines	**36.14**	**0.831219**	**0.753040**	-12.000
Ensemble of two models each	35.44	0.829178	0.752420	-

Table 3: English–Japanese translation results.

Note that $h_i'^{(0)}$ is regarded as the concatenation of the source word embedding vector e_{i-1}^s and the attentional hidden state $\tilde{h}_{i-1}'$ at the previous time step: $[e_{i-1}^s : \tilde{h}_{i-1}']$. In this system, the first hidden state $h_1'^{(l)}$ of each layer is initialized by the hidden state $h_{|Y|}^{(l)}$ of the decoder.

The attentional hidden state $\tilde{h}_i'$ is represented as:

$$\tilde{h}_i' = \tanh(W_{a'}[h_i'^{(L)} : c_i] + b_{a'}) \qquad (26)$$

where $W_{a'} \in \mathbb{R}^{r \times 2r}$ is a weight matrix and $b_{a'} \in \mathbb{R}^r$ is a bias vector.

The inverse context vector c_i' is a weighted sum of each hidden state $\tilde{h}_j$ of the decoder on forward translation. It is represented as:

$$c_i' = \sum_{j=1}^{|Y|} \alpha_{ji}' \tilde{h}_j. \qquad (27)$$

Its weight α_{ji} is a normalized probability distribution, which is computed using the dot product of hidden states as follows:

$$\alpha_{ji}' = \frac{\exp(\tilde{h}_j^{\mathrm{T}} h_i'^{(l)})}{\sum_{k=1}^{|Y|} \exp(\tilde{h}_k^{\mathrm{T}} h_i'^{(l)})}. \qquad (28)$$

The conditional probability of the output word $\hat{x}_i$ is computed as:

$$p(\hat{x}_i|X_{<i}, \tilde{h}) = \mathrm{softmax}(W_{p'} \tilde{h}_i + b_{p'}) \qquad (29)$$

where $W_{p'} \in \mathbb{R}^{v_s \times r}$ is a weight matrix and $b_{p'} \in \mathbb{R}^{v_s}$ is a bias vector.

4.3 Training

The objective function is defined as:

$$\mathcal{L}(\theta, \lambda) = \frac{1}{D} \sum_{d=1}^{D} \left\{ \sum_{j=1}^{|Y|} \log p(y_j^{(d)}|Y_{<j}^{(d)}, X^{(d)}, \theta) \right.$$
$$\left. + \sum_{i=1}^{|X|} \log p(x_i^{(d)}|X_{<i}^{(d)}, \tilde{h}^{(d)}, \lambda) \right\}$$
$$(30)$$

where λ is the model parameters in the reconstructor. We applied pre-training to the encoder–decoder using the baseline.

5 Experiments

We experimented with our NMT system on Japanese–English and English–Japanese scientific paper translation subtasks at the WAT 2018.

5.1 Datasets

We used the Japanese–English parallel corpus in the Asian Scientific Paper Excerpt Corpus (ASPEC) (Nakazawa et al., 2016). Japanese sentences were segmented by the morphological analyzer: MeCab[4] (version 0.996, IPADIC) and English sentences were tokenized by tokenizer.perl of Moses[5]. Regarding the training data, we used only the first million

---

[4]https://github.com/taku910/mecab
[5]http://www.statmt.org/moses/

Source	Blood collection is indispensable for glucose level measurement for the diabetes mellitus diagnosis at present.
Baseline	糖尿病診断のためには血糖値測定には採血が不可欠である。
GAN NMT	現在糖尿病診断のための血糖値測定には採血が必須である。
Reconstructor NMT	糖尿病診断のための血糖値測定には採血が必須である。
Ensemble of six baselines	糖尿病診断のための血糖値測定には採血が必須である。
Ensemble of two models each	糖尿病診断のための血糖値測定には採血が必須である。
Reference	糖尿病診断のための血糖値測定は，現在，採血が不可欠である。

Table 4: Example of outputs of English–Japanese translation.

	adequacy	fluency
GAN NMT > Baseline	16	23
GAN NMT = Baseline	72	72
GAN NMT < Baseline	12	5
total	100	100

Table 5: Pairwise evaluation between baseline and GAN NMT.

sentences sorted by sentence-alignment confidence; sentences with more than 60 words were excluded. Table 1 shows the number of sentences in the parallel corpus.

5.2 Network Settings

We conducted the experiment using the following configuration:

- Number of layers: 3

- Number of hidden units: 512

- Word embedding dimensionality: 512

- Source vocabulary size: 100,000

- Target vocabulary size: 30,000

- Minibatch size: 128

- Optimizer: Adam, SGD

- Initial learning rate: 0.01

- Dropout rate: 0.2

- Beam size: 20

Regarding the optimizer, after we train our model using Adam for 20 epochs, we switch to SGD.

5.3 Results

Tables 2 and 3 show the translation accuracy in BLEU (Papineni et al., 2002), RIBES (Isozaki et al., 2010), AMFM (Banchs and Li, 2011), and HUMAN evaluation scores, which are the result of pairwise crowdsourcing evaluation by five different workers at the WAT 2018. In the "Model" column, "Ensemble of two models each" indicates the ensemble of two baselines, two GAN NMTs, and two reconstructor NMTs (ensemble of six models in total).

Regarding Japanese–English translation, the results show that GAN NMT and reconstructor NMT slightly improved BLEU score compared with the baseline. However, in English–Japanese translation, BLEU score of the baseline is higher than the GAN and reconstructor NMTs. In terms of AMFM score, both methods have higher scores than the baseline.

Matsumura et al. (2017) reported that the reconstructor NMT significantly improves BLEU score in English–Japanese translation. This differs from the results in this study. We consider that only by applying the optimization method in this study, the baseline becomes considerably stronger; therefore, the difference of translation accuracy between baseline and reconstructor NMT becomes less.

In both translation subtasks, the ensemble of six baselines achieved the best score in all metrics. The ensemble of two models each is inferior compared with the ensemble of six baselines. The reason for this could be that the ensemble of six baselines considers perfectly independent six models in terms of parameter initialization; however, the ensemble of two models each considers dependent models, i.e., GAN and reconstructor NMTs are pretrained using the baseline. Furthermore, the training of GAN is unstable; therefore, the model that is not trained well may affect the ensemble model adversely.

Table 4 shows an example of outputs of English–Japanese translations. In the baseline, "for the diabetes mellitus diagnosis at present" is translated to "糖尿病診断のためには", but it should be translated to "糖尿病診断のための" when this phrase modify the noun phrase. Other models except GAN NMT slightly under-translate;

"現在 (at present)" is disappeared. However, GAN NMT perfectly translates.

We examine the effect of GAN NMT by the pairwise evaluation between the baseline and GAN NMT. We evaluated 100 sentences extracted randomly in terms of adequacy and fluency. Table 5 shows the numbers of sentence in each case. Regarding adequacy, GAN NMT performed as same as the baseline, but regarding fluency, GAN NMT outperformed the baseline.

6 Conclusion

In this paper, we described our NMT system, which is based on the attention-based NMT. Furthermore, we implemented GAN and reconstructor models in our NMT. We evaluated our NMT system on Japanese–English and English–Japanese translation subtasks at the WAT 2018. The experimental results demonstrates that the ensemble of baseline systems achieved 25.85 and 36.14 points in Japanese–English and English–Japanese translations, respectively, in terms of BLEU scores. Furthermore, we found that GAN NMT can translate fluently.

References

Dzmitry Bahdanau, Kyunghyun Cho, and Yoshua Bengio. 2015. Neural Machine Translation by Jointly Learning to Align and Translate. In *Proceedings of the 3rd International Conference on Learning Representations (ICLR2015)*.

Rafael E Banchs and Haizhou Li. 2011. AM-FM: A Semantic Framework for Translation Quality Assessment. In *Proceedings of the 49th Annual Meeting of the Association for Computational Linguistics: Human Language Technologies*, pages 153–158, Portland, Oregon, USA. Association for Computational Linguistics.

Kyunghyun Cho, Bart van Merrienboer, Caglar Gulcehre, Dzmitry Bahdanau, Fethi Bougares, Holger Schwenk, and Yoshua Bengio. 2014. Learning Phrase Representations using RNN Encoder–Decoder for Statistical Machine Translation. In *Proceedings of the 2014 Conference on Empirical Methods in Natural Language Processing (EMNLP)*, pages 1724–1734, Doha, Qatar. Association for Computational Linguistics.

Hideki Isozaki, Tsutomu Hirao, Kevin Duh, Katsuhito Sudoh, and Hajime Tsukada. 2010. Automatic Evaluation of Translation Quality for Distant Language Pairs. In *Proceedings of the 2010 Conference on Empirical Methods in Natural Language Processing*, pages 944–952, Cambridge, Massachusetts, USA. Association for Computational Linguistics.

Thang Luong, Hieu Pham, and Christopher D Manning. 2015. Effective Approaches to Attention-based Neural Machine Translation. In *Proceedings of the 2015 Conference on Empirical Methods in Natural Language Processing*, pages 1412–1421, Lisbon, Portugal. Association for Computational Linguistics.

Yukio Matsumura, Takayuki Sato, and Mamoru Komachi. 2017. English-Japanese Neural Machine Translation with Encoder-Decoder-Reconstructor. *CoRR*, abs/1706.08198.

Toshiaki Nakazawa, Manabu Yaguchi, Kiyotaka Uchimoto, Masao Utiyama, Eiichiro Sumita, Sadao Kurohashi, and Hitoshi Isahara. 2016. ASPEC: Asian Scientific Paper Excerpt Corpus. In Nicoletta Calzolari (Conference Chair), Khalid Choukri, Thierry Declerck, Sara Goggi, Marko Grobelnik, Bente Maegaard, Joseph Mariani, Helene Mazo, Asuncion Moreno, Jan Odijk, and Stelios Piperidis, editors, *Proceedings of the Tenth International Conference on Language Resources and Evaluation (LREC 2016)*, pages 2204–2208, Paris, France, May. European Language Resources Association (ELRA).

Toshiaki Nakazawa, Shohei Higashiyama, Chenchen Ding, Raj Dabre, Anoop Kunchukuttan, Win Pa Pa, Isao Goto, Hideya Mino, Katsuhito Sudoh, and Sadao Kurohashi. 2018. Overview of the 5th workshop on asian translation. In *Proceedings of the 5th Workshop on Asian Translation (WAT2018)*, Hong Kong, China, December.

Kishore Papineni, Salim Roukos, Todd Ward, and Wei-Jing Zhu. 2002. BLEU: a Method for Automatic Evaluation of Machine Translation. In *Proceedings of 40th Annual Meeting of the Association for Computational Linguistics*, pages 311–318, Philadelphia, Pennsylvania, USA. Association for Computational Linguistics.

Jeffrey Pennington, Richard Socher, and Christopher Manning. 2014. GloVe: Global Vectors for Word Representation. In *Proceedings of the 2014 Conference on Empirical Methods in Natural Language Processing (EMNLP)*, pages 1532–1543, Doha, Qatar, October. Association for Computational Linguistics.

Ilya Sutskever, Oriol Vinyals, and Quoc V Le. 2014. Sequence to Sequence Learning with Neural Networks. In Z Ghahramani, M Welling, C Cortes, N D Lawrence, and K Q Weinberger, editors, *Advances in Neural Information Processing Systems 27 (NIPS2014)*, pages 3104–3112. Curran Associates, Inc.

Zhaopeng Tu, Yang Liu, Lifeng Shang, Xiaohua Liu, and Hang Li. 2017. Neural Machine Translation with Reconstruction. In *Proceedings of the Thirty-First AAAI Conference on Artificial Intelligence (AAAI-17)*, pages 3097–3103, San Francisco, California, USA.

Ashish Vaswani, Noam Shazeer, Niki Parmar, Jakob Uszkoreit, Llion Jones, Aidan N Gomez, Ł ukasz Kaiser, and Illia Polosukhin. 2017. Attention is All you Need. In I. Guyon, U. V. Luxburg, S. Bengio, H. Wallach, R. Fergus, S. Vishwanathan, and R. Garnett, editors, *Advances in Neural Information Processing Systems 30*, pages 5998–6008. Curran Associates, Inc.

Zhen Yang, Wei Chen, Feng Wang, and Bo Xu. 2018. Improving Neural Machine Translation with Conditional Sequence Generative Adversarial Nets . In *Proceedings of the 2018 Conference of the North American Chapter of the Association for Computational Linguistics: Human Language Technologies, Volume 1 (Long Papers)*, pages 1346–1355, New Orleans, Louisiana, USA. Association for Computational Linguistics.

Osaka University MT Systems for WAT 2018:
Rewarding, Preordering, and Domain Adaptation

Yuki Kawara[†] **Yuto Takebayashi**[†] **Chenhui Chu**[‡] **Yuki Arase**[†]

[†]Graduate School of Information Science and Technology, Osaka University
[‡]Institute for Datability Science, Osaka University
{kawara.yuki,takebayashi.yuto,arase}@ist.osaka-u.ac.jp
chu@ids.osaka-u.ac.jp

Abstract

In this paper, we present Osaka University MT systems submitted to WAT 2018 shared translation tasks and analysis of their performances. For the ASPEC Japanese-English task, we use our rewarding model on neural machine translation (NMT) and preordering model on phrase-based statistical machine translation (PBSMT). For the Myanmar-English task, we further apply our mixed fine tuning method for domain adaptation on NMT. We report the translation results on these two tasks, where the rewarding model performs the best.

1 Introduction

This paper describes our systems submitted to WAT 2018 shared translation task (Nakazawa et al., 2018) and analyzes these systems. This year, Osaka University participated in two tasks: the ASPEC Japanese-English and Myanmar-English tasks. We use three different methods that we have been proposed in the past.

For the first system, we use the rewarding model boosting target words in the decoder of NMT (Takebayashi et al., 2018). It predicts target words that are promising to be used in a correct translation and rewards them to give them better chances to be output. For the second system, we preorder source sentences before translation so that the word order becomes similar to target sentences, which is applied to PBSMT (Kawara et al., 2018). For the third system, we use our mixed fine tuning method (Chu et al., 2017). It is a domain adaptation method that

uses out-of-domain data to leverage for in-domain translation. The rewarding and preordering models are applied to both the ASPEC Japanese-English and Myanmar-English tasks, while mixed fine tuning is only applied to the Myanmar-English task because it is designed for low-resource translation.

We first describe statistics of datasets provided in the translation tasks in Section 2. Then, we present the details of the rewarding model, preordering model, and mixed fine tuning, as well as our internal evaluation results in Sections 3, 4, and 5, respectively. Finally, we analyze the official results of the shared tasks in Section 6 and conclude this paper in Section 7.

2 Datasets

We conduct English-to-Japanese, Japanese-to-English, English-to-Myanmar, and Myanmar-to-English translation, referred to as *En-Ja*, *Ja-En*, *En-My*, and *My-En* for short, hereafter.

Table 1 shows statistics of the datasets provided in the ASPEC (Asian Scientific Paper Excerpt Corpus) (Nakazawa et al., 2016) Japanese-English and Myanmar-English tasks. The ASPEC Japanese-English task is of a scientific domain, providing 3M, 1,790, and 1,812 sentences for training, development, and test, respectively. The Myanmar-English task provides two corpora, namely, the ALT (Asian Language Treebank) and UCSY (NLP Lab, University of Computer Studies, Yangon). The ALT corpus extracted from the Wikinews, providing 18k, 993, and 1,007 sentences for training, development, and test, respectively. The UCSY is a mixed domain corpus, which is supplementary for this task and pro-

Corpus name	ASPEC	ALT	UCSY
Language	En-Ja/Ja-En	En-My/My-En	
Train	$3,008,500$	$17,965$	$208,638$
Dev	$1,790$	993	N/A
Test	$1,812$	$1,007$	N/A

Table 1: Data statistics of the WAT 2018 ASPEC and Myanmar-English tasks.

vides 208k sentences for training only.

3 Rewarding Model

3.1 Model

We employed the rewarding model using bilingual dictionaries (Takebayashi et al., 2018) to address the adequacy problem in NMT. Our model *rewards* target words that are promising to be used in correct translations by boosting their probabilities to be output by a decoder as shown in Figure 1.

Specifically, it first predicts a set of target words D_{f2e} that are promising to be used in translations by looking up bilingual dictionaries. Then, it *rewards* a target word y_j if it is contained in D_{f2e} by adding weight to the logarithm of the posterior probability $p(\cdot)$ of the decoder given a source sentence X:

$$Q(y_j|y_{<j}, X) = \log p(y_j|y_{<j}, X) + \lambda r_{y_j}, \quad (1)$$

where λ is the weight of reward that will be tuned using a development set. This means that our model boosts the probabilities of predicted words that might have been slipped away during beam search in the conventional decoder. We use a simple binary rewarding that performed the best in Takebayashi et al. (2018):

$$r_{y_j} = \begin{cases} 1 & (y_j \in D_{f2e}), \\ 0 & (\text{otherwise}). \end{cases} \quad (2)$$

Finally, a target word is output as:

$$y_j = \arg\max_{y_j} Q(y_j|y_{<j}, X).$$

3.2 Experiments

For the ASPEC Japanese-English task, we used the first 2M parallel sentence pairs among the entire 3M pairs sentences for training following Morishita et al. (2017), because the remaining 1M sentences were noisy. As preprocessing, we segmented

Japanese sentences using MeCab,[1] and tokenized and truecased the English sentences with the *truecase.perl* script in Moses[2]. We further split the words into sub-words using joint BPE (Sennrich et al., 2016) with $32,000$ merge operations. The vocabulary sizes of the Japanese and English side were $28,852$ and $22,340$, respectively. For the Myanmar-English task, we simply concatenated the available ALT and UCSY corpora for training. We tokenized and truecased the English corpus, and used the tokenized and romanized Myanmar corpus released by the organizers.

We used the mlpnlp-nmt system[3] that is an LSTM based encoder-decoder NMT model with attention, which achieved the best translation performance in human evaluations for both the Ja-En, and En-Ja tasks at WAT 2017 (Nakazawa et al., 2017). We implemented our rewarding model on top of the mlpnlp-nmt system. We followed the hyper-parameter settings of Morishita et al. (2017). We used 2-layer LSTMs for both the encoder and decoder with the beam size of 5. Stochastic gradient descent was used as the learning algorithm, with an initial learning rate of 1.0. The mini batch size was 128.

For the rewarding model, accurate prediction of D_{f2e} is crucial. We used the GIZA++ toolkit[4] on the training corpus to automatically create a bilingual dictionary. We applied the "grow-diag-final-and" heuristic and obtained lexical translation probabilities using Moses.[5] We then pruned translation pairs with low probabilities by δ. λ in Equation (1) was tuned on the development sets from 0.1 to 1.0 by 0.1 interval. The threshold δ was tuned on 0, 0.0001, 0.001, 0.01 and 0.1 for the Japanese-English task and 0 and 0.001 for the Myanmar-English task. We selected the best combination among all combinations of δ and λ on the development set for each model.

Table 2 shows the BLEU scores of each task on the test sets. We can see that the rewarding model improves the BLEU score for 0.57 points and 1.07

---

[1] https://github.com/taku910/mecab
[2] https://github.com/moses-smt/mosesdecoder/blob/master/scripts/recaser/truecase.perl
[3] https://github.com/mlpnlp/mlpnlp-nmt/
[4] http://code.google.com/p/giza-pp
[5] http://www.statmt.org/moses/

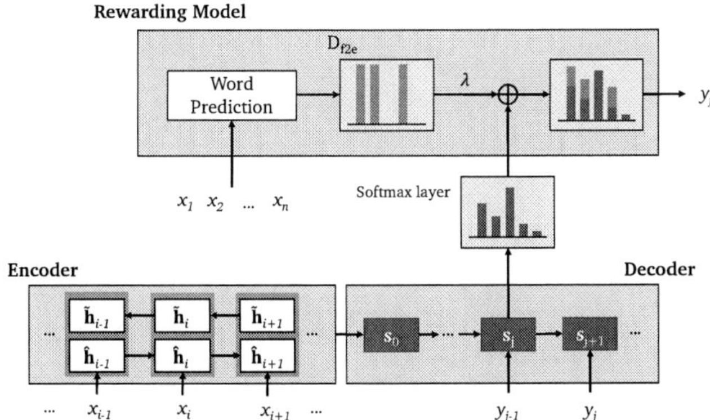

Figure 1: Rewarding model at decoding step j: predicted target words D_{f2e} are rewarded to have better chances to be output at each decoding time step. Note that the attention model is omitted for clarity.

	En-Ja	Ja-En	En-My	My-En
Mlpnlp-nmt	39.50	27.21	**22.34**	13.67
Rewarding	**40.07**	**28.28**	22.33	**13.79**

Table 2: Mlpnlp system and rewarding results (BLEU-4) on the WAT 2018 ASPEC and Myanmar-English tasks.

	En-Ja		Ja-En	
	pre.	rec.	pre.	rec.
Mlpnlp-nmt	73.90	69.03	66.42	61.66
Rewarding	72.87	70.22	66.06	63.09

Table 3: The precision and recall of unigram calculated by comparing the translation hypotheses against the reference translations on WAT 2018 ASPEC task.

points in the En-Ja and Ja-En tasks, respectively. However, there are no significant differences between the mlpnlp-nmt and the proposed model in the En-My and My-En tasks. We think the reason for this is that word alignments between English and Myanmar are not reliable because the size of the corpus is too small, which significantly degrades the word prediction quality. Hence, the rewarding model could not reward correct words. Table 3, 4 show that the precision and recall of unigram calculated by comparing the translation hypotheses against the reference translations on WAT 2018 ASPEC Japanese-English and Myanmar-English tasks, respectively. We can see that the recall increase 1.19 and 1.43 in exchange of decreasing the precision on En-Ja and Ja-En tasks, respectively. However, there are no significant differences between the mlpnlp-nmt and the proposed model in the En-My and My-En tasks.

	En-My		My-En	
	pre.	rec.	pre.	rec.
Mlpnlp-nmt	67.65	48.35	56.44	46.31
Rewarding	67.61	48.34	56.23	46.29

Table 4: The precision and recall of unigram calculated by comparing the translation hypotheses against the reference translations on WAT 2018 Myanmar-English task.

4 Preordering Model

4.1 Model

The word order between source and target languages significantly influences the translation quality in MT. Preordering, arranging words of source sentences so that the order is similar to that of the target language before translation, can effectively address this problem and significantly improves BLEU score of PBSMT (Nakagawa, 2015). Although NMT has been shown its strong performance in translation, it requires a large amount of training corpus, which is not the case for the Myanmar-English task. Hence, we use our preordering model with PBSMT for WAT submission.

We applied the preordering model based on recursive neural networks (RvNN) (Kawara et al., 2018) to En-Ja and Ja-En translation for ASPEC and En-My translation for the Myanmar-English tasks.[6] We first parse source sentences to obtain their syntax trees with a parser, then assign either *Inverted (I)* or *Straight (S)* labels at each node of the source syn-

---

[6]We could not conduct experiments on the My-En translation because parsers are unavailable for Myanmar.

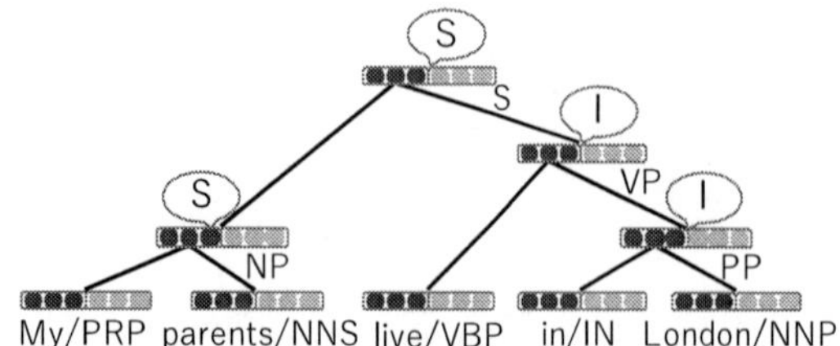

Figure 2: Preordering an English sentence "My parents live in London" with RvNN for Japanese. (*I* indicates to reorder the child nodes, and *S* indicates not to reorder the child nodes.)

tax tree to indicate whether the node should be reordered or not. Gold labels are automatically determined to achieve the highest Kendall's τ computed based on word alignment links. RvNN predicts labels at the node in test time and reorders source sentences. We then train a PBSMT system with reordered source sentences.

Figure 2 shows an example of the labeled parse tree of the English sentence "My parents live in London." RvNN learns to predict correct labels for nodes of a source syntax tree. For example, at the VP node of "live in London," its child nodes of "live" and "in London" are inverted to have the same word order with the Japanese counterpart.

4.2 Experiments

We used Stanford CoreNLP[7] for tokenization and POS tagging, Enju[8] for parsing of English, and MeCab[9] for tokenization and Ckylark for parsing[10] of Japanese. Myanmar corpus was tokenized and romanized by organizers. For the En-My translation, we concatenated the ALT and UCSY corpora for training. For word alignment, we used MGIZA.[11] Source-to-target and target-to-source word alignments were calculated using IBM model 1 and hidden Markov model, and they were combined with the intersection heuristic following Nakagawa (2015). We used 100k sentences sampled from training corpus for preordering. The embedding size and hidden size were set to 200. The vocabulary size was set to 50k. We used

---

[7]http://stanfordnlp.github.io/CoreNLP/

[8]http://www.nactem.ac.uk/enju/

[9]http://taku910.github.io/mecab/

[10]http://odaemon.com/?page=tools_ckylark

[11]http://github.com/moses-smt/giza-pp

	En-Ja	Ja-En	En-My
Moses PBSMT	24.54	15.31	19.71
Preordering	**29.16**	**17.30**	**20.93**

Table 5: PBSMT results (BLEU-4) with and without preordering on the WAT 2018 ASPEC and Myanmar-English tasks.

Adam (Kingma and Ba, 2015) with a weight decay (10^{-4}) and gradient clipping (5) for optimization. The mini batch size was set to 500.

For PBSMT, we used Moses.[12] We trained the 5-gram language model on the target side of the training corpus with KenLM.[13] Tuning was performed by minimum error rate training (Och, 2003). We repeated tuning and testing of each model 3 times and reported the average of scores. The distortion limit of PBSMT system trained by preordered sentences was set to 0, while that without preordering was set to 20.

Table 5 shows the results. We can see that the preordering model improves the results on the PBSMT (4.62, 1.99, 1.22 for En-Ja, Ja-En, En-My, respectively). Translation quality of the En-My task is improved less than the En-Ja task (1.22 point and 4.62 point, respectively). We think this is caused by unbalanced corpus sizes of ALT and UCSY. The ALT corpus, from which the test set was derived, is significantly smaller than the UCSY corpus. This makes the English-Myanmar translation task difficult.

5 Domain Adaptation

5.1 Method

It has been known that vanilla NMT performs poorly for domain specific translation in low-resource scenarios (Chu and Wang, 2018). The WAT 2018 Myanmar-English task is a low-resource setting that only contains 18k in-domain training sentences for the ALT task. However, it also provides the UCSY out-of-domain corpus, containing 208k training sentences. This is a proper domain adaptation setting, where out-of-domain data can be leveraged for in-domain translation.

---

[12]https://github.com/moses-smt/mosesdecoder

[13]http://github.com/kpu/kenlm

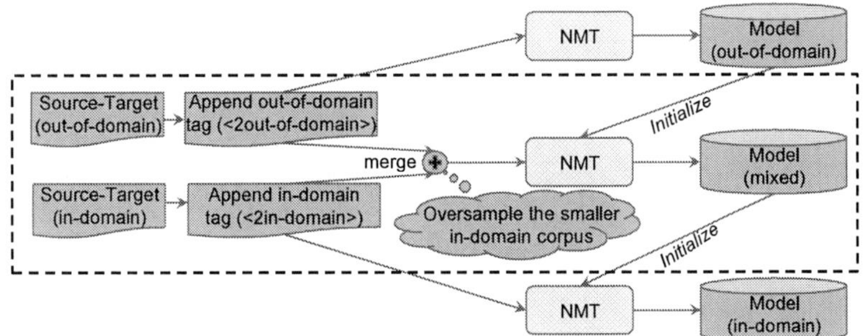

Figure 3: Mixed fine tuning with domain tags for domain adaptation.

In this work, we applied the domain adaptation method of mixed fine tuning (see Figure 3) for the WAT 2018 Myanmar-English task. Mixed fine tuning is a transfer learning based approach proposed by Chu et al. (2017). We first train an NMT model on the resource-rich out-of-domain (*i.e.*, UCSY) corpus till convergence. Then we resume training on the in-domain (*i.e.*, ALT) and out-of-domain (*i.e.*, UCSY) mixed corpus, which simply concatenates the corpora of two domains by appending artificial tokens that indicate the domains and by oversampling the corpus of the resource-poor domain (*i.e.*, ALT). This prevents over-fitting and enables smooth domain transition.

5.2 Experiments

For English, we tokenized and true-cased the sentences using the *tokenizer.perl* and *truecase.perl* scripts in Moses. For Myanmar, we used the transcribed and tokenized data released by the organizers. For the NMT system, we used the open source implementation of the Transformer model (Vaswani et al., 2017) in *tensor2tensor*[14]. We used the Transformer because it is the current state-of-the-art NMT model. For training, we used the default model settings corresponding to *transformer_base_single_gpu* in the implementation and to *base model* in (Vaswani et al., 2017). We compared the MT performance with vanilla NMT, which was trained on the in-domain data only using the Transformer. We trained 100k steps for the vanilla NMT system. For mixed fine tuning, we trained the out-of-domain and fine tuning models for 200k and 200k steps, respectively. As development and test data were not provided for

	En-My	My-En
Transformer	**12.28**	0.45
Mixed fine tuning	9.45	**11.63**

Table 6: Transformer and mixed fine tuning results (BLEU-4) on the WAT 2018 Myanmar-English task.

the UCSY corpus, we randomly sampled $1,043$ and $1,043$ sentences from the corpus for development and test, respectively. Note that we removed the development and test sentences from the UCSY corpus for training.

Table 6 shows the results. We can see that mixed fine tuning significantly improves the results on the My-En direction (10.18 BLEU points higher) but performs worse than vanilla NMT on the En-My direction (2.83 BLEU points lower). We think the reason for this is that Myanmar sentences were tokenized into writing units and romanized and thus has a very small vocabulary. This makes the output word embeddings good enough for the En-My translation direction when training on the in-domain data only. Mixed fine tuning on the mixed data decreases the quality of word output word embeddings due to the mix of domains, leading to the drop in BLEU scores.

6 Official Results on WAT 2018

Table 7 shows the official results of our systems, organizer's systems, and the best systems on the WAT 2018 ASPEC and Myanmar-English tasks.[15] Translation qualities were evaluated with both automatic evaluation metrics (BLEU, RIBES, and AMFM) and human annotations. BLEU is calculated based on the proportion of matched n-gram between output

---

[14] https://github.com/tensorflow/tensor2tensor

[15] http://lotus.kuee.kyoto-u.ac.jp/WAT/evaluation/index.html

		En-Ja	Ja-En	En-My	My-En
Rewarding	BLEU	**38.01**	**26.19**	**22.33**	**11.38**
	RIBES	**82.51**	**74.98**	**66.86**	**65.56**
	AMFM	**76.31**	**58.83**	74.08	51.09
	human	**4.50**	**−37.00**	**3.00**	**−57.00**
Preordering	BLEU	23.24	13.97	20.88	-
	RIBES	71.69	66.54	63.95	-
	AMFM	70.51	57.14	**77.48**	-
	human	−82.25	−95.75	−23.50	-
Mixed fine tuning	BLEU	-	-	9.45	9.99
	RIBES	-	-	58.19	64.89
	AMFM	-	-	66.54	**55.20**
	human	-	-	-	−99.50
Organizer baseline (PBSMT)	BLEU	27.48	18.45	-	-
	RIBES	68.37	64.51	-	-
	AMFM	73.64	59.10	-	-
Organizer baseline (NMT with attention)	BLEU	36.37	26.91	22.42	14.44
	RIBES	82.50	76.50	66.74	69.69
	AMFM	75.99	59.54	74.56	52.60
Organizer baseline (Transformer)	BLEU	40.79	28.06	-	-
	RIBES	84.49	76.76	-	-
	AMFM	76.86	59.56	-	-
Best system	BLEU	*43.43*♣	*30.59*♢	*32.30*♠	*29.14*♠
	RIBES	*85.03*♢	*77.79*♢	*74.65*♠	*79.40*♠
	AMFM	*78.10*♢	*61.94*♢	*81.65*♠	*65.59*♠
	human	*28.50*♡	*15.75*♭	*61.00*♮	*22.25*♯

Table 7: Official results of the WAT 2018 ASPEC and Myanmar-English tasks. Best systems are from different teams as indicated by the following symbols. ♣: Transformer with relative position, ensemble of 4 models, rerank, ♢: Transformer with relative position, ensemble of 3 models, ♠: many PBSMT and NMT n-best lists combined and reranked using Wikipedia data for back-translation and language model trainings, ♡: big bidirectional Transformer using 1.5M sentences only, ♭: Transformer vanilla model using 3M sentences, ♮: 4 models ensemble, ♯: NMT baseline, ensemble (system descriptions are borrowed from Nakazawa et al. (2018)).

and reference sentences. RIBES is calculated based on uni-gram precision and similarity the word order between system output and reference sentence. AMFM is calculated based on both adequacy and fluency, which is designed to decouple semantic and syntactic components of the translation process to provide a balanced view of translation quality. Because human evaluation was restricted to 2 systems of each team, we report human evaluation results of ASPEC En-Ja and Ja-En tasks for the rewarding and preordering systems, and a result of the My-En task for the rewarding and mixed fine tuning systems, and En-My tasks for all systems.

We can see that in terms of BLEU score and human evaluation, the rewarding model performed best among our three systems for all languages. In terms of AMFM, preordering and mixed fine tuning achieved 3.4 and 4.11 points higher scores than the rewarding model in the En-My and My-En tasks, respectively.

Our rewarding model outperformed the organizer's baseline of NMT with attention for 1.64 BLEU points on En-Ja task. However, the organizer's baseline of the Transformer achieved 2.78 and 1.87 higher BLEU points than the rewarding model on En-Ja and Ja-En, respectively. Because the rewarding model can be easily applied to different NMT decoders, we will apply it to the Transformer for further improvement. For En-My and My-En translations, our rewarding model is comparable to the organizer's baseline (En-My) and 3.06 BLEU points lower (My-En) due to the poor word alignment quality as discussed in Section 3.2.

There are significant gaps between our results and those of the best systems. These best systems ensemble multiple systems, while all of our results are from a single system. Ensembling multiple systems would improve our results, which is the future work.

7 Conclusion

We have described our systems submitted to WAT 2018 shared translation tasks. Among which, the rewarding model showed the best performance. As future work, we first plan to conduct system combination of these three systems. Secondly, we will apply the rewarding model to the decoder of the Transformer in order to further improve its translation quality.

Acknowledgments

This work was supported by NTT communication science laboratories and Grant-in-Aid for Research Activity Start-up #17H06822, JSPS.

References

Chenhui Chu and Rui Wang. 2018. A survey of domain adaptation for neural machine translation. In *Proceedings of the International Conference on Computational Linguistics (COLING)*, pages 1304–1319, Santa Fe, USA, August.

Chenhui Chu, Raj Dabre, and Sadao Kurohashi. 2017. An empirical comparison of domain adaptation methods for neural machine translation. In *Proceedings of the Annual Meeting of the Association for Computational Linguistics (ACL)*, pages 385–391, Vancouver, Canada, July.

Yuki Kawara, Chenhui Chu, and Yuki Arase. 2018. Recursive neural network based preordering for english-to-japanese machine translation. In *Proceedings of the Annual Meeting of the Association for Computational Linguistics (ACL), Student Research Workshop*, pages 21–27, Melbourne, Australia, July.

Diederik P. Kingma and Jimmy Ba. 2015. Adam: A method for stochastic optimization. In *Proceedings of the International Conference for Learning Representations (ICLR)*, San Diego, USA, December.

Makoto Morishita, Jun Suzuki, and Masaaki Nagata. 2017. NTT neural machine translation systems at WAT 2017. In *Proceedings of the Workshop on Asian Translation (WAT)*, pages 89–94, Taipei, Taiwan, November.

Tetsuji Nakagawa. 2015. Efficient top-down BTG parsing for machine translation preordering. In *Proceedings of the Annual Meeting of the Association for Computational Linguistics and International Joint Conference on Natural Language Processing (ACL-IJCNLP)*, pages 208–218, Beijing, China, July.

Toshiaki Nakazawa, Manabu Yaguchi, Kiyotaka Uchimoto, Masao Utiyama, Eiichiro Sumita, Sadao Kurohashi, and Hitoshi Isahara. 2016. ASPEC: Asian scientific paper excerpt corpus. In *Proceedings of the Ninth International Conference on Language Resources and Evaluation (LREC)*, pages 2204–2208, Portoro, Slovenia, May.

Toshiaki Nakazawa, Shohei Higashiyama, Chenchen Ding, Hideya Mino, Isao Goto, Hideto Kazawa, Yusuke Oda, Graham Neubig, and Sadao Kurohashi. 2017. Overview of the 4th workshop on asian translation. In *Proceedings of the Workshop on Asian Translation (WAT)*, pages 1–54, Taipei, Taiwan, November.

Toshiaki Nakazawa, Shohei Higashiyama, Chenchen Ding, Raj Dabre, Anoop Kunchukuttan, Win Pa Pa, Isao Goto, Hideya Mino, Katsuhito Sudoh, and Sadao Kurohashi. 2018. Overview of the 5th workshop on asian translation. In *Proceedings of the 5th Workshop on Asian Translation (WAT)*, Hong Kong, China, December.

Franz Josef Och. 2003. Minimum error rate training in statistical machine translation. In *Proceedings of the Annual Meeting of the Association for Computational Linguistics (ACL)*, pages 160–167, Sapporo, Japan, July.

Rico Sennrich, Barry Haddow, and Alexandra Birch. 2016. Neural machine translation of rare words with subword units. In *Proceedings of the Annual Meeting of the Association for Computational Linguistics (ACL)*, pages 1715–1725, Berlin, Germany, August.

Yuto Takebayashi, Chenhui Chu, Arase Yuki, and Masaaki Nagata. 2018. Word rewarding for adequate neural machine translation. In *Proceedings of the International Workshop on Spoken Language Translation (IWSLT)*, pages 14–22, Bruges, Belgium, October.

Ashish Vaswani, Noam Shazeer, Niki Parmar, Jakob Uszkoreit, Llion Jones, Aidan N Gomez, Ł ukasz Kaiser, and Illia Polosukhin. 2017. Attention is all you need. In *Advances in Neural Information Processing Systems (NIPS)*, pages 5998–6008. Long Beach, USA, December.

UCSYNLP-Lab Machine Translation Systems for WAT 2018

[1]Yi Mon Shwe Sin, [1]Thazin Myint Oo, [1]Hsu Myat Mo, [1]Win Pa Pa, [1]Khin Mar Soe and
[2]Ye Kyaw Thu

[1]Natural Language Processing Lab., University of Computer Studies, Yangon, Myanmar
[2]Language and Speech Science Research Lab., Waseda University, Japan
{yimonshwesin, thazinmyintoo, hsumyatmo, winpapa, khinmarsoe}@ucsy.edu.mm,
wasedakuma@gmail.com

Abstract

In this description, we report the experimental results of Machine Translation models conducted by a team from University of Computer Studies, Yangon (UCSY) for the translation tasks of WAT 2018. Generally, our models are based on neural methods and statistical methods for both Myanmar-English and English-Myanmar direction of languages pair. For the neural method experiments, attention-based neural machine translation (NMT) that uses word level segmentation and Transformer that uses sub-word level segmentation have been carried out. In the portion of statistical machine translation (SMT), we used three different statistical approaches: phrase-based, hierarchical phrase-based, and the operation sequence model (OSM). Different Machine Translations are conducted on the ALT and UCSY datasets and the best scores from the experiments are described in this system description.

1   Introduction

Machine Translation (MT) which is also known as Computer Aided Translation is the task of specifically designing to translate both verbal and written texts between natural languages by a computer system. MT uses a machine translation engine to perform substitution of words or phrases or any other in one language for words or phrases or any other in another language. MT is widely used in Natural Language Processing (NLP) tasks such as online translation services applications in information extraction, document retrieval, intelligence analysis, electronic mail, and much more. A few different types of MT are available in the market today, the most widely used are Statistical Machine Translation (SMT), Rule-Based Machine Translation (RBMT), Hybrid Systems, which combine RBMT and SMT and Neural Machine Translation (NMT). However, there are still many challenges for high-quality translations in real-world applications.

To date, there have been very few studies on the MT from Myanmar language to other languages (T.Zin, 2011), (W. Pa, 2016). And Myanmar MT is still in its early stages and researchers are faced with many difficulties such as the lack of resources. Existing research on Myanmar MT has been either rule-based or more recently statistical-based have been tried. There have been some studies on the SMT of Myanmar language. Ye Kyaw Thu et al. (2016) presented the first large-scale study of the translation of the Myanmar language. A total of 40 language pairs were used in the study that included languages both similar and fundamentally different from Myanmar. The results show that the hierarchical phrase-based SMT (HPBSMT) approach gave the highest translation quality in terms of both the BLEU and RIBES scores. Win Pa Pa et al (2016)   presented the first comparative study of five major machine translation approaches applied to low-resource languages, PBSMT, HPBSMT, tree-to-string (T2S), string-to-tree (S2T) and OSM translation methods to the translation of limited quantities of travel domain data between English and {Thai , Laos, Myanmar} in both directions. The experimental results indicate that in terms of adequacy (as measured by BLEU score), the PBSMT approach produced highest quality translations. From their RIBES scores, we noticed that OSM approach achieved best machine translation performance for Myanmar to English translation. There was also a study of SMT on word segmented and syllable segmented data for

Myanmar language by (Ye Kyaw Thau et al., 2016) and they proved word information had large effect in MT.

We have prepared 200K of parallel corpus and tries on both statistical machine translation system and neural machine translation system. In the experiments, there are two different NMT models, NMT with attention and NMT with Transformer model and two SMT models, OSM, PBSMT and HPBSMT and we will refer them as two NMT models as NMT1, NMT2 in the rest of the sections.

The toolkits we used for NMT1 is PyTorch OpenNMT[1] for NMT1 and Sockey Sequence-to-sequence Framework[2] for NMT2. NMT1 is a simple NMT model with an attention mechanism. We implement NMT1 with word level segmentation. For word level segmentation of Myanmar language, we use UCSY_NLP lab segmenter[3].

To build SMT models, we used the Moses (P. Koehn, 2007) which is the de facto tool among the numerous MT tools. Language Modeling is trained by using kenLM using 5-grams, with modified Kneser-Ney discounting (smoothing). Alignment with GIZA++[4] implementation of IBM word alignment model 4 with grow-diagonal-final- and heuristic for phrase-extraction. The lexicalized reordering model was trained with the msd-bidirectional-fe option. Minimum error rate training (MERT) was used to tune the decoder parameters and the decoding was done using the Moses decoder (version 2.1.1).

In this report, section 2 will describe our MT systems. In section 3, the experimental setup will be described. In section 4, the results of our experiments will be reported followed by the conclusion in section 5.

2 System Description

NMT systems and SMT systems are used for Myanmar-English translations in both directions. To reduce the vocabulary size, we apply byte pair encoding (BPE; Sennrich et al., 2016) which breaks all words into sub-word units in

Transformer model and SMTs, with different number of BPE segmentations.

The NMT1 model is based on the standard encoder-decoder architecture with attention as proposed by (Bahdanau et al., 2015). The encoder is a bidirectional recurrent neural network (BiRNN) using Gated Recurrent Units. In each step, it takes an embedded token from the input sequence and its previous output and outputs a representation of the token. The encoder works in both directions; the resulting vector representations at corresponding positions are concatenated. Additionally, the final outputs of both the forward and backward run are concatenated and used as the initial state of the decoder. At each decoding step, it takes its previous hidden state and the embedding of the token produced in the previous step as the input and produces the output vector. This vector is used to compute the attention distribution vector over the encoder outputs. The RNN output and the attention distribution vector are then used as the input of a linear layer to produce the distribution over the target vocabulary. During training, the previously generated token is replaced by the token present in the reference translation.

For building NMT2, we applied Transformer NMT that based on self-attention mechanism. The architecture is single layer encoder and decoder. The model is trained with a sub-word vocabulary and we apply it to all the training and evaluation data.

In the experiment description of SMT, we trained PBSMT and OSM models for English to Myanmar translation and HPBSMT and OSM for Myanmar to English. In this system description, we propose a simple phrase-based translation model consisting of phrase pair probabilities extracted from corpus and a basic reordering model, and an algorithm to extract the phrased to build a phrase table. We model it using 5-gram language model under the PBMT paradigm. The hierarchical phrase-based SMT approach is a model based on synchronous context free grammar and the model is able to learn from corpus of unannotated parallel text. The benefit of this technique is that the hierarchical structure is able to represent the word reordering process. As a

---

[1] http://github.com/OpenNMT/OpenNMT-py

[2] https://awslabs.github.io/sockeye

[3] http://nlpresearch-ucsy.edu.mm/NLP_UCSY/wordsegmentation.html

[4] http://www.statmt.org/moses/giza/GIZA++.html

consequence of this advantage, this makes particularly applicable to language pairs that requires long distance reordering in the case of Myanmar-English translation process. The OSM combines the benefits of phrase-based and N-gram based SMT. It is based on minimal translation units, capture source and target context across phrasal boundaries and simultaneously generate source and target units. OSM motivates better reordering mechanism that uniformly handles local and non-local reordering and strong coupling of lexical generation and reordering. It means that OSM can handle both short and long distance reordering. The list of operations can be divided into two groups and there are five translation operations Generate(X, Y), Continue Source Cept, Generate Identical, Generate Source Only (X) and Generate Target Only (Y) and three reordering operations such as Insert Gap, Jump Back (N) and Jump Forward.

3 Experimental Setup

3.1 Datasets and preprocessing

The parallel data for Myanmar-English and English-Myanmar translation tasks at WAT2018 consists of two corpora: the ALT corpus and the UCSY corpus. The ALT corpus is one part from the Asian Language Treebank (ALT) Project, consisting of twenty thousand Myanmar-English parallel sentences from Wiki news articles. The UCSY corpus is constructed by the NLP Lab, University of Computer Studies, Yangon (UCSY), Myanmar, aiming to promote machine translation research on Myanmar language. This corpus consists of 200K Myanmar-English parallel sentences collected from different domains, including local news articles and textbooks (Yi Mon et.al, 2018). The UCSY corpus and a portion of the ALT corpus are used as training data, which are around 220,000 lines of sentences and phrases. The development and test data are from the ALT corpus. Therefore, the training data for Myanmar-English and English-Myanmar translation tasks is a mix domain data collected from different sources. Table 1 shows data statistics used for the experiments.

Data Type	File Name	Number of Sentences
TRAIN	train.ucsy.[my|en]	208,638
	train.alt.[my|en]	17,965
DEV	dev.alt.[my|en]	993
TEST	test.alt.[my|en]	1,007

Table 1: Statistics of Datasets

Due to Myanmar Language being an unsegmented language with no clear definition of word boundaries, proper text segmentation is essential. Although the Myanmar textual data given form the WAT2018 have been segmented into writing units and Romanized, the data provided was segmented into word level. Moses tokenizer is used for English side of parallel data in NMT1.

In experiment of SMT, byte pair encoding (BPE) is trained using the source and target side of the data. A technique is to segment words into smaller sub-word unit. BPE word segmenter conceptually proceeds by first splitting all words in the whole corpus into individual characters. The most frequent adjacent pairs of symbols are then consecutively merged, until a specified limit of merge operations has been reached. The merge operations learned on a training corpus and that is purely frequency-based. The frequent sequence of characters will be joined through the merge operations, resulting the common words not being segmented. Words containing rare combination of characters will not be fully merged from the characters splitting all the way back to their original form. They will remain split into two or more sub-word units in the BPE segmented data.

3.2 Training

Table 2 shows the settings of network hyper-parameters for NMT models, and Table 3 for SMT models. The experiments were run on Tesla K80 GPU. Based on different parameter settings, the training time is different.

Hyper-parameter	NMT1 Settings	NMT2 Setting
Source Vocabulary size	25,087	10,000
Target vocabulary size	50,004	10,000
Number of hidden units	500	512
Encoder layer	2	1
Decoder layer	2	1
Learning rate	1.0	0.002
Dropout rate	0.3	0.2
Mini-batch size	64	100

Table 2: Hyper-parameter of NMT models

Alignment model	Grow–diag-final and heuristic
Lexicalized reordering model	Msd-bidirectional-fe
Language Model	kenLM (5-gram)
Smoothing	Modified Knerser-Ney discounting
Decoding	Moses decoder
Tuning	Minimum Error Rate Tuning (MERT)

Table 3: Moses settings

3.3 Experimental Results

Table 4 and the Table 5 show the different evaluation metrics such as Bilingual Evaluation Understudy (BLEU), Rank-based Intuitive Bilingual Evaluation Score (RIBES) and Adequacy-Fluency Metrics (AMFM) (Banchs et al., 2015) for Myanmar- English and English-Myanmar translation pairs. We also investigated how segmentation level affects the MT performance in all experiments. The experimental results reveal that word level segmentation can

give better performance for attention-based NMT while sub-word level works better with Transformer. Moreover, experiments are conducted by tuning different parameter settings for all NMT1, NMT2 and SMT. Best scores among those of the experimental results are submitted in this description.

Method	BLEU	RIBES	AMFM
NMT1	19.19	0.671,461	0.717,480
NMT2	21.19	**0.679,800**	**0.756,710**
OSM	**22.78**	0.549,883	0.751,180
PBSMT	22.40	0.544,395	0.749,080

Table 4: English to Myanmar Translation

Method	BLUE	RIBES	AMFM
NMT1	**9.56**	**0.642,309**	0.518,990
HPBSMT	8.91	0.583,956	0.560,800
OSM	8.84	0.553,786	**0.594,800**

Table 5: Myanmar to English Translation

In the direction of Myanmar to English, Table 5 show only 3 system results. Experimental result of NMT2 was not able managed to submit in time. In Myanmar to English translation, NMT1 with outperforms HPBSMT and OSM models in terms of BLEU score and the RIBES score. However, OSM gets highest score in AMFM. In English to Myanmar translation, the OSM model performs better than the other models in terms of BLEU score but NMT2 model is better than the others in RIBES and AMFM score. We used Byte Pair Encoding (BPE) segmentation for SMT experiments. Generally says that OSM is the best method for bi-directional translations. In the results of English to Myanmar translation as shown in Table 4, we got the highest BLEU score in the method of OSM and the RIBES and AMFM scores is nearly the same with PBSMT. Interestingly, we got highest AMFM in the method of OSM in Myanmar to English translation and there is little difference in scores of BLEU and RIBES with comparison of HPBSMT.

Conclusion

In this system description for WAT2018, we submitted our NMT systems, which are NMT with attention and NMT with sockey. And we also submitted SMT systems, which are PBSMT, HPBSMT and OSM. We evaluated our systems on Myanmar-English and English-Myanmar translations at WAT 2018. Our team is the first time of competition in WAT and there are so many weaknesses to fulfillment of our destination. In the future, we will collect the more parallel sentences to get a large-sized MT corpus. And we will remove the noise to clean the existing corpus because it contained a lot of parallel sentences with different content. Moreover, we also intend to do more and more experiments with more recent evolutions of the translation models.

References

Dzmitry Bahdanau, Kyunghyun Cho, and Yoshua Bengio. Neural machine translation by jointly learning to align and translate. *In Proceedings of ACL – IJCNLP 2015*, Volume 1: Long Papers (2015). arXiv preprint arXiv:1409.0473.

Fabien Cromieres, Fabien Cromieres, Toshiaki Nakazawa and Toshiaki Nakazawa. Kyoto University Participation to WAT 2017, Proceedings of the 4th Workshop on Asian Translation, pages 146–153, Taipei, Taiwan, November 27, 2017. © 2017AFNLP.

Guillaume Klein, Yoon Kim, Yoon Kim, Jean Senellart, Alexander M. Rush, SYSTRAN and Harvard SEAS. OpenNMT: Open-Source Toolkit for Neural Machine Translation. (2017). Proceedings of the 55th Annual Meeting of the Association for Computational Linguistics-System Demonstrations, pages 67–72 Vancouver, Canada, July 30- August 4, 2017. ©2017 Association for Computationsl Linguistics http://doi.org/10.18653/v1/P17-4012

Makoto Morishita, Jun Suzuki and Masaaki Nagata. NTT Neural Machine Translation Systems at WAT 2017. Proceedings of the 4th Workshop on Asian Translation, pages 89–94, Taipei, Taiwan, November 27, 2017. © 2017 AFNLP.

Minh-Thang Luong, Hieu Pham and Christopher D. Maiining. Effective Approaches to Attention-based Neural Machine Translation. Proceedings of the 2015 Conference on Empirical Methods in Natu-ral Language Processing, pages 1412-1421(2015).

Rafael E Banchs, Luis F D'Haro, and Haizhou Li. 2015. Adequacy-fluency metrics: Evaluating mt in the continuous space model framework. IEEE Transactions on Audio, Speech, and Language Processing, 23(3):472-482.

Rico Sennrich, Barry Haddow, and Alexandra Birch. 2016. Improving neural machine translation models with monolingual data. In Proceedings of the Annual Meeting of the Association for Computational Linguistics, pages 86–96.

Rico Sennrich, Barry Haddow and Alexandra Birch (2016): Neural Machine Translation of Rare Words with Subword Units Proceedings of the 54th Annual Meeting of the Association for Computational Linguistics (ACL 2016). Berlin, Germany

Sandhya Singh, Ritesh Panjwani, Anoop Kunchukuttan and Pushpak Bhattacharyya. Comparing Recurrent and Convolutional Architectures for English-Hind Neural Machine Translation. Proceedings of the 4th Workshop on Asian Translation, pages 167–170, Taipei, Taiwan, November 27, 2017. ©2017 AFNLP.

Thet Thet Zin, Khin Mar Soe and Nilar Thein. Myanmar Phrases Translation Model with Morphological Analysis for Statistical Myanmar to English Translation System. 25th Pacific Asia Conference on Language, Information and Computation, pages 130-139(2011).

Ye Kyaw Thu, Andrew Finch, Win Pa Pa, and Eiichiro Sumita, " A large scale study of Statistical Machine Translation Methods for Myanmar Language ", in Proc. Of SNLP2016, February 10-12, 2016

Win Pa Pa, Ye Kyaw Thu, Andrew Finch and Eiichiro Sumita. A Study of Statistical Machine Translation Methods for Under Resourced Languages. 29th Pacific Asia Conference on Language, Information and Computation pages 259-269(2016).

P. Koehn, F. J. Och, and D. Marcu, "Statistical phrase-based translation." in Proc. of HTL-NAACL, 2003, pp. 48–54.

Chiang, D., "Hierarchical phrase-based translation", Computational Linguistics 33(2), 2007, pp. 201-228.

Nadir Durrani, Helmut Schmid, Alexander M. Fraser, Philipp Koehn and Hinrich Schutze, "The Operation Sequence Model - Combining N-Gram-Based and Phrase-Based Statistical Machine Translation", Computational Linguistics, Volume 41, No. 2, 2015, pp. 185-214.

Prachya, Boonkwan and Thepchai, Supnithi, "Technical Report for The Network-based ASEAN Language Translation Public Service Project", Online Materials of Network-based ASEAN Languages Translation Public Service for Members, NECTEC, 2013

Philipp Koehn, Hieu Hoang, Alexandra Birch, Chris Callison-Burch, Marcello Federico, Nicola Bertoldi, Brooke Cowan, Wade Shen, Christine Moran, Richard Zens, Chris Dyer, Ondrej Bojar, Alexandra Constantin, Evan Herbst, Moses: Open Source Toolkit for Statistical Machine Translation, Annual Meeting of the Association for Computational Linguistics (ACL), demonstration session, Prague, Czech Republic, June 2007.

Och Franz Josef and Ney Hermann, "Improved Statistical Alignment Models", in Proc. of the 38th Annual Meeting on Association for Computational Linguistics, Hong Kong, China, 2000, pp. 440-447.

Tillmann Christoph, "A Unigram Orientation Model for Statistical Machine Translation", in Proc. of HLT-NAACL 2004: Short Papers, Stroudsburg, PA, USA, 2004, pp. 101-104.

Heafield, Kenneth, "KenLM: Faster and Smaller Language Model Queries", in Proc. of the Sixth Workshop on Statistical Machine Translation, WMT '11, Edinburgh, Scotland, 2011, pp. 187-197.

Chen Stanley F and Goodman Joshua, "An empirical study of smoothing techniques for language modeling", in Proc. of the 34th annual meeting on Association for Computational Linguistics, 1996, pp. 310-318.

Och Franz J., "Minimum error rate training in statistical machine translation", in Proc. of the 41st Annual Meeting n Association for Computational Linguistics – Volume 1,Association for Computer Linguistics, Sapporo, Japan, July, 2003, pp.160-167.

Felix Hieber, Tobias Domhan, Michael Denkowski, David Vilar, Artem Sokolov, Ann Clifton and Matt Post. 2017. Sockeye: A Toolkit for Neural Machine Translation. ArXiv e-prints.

Yi Mon Shwe Sin and Khin Mar Soe, "Large Scale Myanmar to English Neural Machine Translation System". Proceeding of the IEEE 7th Global Conference on Consumer Electronic (GCCE 2018).

XMU Neural Machine Translation Systems
for WAT2018 Myanmar-English Translation Task

Boli Wang, Jinming Hu, Yidong Chen and **Xiaodong Shi**[*]

School of Information Science and Engineering, Xiamen University, Fujian, China

`{boliwang, todtom}@stu.xmu.edu.cn`

`{ydchen, mandel}@xmu.edu.cn`

Abstract

This paper describes the Neural Machine Translation systems of Xiamen University for the Myanmar-English translation tasks of WAT 2018. We apply Unicode normalization, training data filtering, different Myanmar tokenizers, and subword segmentation in data pre-processing. We try to train NMT models with different architectures. The experimental results show that the RNN-based shallow models can still outperform Transformer models in some settings. And we also found that replacing the official Myanmar tokenizer with syllable segmentation does help improve the result.

1 Introduction

In recent years, Neural Machine Translation (NMT) (Bahdanau et al., 2015; Cho et al., 2014; Sutskever et al., 2014) has achieved state-of-the-art performance on various language pairs (Sennrich et al., 2016a; Wu et al., 2016; Zhou et al., 2016; Vaswani et al., 2017). This paper describes the NMT systems of Xiamen University (XMU) for the WAT 2018 evaluation (Nakazawa et al., 2018). We participated in Myanmar→English and English→Myanmar translation subtasks.

In both two translation directions, we compare state-of-the-art Transformer models (Vaswani et al., 2017) with our reimplementation of RNN-based dl4mt models[1]. In pre-processing, We try Unicode

---

[*]Corresponding author.

[1]`https://github.com/nyu-dl/dl4mt-tutorial`

normalization, data filtering and Myanmar syllable segmentation. We also use Byte Pair Encoding (BPE) (Sennrich et al., 2016b) to achieve open-vocabulary translation.

The remainder of this paper is organized as follows: Section 2 describes architecture of NMT we use, including the training details. Section 3 describes the processing of the data. Section 4 shows the results of our experiments. Finally, we conclude in section 5.

2 Baseline System

We compare two NMT architectures:

- DL4MT: We use an in-house reimplementation of dl4mt-tutorial model with minor changes and new features such as dropout (Srivastava et al., 2014).

- Transformer: We use the reimplementation of Transformer model in THUMT toolkit (Zhang et al., 2017).

For both two subtasks, we train our models with almost the same hyper-parameters. For DL4MT, we use word embeddings of size 512 and hidden layers of size 1024. We use mini-batches of size 128 and adopt Adam (Kingma and Ba, 2015) ($\beta_1 = 0.9$, $\beta_2 = 0.999$ and $\epsilon = 1 \times 10^{-8}$) as the optimizer. The initial learning rate is set to 5×10^{-4}. During the training process, we halve the learning rate after every 10K batches. As a common way to train RNN models, we clip the norm of gradients to a predefined value 1.0 (Pascanu et al., 2013). We use dropout to avoid over-fitting with a keep probability of 0.8.

For Transformer, we set both word embeddings and hidden layers as 512 dimension. Transformer models are trained on 8 Nvidia GeForce GTX 1080 Ti graphics cards with batch size of 6400 tokens each card. The initial learning rate is set to 1.0 and Linear Warm-up RSqrt decay function is used with 5000 warm-up steps.

During the training process, we save the parameters as checkpoints for every 5K steps and evaluate the intermediate models on validation set. We train DL4MT models for 40K steps and Transformer models for 100K steps.

3 Data Processing

We use all training data provided by ALT corpus and UCSY corpus and the data processing in both Myanmar→English and English→Myanmar are almost the same. We normalize both Myanmar and English texts by converting Normalization Form Canonical Decomposition to Normalization Form Canonical Composition and applying a modified version of Moses[2] `normalize-punctuation.perl` script with more punctuation normalization rules.

On the Myanmar side, the original training set is pre-tokenized and -Romanized with the official tokenizer `myan2roma.py`. However, as illustrated in Figure 1, we found a number of worse tokenized word types with multiple syllables in the long tail of Myanmar vocabulary, which intensify data sparsity. Therefore, we try to import Myanmar syllable segmentation before Romanization. We first recover the original Myanmar texts using official `myan2roma.py` script and then segment Myanmar syllables with `MyanmarParser` toolkit[3]. Finally, we use `myan2roma.py` to Romanize the syllabificated Myanmar texts, without futher tokenization. On the English side, Moses tokenizer and truecaser are applied.

Furthermore, we found that the official Myanmar tokenizer `myan2roma.py` split numbers into sequences of digits and Latin words into sequences of letters, which makes the sentences become longer

Romanized	Myanmar	Frequency
NNY|103D|103E|103E|UU|103A|N|XH	ညွှင့်နှိုင်း	2
M|103D|103E|103E|UU|103A|XH|N	မွှိုင်းနှ	1
|103B|103C|103D|103D|103E	ျြိုိုိ	1
Q|A|XH|103C|103D|103E|UU	အားြိုို	1
NNY|E|AA|103B|103C|E|E|I	ညေါျြေေဆ	1
NG|103A|XT|103B|103C|E	င်ျြေ	1
PXR|II|XH|103C|103D|E	ြို့ြေ	2
M|103A|XH|103C|103D|E	မ်းြေ	3
NNY|103A|XH|103C|103D	ည်းြို	1
NNY|103A|XH|103B|A|XH	ည်းျာား	1
MXY|A|XH|103C|103D|E	များြေ	1
NG|103D|103B|103E|XH	ငျွိုား	2
Y|AUH|NG|X|KXY|A|XH	ယောက်ျား	12
NXH|A|103B|103D|103E	နှာျိုို	1
TXW|E|103D|103E|E|XT	တွေိုိုေ	1

Figure 1: Some mistokenized word types in the long tail of Myanmar vocabulary.

and inconsistent with the English side. Therefore, we split numbers in English texts into digits and remove sentence pairs which contains Latin words in Myanmar side.

We filter training data in several steps. We first remove duplicated sentence pairs. Secondly, we filter out bad encoded or untranslated sentence pairs. Thirdly, we use Moses `clean-corpus-n.perl` script to remove sentence pairs with too much tokens or imbalanced length ratio. Finally, we use `fast-align` toolkit[4] to train word alignment and filter out bad sentence pairs according to the alignment scores.

To enable open-vocabulary, we apply subword-based translation approaches. In our preliminary experiments, we found that Byte Pair Encoding (BPE) works better than mixed word/character segmentation techniques. As Myanmar texts are already syllabificated, we only apply BPE[5] on English texts with 20K operations.

In the post-processing step, we recover Myanmar sentences using official `myan2roma.py` and then remove all spaces and Romanize sentences again with `myan2roma.py`. For English sentences, we first restore words from subword pieces and then apply Moses detruecaser and detokenizer scripts.

---

[2] `http://statmt.org/moses/`
[3] `https://github.com/thantthet/`
`MyanmarParser-Py`

[4] `https://github.com/clab/fast_align`
[5] `https://github.com/rsennrich/`
`subword-nmt`

4 Results

4.1 Experiments on Myanmar Tokenizers

Table 1 shows the experimental results of different Myanmar tokenization methods. We found that integrating Myanmar syllable segmentation to the official script significantly improve results on Myanmar→English translation, whatever NMT architecture used. This proves that Myanmar syllable segmentation does help alleviate data-sparsity problem. However, Myanmar syllable segmentation underperform the official Myanmar tokenizer on English→Myanmar translation with both two types of NMT architectures. This maybe due to the longer sequences and more ambiguities of target side outputs.

Tokenizer	DL4MT		Transformer	
	EN-MY	MY-EN	EN-MY	MY-EN
M2R	**22.03**	9.90	**21.95**	11.45
MP + M2R	21.23	**13.86**	20.57	**14.22**

Table 1: Experimental results on validation sets of different Myanmar tokenization methods. M2R denotes `myan2roma.py` and MP denotes `MyanmarParser`. Here, we use tokenized case-sensitive BLEU score with `multi-bleu.perl` script of Moses.

System	EN-MY	MY-EN
DL4MT	**22.76**	12.11
Transformer	21.57	**12.71**

Table 2: Experimental results on test sets of different NMT Architectures. Here, we report the online results provided by the automatic evaluation server.

4.2 Experiments on NMT Architectures

In this section, we compare NMT systems with different architectures. The results of online automatic evaluation[6] are shown in Table 2. The deep self-attention based Transformer model beats the shallow RNN-based DL4MT model in Myanmar→English translation with +0.6 BLEU score, while DL4MT outperforms Transformer in English→Myanmar translation with +1.2 BLEU score.

---

[6] `http://lotus.kuee.kyoto-u.ac.jp/WAT/evaluation/index.html`

5 Conclusion

We describe XMU's neural machine translation systems for the WAT 2018 Myanmar→English and English→Myanmar translation tasks. In such a low-resourced settings, experiments show that shallow RNN-based models can still outperform Transformer models and Myanmar syllable segmentation is effective to alleviate data-sparsity.

Acknowledgments

This work was supported by the Natural Science Foundation of China (Grant No. 61573294), the Ph.D. Programs Foundation of Ministry of Education of China (Grant No. 20130121110040), the Foundation of the State Language Commission of China (Grant No. WT135-10), the Outstanding Achievement Late Fund of the State Language Commission of China (Grant No. WT135-38) and the National High-Tech R&D Program of China (Grant No. 2012BAH14F03).

References

Toshiaki Nakazawa and Shohei Higashiyama and Chenchen Ding and Raj Dabre and Anoop Kunchukuttan and Win Pa Pa and Isao Goto and Hideya Mino and Katsuhito Sudoh and Sadao Kurohashi. 2018. Overview of the 5th Workshop on Asian Translation. In *Proceedings of the 5th Workshop on Asian Translation (WAT2018)*.

Dzmitry Bahdanau, KyungHyun Cho, and Yoshua Bengio. 2015. Neural machine translation by jointly learning to align and translate. In *Proceedings of ICLR*.

Kyunghyun Cho, Bart van Merrienboer, Caglar Gulcehre, Dzmitry Bahdanau, Fethi Bougares, Holger Schwenk, and Yoshua Bengio. 2014. Learning phrase representations using rnn encoder–decoder for statistical machine translation. In *Proceedings of EMNLP*, pages 1724–1734.

Diederik Kingma and Jimmy Ba. 2015. Adam: A method for stochastic optimization. In *Proceedings of ICLR*.

Toshiaki Nakazawa, Shohei Higashiyama, Chenchen Ding, Hideya Mino, Isao Goto, Graham Neubig, Hideto Kazawa, Yusuke Oda, Jun Harashima, and Sadao Kurohashi. 2017. Overview of the 4th Workshop on Asian Translation. In *Proceedings of the 4th Workshop on Asian Translation (WAT2017)*, Taipei, Taiwan.

Razvan Pascanu, Tomas Mikolov, and Yoshua Bengio. 2013. On the difficulty of training recurrent neural networks. In *Proceedings of ICML*, pages 1310–1318.

Rico Sennrich, Alexandra Birch, Anna Currey, Ulrich Germann, Barry Haddow, Kenneth Heafield, Antonio Valerio Miceli Barone, and Philip Williams. 2017. The University of Edinburgh's Neural MT Systems for WMT17. *arXiv preprint arXiv:1708.00726*.

Rico Sennrich, Barry Haddow, and Alexandra Birch. 2016a. Edinburgh neural machine translation systems for wmt 16. *arXiv preprint arXiv:1606.02891*.

Rico Sennrich, Barry Haddow, and Alexandra Birch. 2016b. Neural machine translation of rare words with subword units. In *Proceedings of ACL*, pages 1715–1725.

Nitish Srivastava, Geoffrey Hinton, Alex Krizhevsky, Ilya Sutskever, and Ruslan Salakhutdinov. 2014. Dropout: A simple way to prevent neural networks from overfitting. *The Journal of Machine Learning Research*, 15(1):1929–1958.

Ilya Sutskever, Oriol Vinyals, and Quoc V Le. 2014. Sequence to sequence learning with neural networks. In *Advances in neural information processing systems*, pages 3104–3112.

Yonghui Wu, Mike Schuster, Zhifeng Chen, Quoc V Le, Mohammad Norouzi, Wolfgang Macherey, Maxim Krikun, Yuan Cao, Qin Gao, Klaus Macherey, et al. 2016. Google's neural machine translation system: Bridging the gap between human and machine translation. *arXiv preprint arXiv:1609.08144*.

Jie Zhou, Ying Cao, Xuguang Wang, Peng Li, and Wei Xu. 2016. Deep recurrent models with fast-forward connections for neural machine translation. *Transactions of the Association for Computational Linguistics*, 4:371–383.

Ashish Vaswani, Noam Shazeer, Niki Parmar, Jakob Uszkoreit, Llion Jones, Aidan N. Gomez, Lukasz Kaiser, and Illia Polosukhin. 2017. Attention Is All You Need. *arXiv preprint arXiv:1706.03762*.

Jiacheng Zhang, Yanzhuo Ding, Shiqi Shen, Yong Cheng, Maosong Sun, Huanbo Luan, Yang Liu. 2017. THUMT: An Open Source Toolkit for Neural Machine Translation *arXiv preprint arXiv:1706.06415*.

32nd Pacific Asia Conference on Language, Information and Computation
The 5th Workshop on Asian Translation
Hong Kong, 1-3 December 2018

AUTHOR INDEX

Arase, Yuki 117

Banerjee, Tamali 105

Bhattacharya, Pushpak 105

Bhattacharyya, Pushpak 100

Bojar, Ondrej 42

Chen, Yidong 130

Chowdhury, Koel Dutta 95

Chu, Chenhui 117

Dabre, Raj 1, 49

Ding, Chenchen 1, 69

Dong, Bin 58

Ehara, Terumasa 63

Ekbal, Asif 100

Fujita, Atsushi 49, 72

Goto, Isao 1

Gupta, Kamal Kumar 100

Han, Nway Nway 85

Higashiyama, Shohei 1

Hu, Jinming 130

Jawahar, C. V. 90

Jiang, Shanshan 58

Katsumata, Satoru 109

Kawara, Yuki 117

Kocmi, Tom 42

Komachi, Mamoru 78, 109

Kunchukuttan, Anoop 1, 49, 105

Kurohashi, Sadao 1

Li, Yihan 58

Liu, Boyan 58

Liu, Chao-Hong 95

Marie, Benjamin 72

Matsumura, Yukio 109

Mino, Hideya 1

Mo, Hsu Myat 124

Nakazawa, Toshiaki 1

Namboodiri, Vinay P. 90

Ojha, Atul Kr. 95

Oo, Sheinn Thawtar 85

Oo, Thazin Myint 124

Pa, Win Pa 1, 124

Parida, Shantipriya 42

Philip, Jerin 90

Saxena, Karan 95

Sen, Sukanta 100

Shi, Xiaodong 130

Sin, Yi Mon Shwe 124

Soe, Khim Mar 124

Sudoh, Katsuhito 1

Sumita, Eiichiro 49, 69, 72

Takebayashi, Yuto 117

Thida, Aye 85

Thu, Ye Kyaw 124

Tong, Yixuan 58

Utiyama, Masao 69

Wang, Boli 130

Wang, Rui 69

Zhang, Longtu 78

Zhao, Yuting 78